Rainer Maria Rilke

SELECTED WORKS

VOLUME II POETRY

By the same Author

*

REQUIEM AND OTHER POEMS
Translated with an Introduction
by J. B. Leishman

THE BOOK OF HOURS
Translated by A. L. Peck

DUINO ELEGIES
The German text with an
English translation, Introduction
and Commentary by J. B. Leishman
and Stephen Spender

SONNETS TO ORPHEUS
The German text with an
English translation, Introduction
and Commentary by J. B. Leishman

FROM THE REMAINS OF COUNT C.W.
The German text with an
English translation and Introduction
by J. B. Leishman

CORRESPONDENCE IN VERSE WITH
ERIKA MITTERER
The German text with an
English Translation by N. K. Cruickshank,
and an Introduction by J. B. Leishman

POEMS 1906–1926
Translated with an Introduction
by J. B. Leishman

NEW POEMS
The German text with a translation
Introduction and Notes by J. B. Leishman

*

THE NOTEBOOK OF MALTE LAURIDS BRIGGE
Translated by John Linton

SELECTED WORKS: PROSE
Translated by G. Craig Houston
with an Introduction by J. B. Leishman

LETTERS TO BENVENUTA
Translated by Heinz Norden
with a Foreword by Louis Untermeyer

LETTERS TO FRAU GUDI NÖLKE
Translated by Violet M. MacDonald

THE LETTERS OF RAINER MARIA RILKE AND
PRINCESS MARIE VON THURN UND TAXIS
Translated and Introduced by Nora Wydenbruck

RAINER MARIA RILKE

SELECTED WORKS

VOLUME II
POETRY

Translated by
J. B. LEISHMAN

1980

THE HOGARTH PRESS

LONDON

PUBLISHED BY
THE HOGARTH PRESS LTD
40 WILLIAM IV STREET
LONDON W.C.2

*

CLARKE, IRWIN AND CO LTD
TORONTO

FIRST PUBLISHED 1960
SECOND IMPRESSION 1967
THIRD IMPRESSION 1976
FOURTH IMPRESSION 1980

ISBN 0 7012 0197 5

PRINTED IN GREAT BRITAIN BY
REDWOOD BURN LIMITED
TROWBRIDGE AND ESHER

CONTENTS

(The bracketed dates are those of the first publication of books from which the poems here translated have been taken. For dates of composition, see the separate title-pages preceding each section of this book. Poems marked with an asterisk are not in *Ausgewählte Werke.*)

THE BOOK OF HOURS (CONTINUED)

SECOND BOOK: THE BOOK OF PILGRIMAGE

THE BOOK OF HOURS (CONTINUED)

THIRD BOOK: THE BOOK OF POVERTY AND OF DEATH

THE BOOK OF HOURS (CONTINUED)

FROM THE BOOK OF IMAGES (1902 AND 1906)

FROM THE BOOK OF IMAGES (CONTINUED)

FROM NEW POEMS (1907 AND 1908)

FROM NEW POEMS (CONTINUED)

FROM NEW POEMS (CONTINUED)

REQUIEM (1909)

THE LIFE OF MARY (1913)

THE LIFE OF MARY (CONTINUED)

DUINO ELEGIES (1923)

SONNETS TO ORPHEUS (1923)

FIRST PART

SONNETS TO ORPHEUS (CONTINUED)

SECOND PART

SONNETS TO ORPHEUS (CONTINUED)

FROM THE UNCOLLECTED POEMS OF 1906 TO 1926

FROM THE UNCOLLECTED POEMS OF 1906 TO 1926 (CONTINUED)

FROM THE UNCOLLECTED POEMS OF 1906 TO 1926 (CONTINUED)

FROM THE UNCOLLECTED POEMS OF 1906 TO 1926 (CONTINUED)

PREFACE

This book is a complete translation of the first volume of the second edition of *Ausgewählte Werke* (Selected Works), edited by Professor Ernst Zinn and published by the Insel-Verlag in 1948. Some years ago I was invited to undertake, or at least to superintend, a complete translation of the two volumes of *Ausgewählte Werke*, and I was fortunately able to persuade my friend the late Miss G. Craig Houston to translate the prose volume, which, completed shortly before her death, was published in 1954. I was at that time too fully occupied with the translation and preparation of *Poems 1906 to 1926* to be able to start the vast amount of revision and new work required for the verse volume of *Ausgewählte Werke*, so it was decided that the prose volume should appear first, with the title *Selected Works: Volume I, Prose*. The present volume contains complete translations of *Das Stunden-Buch* (The Book of Hours), *Requiem*, *Das Marien-Leben* (The Life of Mary), the *Duino Elegies* and the *Sonnets to Orpheus*, together with selections from *Das Buch der Bilder* (The Book of Images), the two Parts of *Neue Gedichte* (New Poems), and the Uncollected Poems written between 1909 and 1926. To Professor Zinn's selection from *The Book of Images* I have added six poems, and to his selection from *New Poems* I have added thirteen poems, which I included in the second edition of *Requiem and Other Poems* (1949), and to his selection from the Uncollected Poems I have added two.

For the translation of *The Book of Hours* my friend Dr A. L. Peck has very kindly allowed me to make use of the first draft of his own version, which will be published by the Hogarth Press. Readers of it will perceive how deeply I have been indebted to him. I have followed what seems to me his excellent procedure in numbering the poems in each of the three parts; I recommend all possessors of the German text to do likewise, and hope that an excessive piety will not prevent the German publishers from eventually doing so too. A reference to, for example, II 25, ll. 10-11 could then be immediately identified in any edition, just as can a reference to Horace, *Odes*, II, xvi, 19-20, or to *Hamlet* III, ii, 414.

The translation of *The Life of Mary* is by Miss N. K. Cruickshank, to whom, as well as to its original publishers, Messrs Oliver and Boyd, my publishers and I are most grateful for permission to include it.

The translation of the *Duino Elegies* was originally made in collaboration with Mr Stephen Spender and published in 1939. In the third edition (1948) I made very extensive revisions, and the version here included has again been thoroughly revised.

The translation of *Requiem* is a considerably revised version of that which I published in 1949 in *Requiem and Other Poems*, and that of the *Sonnets to Orpheus* a slightly revised version of that which I published in the second edition of 1946.

In this large volume there has been no space for elaborate introductions and commentaries, but in *The Book of Hours* and the *Duino Elegies* I have occasionally added what seemed to me indispensable footnotes, and on the half-title pages preceding each of the two Requiems, *The Life of Mary*, the *Duino Elegies* and the *Sonnets to Orpheus* various kinds of indispensable information will be found.

Having now dealt with the five complete translations in this volume, I must add some more detailed remarks about the three series of selections.

Rilke divided the second edition of the *Buch der Bilder* (Book of Images) into two books, each consisting of two parts. Neither in the divisions into books and parts nor in the arrangement of poems within each part is it possible to detect any clear or consistent principle, and Professor Zinn therefore followed in his selection (with, I think, only one exception) the order in which the poems appear in the complete book. This order I too have followed, and I have inserted the six poems omitted by Professor Zinn in the same relative positions as they occupy in Rilke's book. For the two volumes (1907 and 1908) of *New Poems* Rilke adopted a much more systematic and discernible, though not rigidly consistent, principle of arrangement. In each volume there is something like a progress through the centuries, a kind of panorama of scenes and incidents from mythical Antiquity, from the Old and New Testaments, from the Middle Ages, the Renaissance and the 'Baroque', up to the present day, which provides subjects for the majority of poems in each volume. This 'historical' procession is often interrupted and diversified by various evocations of landscapes, animals and flowers and by various 'Poems founded on the Affections' (to borrow one of Wordsworth's classifications) of a more or less timeless sort. And, although each volume begins with a fairly consistently chronological progress through the centuries, Rilke, when once he has reached his own age, does not wholly remain there, but often returns to the evocation of scenes and incidents from earlier periods. Accordingly, in his selection from the two volumes of *New Poems*, Professor Zinn very sensibly adopted an arrangement more or less according to subject, placing, for example, together the 'Classical', 'Biblical' and 'Medieval' poems with which both volumes begin and which he selected from both. Of the five blank verse poems with which Rilke concluded the first volume Professor Zinn rightly placed the three he chose at the end of his selection, and I have followed his example, adding translations of the two which he omitted. The other eleven poems which I have added to Professor Zinn's selection I have inserted at what seemed to me the most appropriate places.

All the poems from the *Book of Images* and *New Poems* which I published in the second edition of *Requiem and Other Poems* are here included, with larger or smaller revisions, but by far the greater number of my translations from these two books now appear for the first time.

The only respect in which I have here departed from Professor Zinn's procedure, or rather, perhaps I should say, the only innovation I have ventured to introduce, is that, as in my complete translation of the uncollected *Poems 1906 to 1926*, I have added in smaller type at the end of each poem the date and place of composition, and also very occasionally, a note. To do this with either the original or translated version of a complete book which Rilke himself had arranged and published might perhaps be an unwarrantable intrusion, but I can see no objection to doing it with selections from such books. Nothing is lost and much, it seems to me, is sometimes gained. Most of what has been written about *New Poems* greatly exaggerates their impersonality and objectivity, and fails to perceive to what an extent Rilke has often found, without being directly confessional, 'objective correlatives' for his own situation, as from time to time he experienced it. It is therefore worth knowing that, for examples the poem *David sings before Saul* (p. 149) was written while he was still living in the little cottage in Rodin's garden at Meudon and acting as a kind of secretary to his boundlessly admired Master, and that *The Departure of the Prodigal Son* (p. 153) and *The Olive Garden* (p. 154) were written just after his stormy dismissal in May 1906, as the result of an unfortunate misunderstanding about a letter. It is also perhaps worth knowing that the beautiful poem *The Apple Orchard* (p. 183) is a 'recollection in tranquillity', written three years after Rilke had stayed with Hanna Larsson and the painter Ernst Norlind at the Swedish country-house Borgeby-gård.

Where I have ventured to depart entirely from Professor Zinn's arrangement is in the selection from the uncollected poems written between 1909 and 1926. At the time when he made his selection from these poems for the first edition of *Ausgewählte Werke*, published in 1938, their dates and places of composition were only imperfectly known, and, although he entitled his selection 'From the Years 1913-1926', the earliest poem he included was, as a matter of fact, written in 1909. For the second edition of 1948 he added twenty-two more poems from the material he was still in process of discovering, but the places at which they were inserted seem to have been dictated largely by typographical considerations. I have therefore rearranged all these poems in a strictly chronological order, as in the complete translation of the uncollected poems which I published in

1957, and, as in that book, I have added dates, places of composition, and occasional notes. In my Introduction to *Poems 1906 to 1926* I have described the history of the gradual discovery and publication of these poems, a history which ended only with the appearance of Professor Zinn's second volume of the new edition of Rilke's *Sämtliche Werke* in 1957.[1] Professor Zinn himself asked me whether the selection he had made for *Ausgewählte Werke* could any longer be considered adequate, and whether I ought not to enlarge it. Since, however, it seems to me an admirable selection, and since I have already published a complete translation of the uncollected poems, I have contented myself with adding two of the most remarkable of Professor Zinn's many remarkable discoveries, the *Ode to Bellman* (1915) and *Mausoleum* (1924).

For the convenience of readers who may wish to turn to or from the German text either of *Ausgewählte Werke* or of the first two volumes of the new edition of Rilke's *Sämtliche Werke*, I have added two pairs of indexes: first, a German and an English index of the First Lines of poems in *The Book of Hours*, and then a German and an English index of Titles and First Lines of all the other poems in this book.

In Prefaces to previous volumes I have expressed my gratitude to the friends who, during these many years, have assisted me in this most difficult task. In the preparation of this volume, as in that of its immediate predecessor, I have received invaluable assistance from Dr George Hill, who carefully read through both the new work it contains and the greater portion of the old, and helped me to correct many errors and to make many improvements.

Except, perhaps, for a possible attempt at a bilingual edition of the surviving first drafts and *brouillons* of the *Duino Elegies*, and for any future discoveries that may require to be added to the uncollected *Poems 1906 to 1926*, it is unlikely that I shall now publish any further new translations of Rilke's poems. On the other hand, I shall never, I hope, completely rest from the attempt to make less imperfect the many poems I have already translated, and to consider carefully any suggestions for improvement that may reach me from any quarter. It is not only a matter of finding a more adequate, or less inadequate, expression for something which I think I have completely understood; it is sometimes a matter of coming to understand, or of thinking that I have come to understand, the original for the first time. For such late understanding I do not feel it necessary to apologise, since I am well aware that many of the formidable grammatical, syntactical and semantic difficulties of Rilke's poetry are no less formidable to competent German readers than they are to me. Apart

[1] Although this volume bears the date 1956, it did not actually appear until the summer of 1957.

altogether from questions of general interpretation, many distinguished and devoted scholars have proposed interpretations of the most primary and prose sense of particular phrases and passages which to other scholars, no less distinguished and devoted, have seemed clearly impossible. Some would maintain that no poet ought to seem so difficult as this to his contemporaries, and they may be right. Nevertheless, whatever his defects and limitations, Rilke remains a very great poet, perhaps the greatest of our time; we must take him as he is, and, above all, try to see him as he is.

Various phrases in my translations have from time to time been objected to as 'un-English'. Here I will appeal to the authority of Rilke himself, and allow his words to conclude this Preface. Writing on 17 November 1912 to Princess Marie von Thurn und Taxis, who had been translating some of his poems into her native Italian, he congratulated her on certain audacities and urged her to pay no attention to those who might object to them as 'un-Italian': *Remember that any language-superintendant on the German side, to whom the corresponding passage in my version was submitted, would certainly protest that it was impossible, un-German, un-intelligible, un- un- un-*. There is a lot of *un-ness* in Rilke's poetry, just as there was in Rilke himself, and to fail to reproduce at least some of it would be to distort the original.

J. B. L.

Oxford, *January 1959*

THE BOOK OF HOURS

CONTAINING THE THREE BOOKS:
OF THE MONASTIC LIFE
OF PILGRIMAGE
OF POVERTY AND DEATH

Written in 1899, 1901 and 1903; revised April-May 1905; published Christmas 1905

Placed in the hands of Lou

FIRST BOOK
THE BOOK OF THE MONASTIC LIFE

First version written at Berlin-Schmargendorf, 20 September to 14 October 1899. Final version completed at Worpswede, 24 April to 16 May 1905. The order of the poems in the book is that of their composition. The numbering of the poems has been introduced by the translator.

In the spring of 1899 Rilke had visited Russia for the first time with Lou Andreas-Salomé and her husband; it was one of the most important experiences in his life, and the meditations in this book are supposed to be those of a Russian monk. He had spent April and May of 1898 in Florence, having previously studied the history of art in general, and of Renaissance art in particular, at the universities of Prague, Munich and Berlin. This first direct experience of Italian Renaissance art is also, like the more overwhelming Russian experience, reflected in *The Book of the Monastic Life*.

On 14 May 1911 Rilke gave an important description of the origin of this First Part of *The Book of Hours* in a reply to a correspondent, Marlise Gerding, who had presumably asked him in what sense it was to be regarded as 'religious'. He declared that, at a time when he was occupied with other tasks, words, 'prayers, if you like', suddenly began to come to him when he awoke in the morning and during the stillness of the evening, words which he at first merely recited, but which gradually developed into an 'inner dictation' of such strength, that he began to write them down. The act of writing them down strengthened and summoned inspiration, and to his instinctive pleasure in an inner excitement was added delight in what had now become a new piece of work. The work, it is true, had been, as it were, 'given' to him, but *qua* work, 'it has the delight of all art in itself and is thereby different from prayer, has a vanity which prayer does not possess. But what is prayer, – do we know?' Rilke then proceeds to declare that all piety is either inexplicable or indifferent to him that does not contain something of invention, and that, for him, our relationship to God presupposes a certain 'creativity', a certain 'inventive genius', which he can imagine as being pushed so far that 'one suddenly does not understand what is meant by the name of God, so that one allows oneself to repeat it, to recite it, ten times over, without understanding it, simply in order to search for it entirely anew, somewhere at its origin, at its source. This perhaps is the admixture of unbelief in the Book of Hours, unbelief not as the result of doubt but as the result of not-knowing and beginnership' (*Ausgewählte Briefe*, 1950, I, pp. 303-4).

I

With strokes that ring clear and metallic, the hour
to touch me bends down on its way:
my senses are quivering. I feel I've the power –
and I seize on the pliable day.

Not a thing was complete till by me it was eyed,
every kind of becoming stood still.
Now my glances are ripe and there comes like a bride
to each of them just what it will.

There's nothing so small but I love it and choose
to paint it gold-groundly and great
and hold it most precious and know not whose
soul it may liberate . . .

2

I live in expanding rings that are weaving
over these things below.
The last, perhaps, is beyond my achieving,
I'll make an attempt at it though.

Round God, the old tower, my gyres I perform,
and I've gyred there centuries long;
and don't know whether I'm falcon or storm
or, maybe, a mighty song.

3

I've many brethren in the life of prayer
in Southern cloisters where the laurel grows.
They give Madonnas such a human air,
I often dream of youthful Titians there,
through whom their God as fervour flows.

How, though, into my self I keep inclining!
My God is dark and like a deep-extended
cluster of hundred roots still springs are laving.
More than that from his warmth I have ascended
I know not, for my boughs are all reclining
deep down and only in the winds are waving.

4

We dare not paint you at our own dictation,
you maiden-dawn from whom the morning grew.
From pigments of an older generation
we fetch those strokes, that same irradiation
with which long since the saint secreted you.

We've built up images like walls before you,
till now you're hemmed with thousands of ramparts.
For to your veils our pious hands restore you
whenever you are open to our hearts.

5

I love the darker hours of my existence,
wherein, as in old letters, I discover
my daily life already lived and over
and like some legend lost in farthest distance.

I learn from them that space is granted me
for yet a second, ampler life, in time uncharted.
And sometimes I am like a tree
which rustlingly above a grave has started
to realise that dream the lad departed
(around whom now its warming root-throng presses)
lost long ago in songs and mournfulnesses.

6

If sometimes, neighbour God, my knocking on
your wall at night disturbs you out of season,
that I've scarce heard you breathing is the reason,
and know you're in your room alone.
And no one's present there to understand
what you are groping for and bring it you:
I'm always listening. Just a rap will do.
I'm close at hand.

Nothing's between us but a slender wall,
fortuitously; for if there came perhaps
from your mouth or from mine a sudden call,
it might collapse
forthwith, quite noiselessly.

It's been constructed from your imagery.

Before you stand your images like names.
And if at times the light in me leaps high,
that light the depths of me discern you by,
it spends itself as radiance on their frames.

And senses which a sudden tiredness lames
homelessly separated from you lie.

7

If only stillness reigned, pure, elemental.
If silence fell on all that's accidental
and casual and the neighbour's laugh were quiet,
if my own senses with their noisy riot
did not so much disturb my concentration –

Then in one thousandfold excogitation
right to your topmost verge I'd come to guess you
and (just the lasting of one smile) possess,
and out to all things living would largess you
like gratefulness.

8

I'm here just when the century's passing by.
By wind from some great leaf the world is stirred
which God and you and I have character'd,
now being turned by unknown hands on high.

A quite new page's radiance is arresting,
where all as yet may come to be.
The silent forces are already testing
their range and eyeing each other sombrely.

9

It's this I seem to hear your Word proclaim, –
I see the story of Creation showing
how warmly and how wisely earliest growing
by those surrounding hands of yours was bounded.

You loudly uttered 'live' and softly sounded
'die', and continually repeated 'be'.
Yet, before death's first coming, murder came.
A rent through your ripe circles then rebounded,
a scream that instantly
out-tore the voices gathering there to frame
those earliest utterings
that should declare you,
that should upbear you,
bridge over each ravine –

Since then their mutterings
fragments have been
of your primeval name.

10

Hear what pale-faced Abel says:

I am no more. My brother has done to me
something my eyes did not see:
He has cloaked from me light's rays.
He has displaced my face
by his own face.
Now he is solitary.
I think he must needs still *be.*
For none inflicts on him my chastisement.
All were going the way I went,
all towards his anger wend,
all through him will meet their end.

I think my big brother's as vigilant
as a judgment court.
Night, my kindly visitant,
gives him no thought.

11

You darkness, whence my lineage came,
I love you more than that bright flame
by which the world is limited,
its shine being shed
only upon some Where
outside of which no creature knows it's there.

Darkness enfolds, though, all things utterly:
figures and flames, dumb creatures and me,
grasps unwithstood
all men, all mights –

And, all unknown, some great force could
be stirring within my neighbourhood.

I believe in nights.

12

I believe in all that's unuttered still.
My devoutest feelings shall have their way.
What no one as yet has dared to will,
I shall involuntarily one day.

If, God, that's presumptuous, pardon me.
This is all I mean by the affirmation:
My best power must function instinctively,
without all anger or hesitation –
don't children love you similarly?

With this onsurging of mine, this ever-
outflowing, wide-armed, to the open sea,
with this increasing recurrency,
I want to confess you, proclaim you, as never
one previously.

And if that's pride, it's for what has none of its own –
pride for my prayer,
so grave and alone
confronting your clouded brow up there.

13

In the world too alone am I, yet not in such solitude
as to hallow each hour going by.
In the world I am far too slight, yet not of such parvitude
as to be like a thing in your sight,
sombre and shrewd.
I will my will and would go with my will as it speeds
on its way to deeds;
and would be in those times of silence, that seem so to linger
here
when something's drawing near,

among those to whom all is known,
or else alone.

I would mirror you in your absolute shape for ever,
and would that blindness or age may never
make your tottering image too heavy for me to hold.
I want to unfold.
I will nowhere suffer a circumscribing,
for wherever I'm bent I am there belied.
And I'd have my meaning abide
true in your sight. I would be describing
myself like some picture I've seen
with gaze long and keen,
like some saying clear for me,
like the jug before me,
like my mother's face and form,
like a ship that bore me
through the deadliest storm.

14

You see my will's wide extent.
Maybe it embraces all:
the darkness of every limitless fall,
the tremulous light-play of every ascent.

So many are living without a trace
of will and are raised to the princeliest place
by their feelings' soon-gratified throngs.

You, though, delight in every face
that serves and that longs.

You delight in all of those who are striving
to use you like an implement.

You are not yet cold, nor is time too spent
for us into your growing depths to be diving,
where Life's so tranquilly evident.

15

With tremulous hands we're trying to upheave you,
one speck on another we cast.
Who, though, can ever achieve you,
Minster vast?

What is Rome? A past
glory, to ruin hurled.
What is the world?
It will disintegrate before
the domes above your turrets soar
and out of mile-lengths of mosaic
your radiating brow shall break.

At times, though, in dreams I can
survey the space you span
from where commences
the deep foundation
up to the roof-top ridge's gilding.

And I see my senses
shaping and building
the topmost decoration.

16

Just because someone has willed you before,
I know that to will you we have permission.
Even though we viewed all depths with suspicion,
if a mountain has gold in store
which none any longer's allowed to unseam,
into the light one day the stream,
grasping the rock that immures,
will swill it.

Even if we don't will it,
God matures.

17

He who can reconcile his life's so many
absurdities and gratefully assemble
them all into a symbol,
he flings
the roisterers from his palace, wins a zest
for different festiveness, and you're the guest
whom he receives on gentle evenings.

You are his solitude's responsive chime,
the peaceful centre he soliloquises;
and every circle round you prises
his outstretched compass out of Time.

18

Why does my brush-hand stray as though unthinking?
God, when I *paint* you, you are scarce aware.

I *feel* you, hesitantly starting where
my senses end, like far-off islands winking;
and for those eyes of yours, so all-unblinking,
as space I'm there.

You now no longer dwell within your shining,
where those angelic dancers' endless twining,
like music, wears away your distantness, –
you're now within your farthest harbouring.
Out into me all Heaven's hearkening
because I hid from you in pensiveness.

19

I am, you worrier. Can't you hear me now
with all my senses up against you surging?
My feelings (unexpected wings emerging)
are circling whitely round your brow.
Can you not see my soul before you, how
she's standing in a robe of silence there?
Is it not ripening, my May-blown prayer,
upon your looking as upon a tree?

When you're the dreamer, what you dream is me.
But when you'ld wake, then I'm your will, assuming
dominion over all sublime,
and arch into a starry silence, looming
over this so-amazing Town of Time.

20

My life's not this steep hour wherein you see
me still interminably run so.
Before my background there I'm just a tree,
I'm only one of all the mouths in me,
one that will close before the rest have done so.

I am the pause between two notes that fall
into a real accordance scarce at all:
for Death's note tends to dominate –

Both, though, are reconciled in the dark interval,
tremblingly.
And the song remains immaculate.

21

If I'd grown up somewhere where every day
was lighter, hours were slimmer, I'd have planned
you some great festival in such a land;
my hands, too, would not hold you in the way
they sometimes do, with such tight anxiousness.

There I'd have had the courage to spend you,
you all-unbounded presentness,
and, like a ball,
into all billowing joys to send you
hurtling, with stroke that brings,
to meet your fall,
one that with lifted hands upsprings,
you thing of things.

Like a sword, I'd have let your lightenings
flash manifold for me.
I'd have had your fire inset in a ring's
purest of gold for me,
fire that ring would have had to hold for me
over a hand that was whiter than all.

I'd have painted you too: not on the wall,
but on that blue ceiling celestial,
and shaped you with art preternatural,
as a giant would do, into mountain tall,
forest fire or sandstorm meridional –

And yet
it may be that after all
I found you once . . .
My friends recede,
of their laughter now I'm scarcely aware;
and you, you've fallen from your nest up there,
a fledgling with yellow claws, and the stare
of your great big eyes makes my heart bleed.
(My hand's too spacious for you indeed.)
And with drop from the spring on my finger I'm waiting
to see if you'll reach for it there in your plight,
and I feel your heart and mine pulsating,
both from sheer fright.

22

I find you thus in all whereon with tender
and brotherly devotedness I wait;
you sun yourself like seed within the slender,
and greatly give yourself within the great.

Such is the marvellous play of forces here,
so servingly through everything they spread:
to grow in roots, in trunks to disappear,
and in the tree-tops rise as from the dead.

23

Voice of a Young Brother

All of me, all of me running hence is,
as sands through fingers run.
I've all of a sudden so many senses,
with a different thirst in each one.
I feel in parts of myself past telling
swelling and smart,
most of all, though, within my heart.

I want to die. Oh, let me be!
I think at last I'll attain
such anxiety,
my pulse will burst with the strain.

24

Look, God, a novice comes to work at you,
who yesterday was still a boy: his two
hands still compressed as they were folded by
women to what's already half a lie.
For now his right already has a craving
to leave his left for warding or for waving
and be on its own arm alone.

Even yesterday his brow was like a stone
within the brook, by days being rounded
that mean no more than waves the wind's uphounded,
days whose ambition by the wish is bounded
just to reflect those skies that chance beclouds;

to-day there crowds
on it a whole world-history
before a court that knows no clemency
and in whose sentence it is lost to view.

Space on a new face has originated.
Before this light no light illuminated,
and how your book begins anew!

25

I love you, gentlest law, through which we yet
were ripening while with it we contended,
you great homesickness we have not transcended,
you forest out of which we've never wended,
you song that from our silence has ascended,
you sombre net
where feelings taking flight are apprehended.

You made yourself a so immense beginning
that day when you began us too, – and we
beneath your suns such ripeness have been winning,
have grown so broadly and deep-rootedly,
that you, in angels, men, madonnas inning,
can now complete yourself quite tranquilly.

Let your right hand on heaven's slope repose
and mutely bear what darkly we impose.

26

We're workmen, all the millions of us, whether
craftsman or prentice, huge Nave, building you.
And sometimes some grave traveller comes hither,
goes like a gleam through all our minds together,
and shows us tremblingly a grip that's new.

Up to the rocking scaffold we are going,
the hammer in our hands hangs heavily,
until some hour upon our brows be blowing
that radiantly, as though it were all-knowing,
comes from you like the wind from sea.

Then hammer upon hammer rings out gaily,
and through the mountains blows reverberate.
We do not let you go till it's grown late:
and now your future contours glimmer greyly.

God, you are great.

27

You are so great that I quite cease to be
when in your neighbourhood I take my station.
You are so dark, my small illumination
lacks sense in your vicinity.
And in your will's vast undulation
each day is drowned as in a sea.

Only my longing's able to get through
and like the tallest angel dares to eye you:
one alien, pallid, still unransomed by you,
holding his pinions out to you.

He yearns for that untrammelled flight no more
where pallid moons in passing would observe him,
and long has known enough of cosmic lore.
His pinions now, like flames, shall merely serve him
to stand before your shadowy countenance
and by their white resplendence see what chance
there is that your grey brows may yet preserve him.

28

So many angels seek you in the light
and, craning up towards the constellations,
would learn of you from all bright emanations.
I feel, though, every time I come to write
about you, they're withdrawing from the might
of your royal mantle folds their contemplations.

For you yourself were but the guest of gold.
Only to please an age (it is reported)
into whose marble prayers you'd been exhorted,
as monarch of the comets you disported,
proud of the rays that from your brow outrolled.

You went home when that age returned to mould.

Dark is your mouth by which I was transported,
and ebonite the hands that you outhold.

29

Those were the days of Michelangelo,
of which from foreign books I know so well.
That was the man whose stature could excel
all measure so,
that he forgot the Incommensurable.

That was the man who always reappears
when any age, to mark its closing years,
strives yet once more to recapitulate.
There's one who still can heave its total weight
and hurl it into his abysmal breast.

His forbears were by joy and pain possessed;
he, though, feels nothing but life's massiveness,
which like one object he encompasses, –
God only still transcends his will, and he
straight loves him with that lofty hate of his
for this unreachability.

30

That bough stretched from God the Tree out over Italy
bloomed long ago.
It would, maybe,
have gladly had early-ripening fruits to show;
in the midst of its bloom it grew weary, though,
and no fruits will it ever render.

Only God's Springtime there occurred,
only his son the Word
reached completeness.
There flocked with fleetness
all forces on earth to that youthful splendour.
All come to tender
gifts to him;
his praises, like cherubim,
all creatures sing.

And his perfuming
is like rose of all roses.
He like a ring
the homeless encloses.
He passes in mantles and metamorphoses
through all the ascending voices of Time.

31

And she, whom angel visitation
to fruit once quickened, adoration
was paid to her, shy, startled maid:
that garden waiting exploration,
that wood a hundred paths pervade.

They let her float aloft and merge in
the youthful season's germinal;
the life of the ministral virgin
grew wondrous and imperial.
Like peals with festive tidings laden,
through every house it was dispersed;
and that once so distracted maiden
was now so inwardly immersed,
so filled with that supernal honour,
so inexhaustible a store,
that all things seemed to shine upon her,
who like a vineyard basked and bore.

32

But as though the weight of carved festoons and the way
that columns and colonnades have fallen in decay
and the singing of hymns day after day
have all oppressed,
there are times when the Virgin, disconsolater,
as still unburdened of one still greater,
to wounds that wait her
has turned her breast.

Her hands, that were so closely clasped before,
hang emptily.
Not yet the greatest was it whom she bore.

And the angels, comforting no more,
surround her alienly and terribly.

33

Such painting of her reached its consummation
in one[1] whose ardentness the sun infused.
Purer for him she grew from all negation,
but ever totaller in tribulation:
his whole life seemed to pass in lamentation
that found its way into the hands he used.

He is her sorrow's loveliest attire,
he whom her mournful lips almost beguile,
as he close-clings to them, into a smile –
and seven angelic candles lack the fire
to force his secret from its domicile.

34

The day is coming when from God the Tree
a bough unlike that over Italy
in summer-ripe annunciance shall glisten;
here in a country[2] where the people listen,
and everyone is solitary like me.

For only solitaries shall behold
the mysteries, and many of that mould
far more than any narrow one shall gain.
For each shall see a different God made plain,
till they acknowledge, near to crying,
that through their so diverse descrying,
through their affirming and denying,
unitingly diversifying,
one God rolls ever-flowingly.

This the conclusive hymn shall be
which then the seers will be singing:
Fruit out of God the Root is springing,
go, smash those bells that you were ringing;
we've reached that quieter season, bringing
the hour to full maturity.
Fruit out of God the Root is springing.
Be grave and see.

[1] Botticelli. [2] Russia.

35

I can't believe that tiny Death, whose head
we overlook in daily observation,
must needs remain for us a care and dread.

I can't believe his threats are warranted;
I'm still alive, with time for some creation,
and longer than the rose my blood is red.

My meaning's deeper than that witty bout
he revels in with our anxiety.
I am the world whence he,
straying, has fallen out.
                    Just so
monks keep on passing; round and round they go;
you dread their reappearance, do not know
if every time it's just the self-same fellow,
or if they're two, ten, hundreds in a row.
That strange, that yellow outstretched hand alone
you recognise, so near you and so bare –
there, there:
as though the sleeve it came from were your own.

36

What will you do, God, if Death takes me?
I am your jug (if someone breaks me?)
I am your drink (if curdling cakes me?)
I am your trim, your trade, – it makes me
think: with me goes your meaning too.

You'll have no house to turn into,
where words, so near and warm, will greet then.
They'll fall from off your weary feet then,
those velvet sandals I'm for you.

Your cloak will slip from off your shoulders.
Your glance, which on my cheek would rest,
warmly as by a pillow pressed,
will come, and, after much vain quest,
sink, as the sun goes down the west,
into some lap of alien boulders.

What will you do, God? I'm distressed.

37

You're that smoked whisperer, extended
on every stove in drowsiness.
Time bounds our comprehendingness.
You are the dark uncomprehended
throughout all everlastingness.

You are that trembler and entreater
who makes all meanings hard to tell.
You're that recurring syllable,
for ever tremulously sweeter
in strong-voiced hymning audible.

Never else apprehensible.

For you're not one whom rich and clever
surround, but one whose simpleness
makes putting-by his chief endeavour:
the peasant with the beard, from everlasting to everlastingness.

38

To the Young Brother

You, almost boy, to whom such chaos came:
oh, may your blood not blindly run to waste!
It isn't lust, it's joy you want to taste;
you're fashioned like a bridegroom, and can claim
no other bride except just this: your shame.

For you too mighty lust conceives desire,
and every arm is on a sudden bare.
On pious canvases an alien fire
in pallid cheeks begins to flare;
and all your senses now like serpents gyre
in the red key's encompassing and spire
up in the drum-vibrated air.

And suddenly you're wholly isolated
with those two hands by which you're hated –
and now, unless with spells your will constrains:
. . . .
But through your dark blood are being circulated
rumours of God as through dark lanes.

39

To the Young Brother

With his instruction let your prayer accord,
who back from chaos came so much restored,
that all in shapes of saintly adoration,
retaining all their being's exaltation,
within a church, on golden tesselation,
he painted beauty, and she held a sword.

He bids you say:
O deepest sense of me,
trust me, that I may be what you require;
though in my blood so much throbs noisily,
I know my being is infinite desire.

Over me spreads a mighty earnestness,
and cooler in its shadow life has grown.
For the first time I'm here with you alone,
my consciousness.
You have such maiden ways.

A woman lived near-by in former days
and waved to me from withering attire.
You, though, with tales of such far lands can fire.
And to outgaze
towards their mountains all my powers aspire.

40

Some hymns I have are not ascending.
There's an erectness, after all,
in which my senses can be bending:
you see me large and I am small.
You but distinguish me obscurely
from other things that bend the knee;
they are like herds that graze securely;
I tend them, and they wander surely
at sunset home in front of me.
I follow them through wold and weald
and hear the darkling bridges creaking,
and in the vapour they're upreeking
my homeward-coming is concealed.

41

It's almost, God, as if I saw you,
that time you placed your voice before you
so that it might grow round in space;
the void was like a wound that tore you,
you used the world to cool the place.

Its healing among us is steady.

Past ages drained the varied breed
of fevers from the invalid,
and we ourselves can feel indeed
the background's gentle pulse already.

Soothingly on the void we're laid
and do not leave one rent there showing;
but more ungraspable you're growing
within your countenance's shade.

42

All those whose hands are still progressing
outside of Time, that town so poor;
who lay them with a light caressing
on spots to which no roads are pressing,
whose very name is still unsure, –
they utter you, you daily blessing,
and softly thus entablature:

There's nothing in the end but prayer:
our hands have been so consecrated,
prayer's risen from all they have created;
were ploughing or portraiture their care,
the tools' mere struggle generated
incipient religion there.

Time is a thing so many-folded.
We hear of Time at times, though we
do timeless things as those of old did;
we know God always has enfolded
us like a beard, a drapery.
Like veins in basalt we are moulded
in God's enduring majesty.

43

Our names are like a light that plays
on foreheads shadelessly.
Before that temporal judgment-place
submissively I bowed my face,
which saw (what since then fills its gaze)
your vast obscurity that weighs
on all the world and me.

You bent me back from Time, wheréto
I'd struggled to ascend;
I bowed after some small ado:
now round your gentle victory you
spread darkness without end.

Whom now you hold you cannot guess,
for nothing but my darkenedness
to your long sight appeared.
You hold me with strange tenderness
and hearken how my hands progress
through your old stream of beard.

44

Your primal word was 'Light', whereat
rose Time. Then, after long cessation,
your next in 'Man' found incarnation
(we darkle still in that vibration).
Now once more long in thought you've sat.

Spare me your third, though, spare me that.

I often pray at night: Be voiceless,
one that by signs alone we ken,
one moved by dreaming mind to pen
the heavy sum of all that's noiseless
on brows of mountains and of men.

Be refuge from that rage whose entry
denied the Ineffable its due.
In Paradise the darkness grew:
be you that horn-uplifting sentry
of whom it's only told: he blew.

45

You come and go. The air, in closing
of doors by you, will scarcely stir.
Of all who tiptoe through reposing
dwellings, not one is quieter.

One grows so much accustomed to you,
over one's book one lingers bowed
when with your passing shadow's blue you
have made its pictured pages proud;
for things are always sounding through you,
though sometimes soft and sometimes loud.

Often when in my thoughts I con it,
your universal shape divides;
you are a deer with dapples on it
and I'm the dark a forest hides.

You are a wheel, I gaze upon it:
of your dark buckets high above me
there's always one that's gathering weight
and nearer to me will rotate,

and all my labourings that love me
with each return accumulate.

46

Divers and towers with envy view you,
deepest and also loftiest.
Through gentle utterance many knew you;
when, though, a coward put questions to you,
through silence you were manifest.

You wood of bristling contradictions!
I rock you like a child, although
fulfilment of your maledictions
whole terror-stricken nations know.

To you first books were dedicated,
your image the first artist drew,
within both pain and love you waited,
your graveness as in bronze was plated
on brows that from the consummated
work of seven days conjectured you.

In thousands died away your fires,
and offerings were no longer warm:
till once more, under lofty spires,
you stirred in golden-gated choirs,
and new-born tremulous desires
engirdled you with shape and form.

47

I know: You are the Enigmatic,
round whom arrested Time would stand.
How finely, though, one hour ecstatic,
I featured you, in some erratic
high-overweeningness of hand!

First outlines had been long debated,
all obstacles anticipated, –
then all my plans went quite askew:
the lines and ovals that I drew
like trailing briars proliferated,
till, deep within me, liberated
by some stroke unpremeditated,
the heavenliest of all forms upflew.

This work of mine I can't review,
and yet I feel it's been perfected.
With eyes, though, otherwhere directed
I'll keep constructing it anew.

48

Such is my labour day by day
beneath my shielding adumbration.
And though I'm but as leaf and clay,
as often as I paint or pray
I turn into a Sabbath-day
Jerusalem in jubilation.

I'm the proud town of Heaven's King,
whose praise with hundred tongues I'm crying;
in me ceased David's psalmodying,
in the harp's twilight I was lying
and breathed the star of evening.

Eastward my streets are all repairing.
And if it's long since folk were faring
along them, greater width I win.
I hear each step in my recesses
and broaden out my lonelinesses
from origin to origin.

49

You many cities still unwrested,
have you not longed to see the foe?
Oh, would that you had been invested
by him for ten long years though!

Till in despairing lamentation,
till hungering you had felt his hand;
like landscape round their crenellation
he crouches, he whose visitation
outsieges all that would withstand.

Up to your roofs! On every acre
look how unbudgeably he waits,
unweakened by a sole forsaker,
and sends no threat- or promise-maker
to parley with your magistrates.

He is that greatest bastion-breaker
whose work in silence culminates.

50

Home from those soarings too sublime
I once more reappear.
I was a hymn, and God, the rhyme,
still rustles in my ear.

I'm once more silent and resigned,
with little to declare;
my face has now been long inclined
in more availing prayer.
For others I was like a gale,
my cry would shake them so.
I roamed far off where angels sail,
high up, where light begins to pale –
God dwells in darkness, though.

The angels are the final gust
around his topmost stem;
that from his branches they were thrust
is but a dream for them.
Their faith is more in light up there
than in God's sombre might;
it was to them that Lucifer
took his rebellious flight.

In light's realm he has dominance,
and with his forehead he
so meets the void's vast radiance
that he, with heat-scorched countenance,
begs for obscurity.
He's Time's bright god, for whom it wakes
clamouring, and since in pain
he often screams and often breaks
into a laughing strain,
to Time, with faith that nothing shakes,
his bliss and power are plain.

Time's like that bordering fadedness
around a beechen leaf.
Time's merely the resplendent dress
God loosened with relief
when his innate profundity,
tiring of flight, withdrew
to where no wheeling year could see,
until his hair deep-rootedly
through all creation grew.

51

By deeds alone you're manifest,
by hands alone uplit;
each meaning's nothing but the guest
of what it longs to quit.

Each meaning has been made with thought,
one feels the seam, so finely wrought
by spinning humanness:
you yield yourself, though, unbesought
and speed their fleetingness.

Where you may be, I care not; let
me hear you all around.
Your apt evangelist will set
down everything and quite forget
to look whence comes the sound.

With my whole gait I'm constantly
going to you, though; for who
are you if you're unknown to me,
I if unknown to you?

52

My life with selfsame robes and hair is waiting
as the last hour of all the ancient Czars.
My power of speech alone was abdicating;
my realms, though, which I'm quietly consummating,
here in my background have been congregating,
and all my senses are still gossudars.[1]

For them the prayer must ever rise anew:
Build, past all measure build, till horror too
be almost into beauty flowering, –
and every kneeling and confessing-to
(to hide it from all others' view)
let many a golden, many a blue
and motley dome be overtowering.

For what, in surging exaltation,
have church and convent ever seemed
but harps, resounding consolation,
through which, for kings' and maids' elation,
move hands already half-redeemed?

53

And God commanded me to write:

Let not your kings lack cruelty,
that angel love is following,
that arch without which there would spring
no causeway into Time for me.

[1] Gossudars: the Russian word for 'rulers'.

And God commanded me to paint:

It's Time that gives most pain to me:
within its hollowness I've laid
the stigmata, the watchful maid,
rich Death (by whom their price is paid),
the anxious prostitutes' parade,
throned monarchs and insanity.

And God commanded me to build:

For Time's imperial lord am I;
for you, though, just the dimly-viewed
grey partner of your solitude.
And I'm the brow-surmounted eye . . .

Watching through all infinitude
over my shoulder from on high.

54

Divines unnumbered have been diving
into your name's primeval night,
and maids awakening to your light,
and silver-armoured youths arriving
to glitter in you, glorious fight.

Within your colonnades' expanses
poets would meet and come to be
kings of resounding consonances
and mild and deep and masterly.

You're the soft evening hour, bringing
all poets into resemblingness;
darkly you crowd into their singing,
and each, with revelation ringing,
surrounds you with resplendentness.

You myriad wing-like harps are waking
out of your taciturnity.
And your primeval winds are taking
to every thing and every making
the effluence of your majesty.

55

Poets have strewn you out in bits
(a storm through all their stammering passed):
I would re-gather you at last
within the vessel that befits.

Against much wind have I inclined;
a thousand times therein you blew.
I'm bringing everything I find:
you served as beaker for the blind,
the servants kept you deep-confined,
the beggar, though, extended you;
and sometimes in a childish mind
was much that you amounted to.

You see, that I'm a seeker too.

An into fore-held hands retreater,
moving in shepherd loneliness
(avert that glance that can distress
him so, the glance of alien meeter),
who dreams of being your completer
and – of his own completedness.

56

Seldom there's sun in the sobór.[1]
Its walls ascend through figurings
midst of whose trials and triumphings
emerges, like unfolding wings,
the golden, the all-kingly door.

And where its flanking columns soar
ikons obliterate the wall;
and, robed in silver one and all,
jewels mount like voices that adore,
till back upon the crowns they fall
in silence lovelier than before.

[1] *Sobór* is the Russian word for cathedral. The last line of this stanza describes the door in the tall choir-screen, or ikonostasis, called in Russian sometimes the holy and sometimes the kingly door – this last with allusion, not to temporal sovereignty, but to Christos Pantokrator, Christ the King of Kings.

And over them, like midnight's blue,
and pale of countenance,
she you delight in hovers too,
the porteress, the morning dew,
round you like mead with ever-new
upspringing flowers a-glance.

The dome, so crowded with your son,
binds all in its embrace.

Deign from your throne to cast but one
glance at my trembling face.

57

And there, a pilgrim, all alone,
I entered, and, dismayed,
felt you against my brow, you stone.
With candles, seven in all, I made
a circle round your darkling throne,
and in each picture saw your own
brownish birthmark displayed.

And there I stood where beggars go,
ragged and saggy-skinned;
and from their swaying high and low
was ware of you, you wind.
I saw the peasant, bent and slow,
bearded like Joachim,
and as I watched his darkness grow,
and his resemblers, row on row,
as never yet I came to know
your mildness, manifested so
wordless in them and him.

You let Time have the rein,
and get there no tranquillity:
the peasant finds your meaning, he
will pick it up and let it be
and pick it up again.

58

As the watchman has a hut that stands there
in the vineyard for his watch and ward,

I am hut, O Lord, within your hands there,
and am night within your night there, Lord.

Vineyard, pasture, ancient apple-fruited
orchard, every Spring upspringing field,
fig-tree that, in hardest rock enrooted,
countless swelling figs will yield:

fragrance from your rounded boughs is blowing.
And you do not ask if I can see;
fearlessly, in mounting saps upflowing,
all your depths are quietly passing me.

59

God speaks to a man but once, just before he makes him,
then silently out of the night he takes him.
But before each begins, these words he hears,
hears these cloudlike words in his ears:

Outsent by your sensibility,
go wherever your longing's verge may be;
give garb to me.

Grow behind all things burningly,
that the shadows of them, expandedly,
may always conceal me quite.

Take all as it comes, beauty and fright.
Only keep on: feeling's range is unbounded.
Let nothing part you from me.
Near is the land
called 'Life' by humanity.

By its gravity
you'll know you have found it.

Give me your hand.

60

I mingled with oldest monks, the painters and fable-reporters,
peacefully gazeteering and runing of deeds renowned.
And I see you in visions appearing with winds and woodlands and waters,

murmuring on Christendom's farthest bound,
you land beyond clearing.

I want to narrate you, I want to describe what I'm seeing,
not with ochre or gold, but with ink that the apple-bark gives;
not even with pearls can I fetter you onto the leaves,
and the tremblingest image my sense in its searching conceives
you would quite overwhelm with the simple effect of your being.

So the things that are in you, I'll merely name them, without
decoration,
give the names of the monarchs, the oldest, and their generation,
and tell of their battles and deeds at the edge of my pages.

For you are the soil. But as summers to you are the ages,
and of near and remote much alike are the memories you hold,
and whether they're deeplier sowing you or manlier cleaving the
mould,
you merely feel softly bestirred by harvests resembling the old,
and your hearing the stride of neither sower nor reaper engages.

61

Patiently you're enduring the walls, you dark foundation,
and will grant, maybe, to the towns yet an hour's continuation,
and permit another two hours to the churches and convents lone,
and let the souls redeemed for five hours longer groan,
and behold for seven more hours the peasant's preoccupation:–

Till you're once more woodland and water and wildering fen
in that hour of incomprehensible fear
when you claim your unfinished image again
from everything that is here.

Give me a little time: such lovingness I'll bear for things as no one
ever bore,
till all partake of your own spaciousness.
I want but seven days, no more,
seven leaves none's written on before,
seven leaves of loneliness.

He whom you give the book they make will then
over those leaves be evermore delighting.
Unless your hand shall seize him as the pen
for your own writing.

62

I only woke in childhood quite
so absolutely sure,
after each terror and each night,
of seeing you once more.
When my thought's measuring, I know
how deep, how long, how wide:–
you are and are for ever, though,
lapped by Time's quivering tide.

I feel as though in me abound
child, boy and man and more,
and that the ring, in coming round,
is richer than before.

I thank you, deepest power, that still
more softly let me know your will,
as though through walls that twine;
at last my work-day's simplified
and like a sacred face supplied
to these dark hands of mine.

63

Are you aware that once I wholly
wasn't? You say no. Whereon I
feel if I just keep going slowly
I never shall have quite gone by.

I'm more than vision dreamt in vision.
Only what yearns for definition
is like a note and like a day;
in search of freer spaciousnesses
alienly through your hands it presses,
which sadly let it fall away.

Darkness remained with you alone,
and up into the empty clearing
a whole world-history went rearing
in piles of ever-blanker stone.
Is there still one who'll add thereto?
Masses for further masses call there,
stones look as though they'd been let fall there,

and not one has been hewn by you . . .

64

The noisy light through your tall tree-top racing
makes all your things seem shrill and ostentatious,
nor can they find you till the day's gone out.
That tenderness of space, the twilight, placing
on thousand heads a thousand hands, with gracious
blessing can make estrangement grow devout.

For in no more possessive fashion do you
embrace the world than with this gentlest gesture.
From its own heavens you reach the earth up to you
and feel it underneath your flowing vesture.

You've such a quiet manner of existence.
And those who name you with a loud insistence
show they've forgotten your proximity.

Down from your hands, those towering eminences,
to give the tabled law to all our senses
descends, dark-browed, your silent potency.

65

You ever-willing, and your grace became
what all the oldest gestures once were showing.
If any his hands so interlace
that they grow tame
and round some little darkness close:–
he all at once feels you within them growing,
and downward goes,
as in a wind, his face
in shame.

And then to lie on stone he tries to learn
from others and, like them, to rise again,
and rocking you to sleep's his chief concern,
for fear he's made your wakefulness too plain.

For one who feels you shrinks from advertising;
he fears for you, and in his anxiousness
avoids all strangers who'd be recognising:

you are that miracle surprising
lone wanderers in the wilderness.

66

Just an hour from the edge of the day,
and the land awaits all may betide.
Soul, say what you're longing for, say:

Be heath and, O heath, be wide.
Have old, old barrows there, growing
huger and hard to place
when it's moonlight over the flowing
land that has lost its face.
Mould yourself, silence, and mould there
things too (they'll show the resignedness
this their childhood allows).
Be heath, heath, heath, and he might
then come, that oldest of old there,
whom I scarce can distinguish from night,
and bring his gigantic blindness
into my hearkening house.

Sitting in thought I've spied him,
in thought that I'm not beneath;
all things exist inside him,
house and heaven and heath.
Only the songs have flitted
he'll nevermore begin;
those from the ears they befitted
time and the wind drank in –
from the ears of the feeble-witted.

67

And yet: I feel that deep
down within me I keep
each of the songs he's seeking.

With quivering beard, unspeaking,
he longs to be regaining
his self from his melodies.
I come up to his knees:

and back into him are raining
all those songs of his.

SECOND BOOK
THE BOOK OF PILGRIMAGE

Written at Westerwede, near Bremen, 18-25 September 1901. Fair copy for Lou Andreas-Salomé made in Paris, early summer 1903. Revised for the press at Worpswede, 24 April – 16 May 1905. The order of the poems in the book is that of their composition. The numbering of the poems has been introduced by the translator.

Between the composition of the first and second books of *The Book of Hours* Rilke had paid a second and longer visit to Russia, this time with Lou Andreas-Salomé alone, from 7 May to 22 August 1900. Immediately after his return he had accepted an invitation to stay with his friend Heinrich Vogeler in the artists' colony of Worpswede, a remote heath village near Bremen. Here he had met, among others, the sculptress Clara Westhoff, a pupil of Rodin's, who in April 1901 had become his wife, and they had set up house in a peasant's cottage in the neighbouring hamlet of Westerwede.

I

You're not astonished by the storm, –
you've watched the way it brews; –
trees scatter. Their escapings form
long-striding avenues.
You know that he, before whose face
they're fleeing, is your goal,
and him, as from your room you gaze,
your senses now extol.

The summer's weeks were standing still,
the trees' blood climbed; to fall,
you feel has now become its will,
into the cause of all.
The force that in the fruit they bore
appeared so manifest
is growing mysterious once more,
and you're once more a guest.

The summer seemed like your own home,
with all that it contains –
out to your heart you now must roam
as into open plains.
Now the great solitude begins,
the days are getting brief,
the wind out of your senses spins
the world like withered leaf.

A sky still yours is peering through
their branches' emptiness:
earth now and evensong be you,
and land for it to bless.
Be humble now and like a thing,
ripe with reality, –
that He whom all was heralding
may grasp you feelingly.

2

Once more, most High, it's you I'm urging
to hear me through the tempest's roar,
because these depths of mine are surging
with phrases never used before.

In bits to many an adversary
my self's been dealt continually.
I've been the mirth of all the merry
and every drinker's swallowed me.

In many a courtyard I have scrabbled
my self from all rejectedness.
With half a mouth to you I've babbled
in your eternal shapeliness.
How my half-hands I've lifted to you
in nameless agonies of prayer,
that those same eyes that used to view you
I yet might light upon somewhere.

Like some half-burnt-out house I've stood,
where only murderers are sleeping,
till hungry penalties come leaping
and hound them from the neighbourhood;
and like a town beside the sea
which some great pestilence oppresses,
and, like a corpse, hangs heavily
upon the children it distresses.

As strange as one I never knew
I've been to my own self, one who
hurt my young mother by some action
while she bore me,
so that her heart, in its contraction,
knocked on my embryo painfully.

Rebuilt now from each splintering
of misachievement suffered by me,
I'm longing for some cord to tie me,
some intellect to unify me
and look me over like a thing, –
for your heart's mighty hands (oh, may you
extend them as you used to do!) –
I count myself up, God: if you
expend me, I will not gainsay you.

3

I'm still the one who knelt before you
as the monastic brethren do,
the Levite living to adore you,
whom you filled, who discovered you, –

voice of that cloistral contemplation
past which the world goes wavering, –
and you are still that undulation
that surges over everything.

Else there is nothing. Just a sea
whence lands have sometimes been ascending.
There's nothing else but a suspending
of psalms where voice and viol were blending,
and the unpsalmodied is he
before whom everything is bending,
bowed down by his strong radiancy.

Are you, then, all? I but the waning
one that surrenders and uprears?
Am I, then, not the all-containing,
am I not all when I'm complaining,
and are you still the one that hears?

Can you hear other sounds than mine?
Do other voices reach to you, then?
Is there a storm? Well, I'm one too then,
and it's to you my woods incline.

Does some song's sickly, tiny tone, then,
distract you from what I implore? –
Well, I'm one also, hear my own then,
lonely and never heard before.

I'm that same palpitating one still
who sometimes asked who you might be.
After each setting of the sun still
left woundedly and orphanedly,
pale and released from all relations,
by every company contemned,
and all things stand like old foundations
within whose cloisters I've been hemmed.
Then I need you, you all-awarer,
kind neighbour of all sore bestead,
you, my affliction's quiet sharer,
you, God, I need you then like bread.
You may not know what awful longness
nights for the slumberless unfold:
then they are all in utter wrongness,
the child, the maid, the oldest old.

Like those who've forfeited life's lease
they fare where darkest shapes assemble,
and their so pallid hands, a-tremble
at what they're tangled in, resemble
hounds woven into a hunting-piece.
The coming of the past they wait there,
and in the future corpses lie,
a cloaked man beats upon the gate there,
and for expectant ear and eye
no sign of daybreak marks the sky,
no cockcrow lifts the silent weight there.
Like some vast dwelling is the night.
And with the strength their terror's lending
doorways into the walls they're rending, –
and then come corridors unending,
and not one gate that leads to light.

Just so, God, is each night; just so
ther're always some awake, who go
and go, and you they cannot find.
Hark, how with footsteps of the blind
they're darkly straying!
Can you, on stairs that downwards wind,
not hear them praying?
Hark how they fall on the black stones! Their crying
you surely hear; their cry there's no denying.

I seek you, since they keep on passing by
my door. I almost see them. Whom should I
invoke but him whose darkness can outvie
the darkest night, – that uncompeered whose head
lies sleepless, with no lamp beside his bed,
yet fears not, – that deep cogitator who
is still unspoiled by light, of whom I know
because from earth in trees he bursts to view,
and because so
softly from earth as scent he mounts into
my bowed face silently?

4

Eternal, you have shown yourself to me.
I love you like a dear son of my own,
who as a child forsook me long ago,
since destiny had called him to a throne
before which all his lands like vales lie low.

And now I'm left behind like one grown grey,
who cannot comprehend his grown-up son,
and little of those novelties can say
on which his offspring's inclinations run.
I tremble for the fortune that you win,
borne in so many ships across the sea;
I sometimes wish you back again in me,
back in that darkness you grew up within.
I sometimes fear that you no more exist
when I'm too lost in temporality.
Then I read of you: the Evangelist
writes everywhere of your eternity.

I am the Father; more, though, is the Son –
not only all the Father was, but one
the Father was not is in him begun:
he is what yet, and what again, shall be,
he is the womb, he is the sea . . .

5

My prayers are no blasphemies for you:
as though I'd searched old books and read therein
that you and I were thousandfold akin.

There's love I'd like to give you . . . and yet who
can love a father? Doesn't one progress
out of his helpless empty-handedness
with hardness in one's look, as you left me?
Doesn't one place his dead words tenderly
between old pages that one seldom reads?
Doesn't one, as from watershed to plain,
flow from his heart to pleasure and to pain?
Isn't the father only what has been:
years long departed, antiquated ways,
gestures outmoded, dress of other days,
hands that have withered, hair that's lost its sheen?
He may have seemed a hero long ago,
he's now the falling leaf that we outgrow.

6

And like a nightmare seems his anxiousness
and like a stone that voice of his to us, –
we'd gladly, when he speaks, be courteous,
but can't hear more than half of what he says.

The drama played by our relationships
makes too much noise for meanings to be clear,
we only see the working of his lips
from which fall syllables that disappear.
Thus we're far further off from him than far,
if still by love remotely interknit;
not till he has to die upon this star
do we perceive that he has lived on it.

That's what a father is for us. And I
must call you father? Why?
That were to part us further than before.
You are my son. I'll know you evermore,
even as one knows one's own beloved child, and can
still know him when he's grown a man, an aged man.

7

Extinguish both my eyes: I can descry you;
slam my ears to: I can attend to you;
without feet I am able to draw nigh you,
without a mouth I still can conjure you.
Break both my arms away, and with my heart,
as with a hand, I'll capture you again;
arrest my heart's, there'll be my brain's pulsation;
and if you cast a fire into my brain,
I'll carry you on my blood's circulation.[1]

8

And my soul is a woman in your sight:
like Naomi's daughter, Ruth the Moabite.
By day she gleans your cornfield while they reap,
like any maid who heavy service plies.
At eventide, though, to the stream she hies
and bathes and clothes herself in comely wise
and comes to you, round whom all peaceful lies,
and nestles in your foot-clothes as you sleep.

If at midnight you question her, with deep
simplicity she says: I'm Ruth the maid.
Outspread those wings of yours above your maid.
You're the inheritor . . .

[1] Lou Andreas-Salomé has recorded that this poem was written in the summer of 1897, before Rilke had thought of *The Book of Hours*, and addressed to her.

And at your feet my sleeping soul is laid
till daylight, warm with you. And is in truth
a woman in your presence. And like Ruth.

9

You're the inheritor.
Sons are inheritors,
since fathers die perforce.
Sons bloom the seasons through.
You're the inheritor.

10

The greenness you inherit too
of vanished gardens and the silent blue
of ruined skies.
A thousand days' fresh dew,
the many summers and the suns they sing,
the smiles and tears of many a candid Spring,
like some young woman's letters, are your prize.
You're heir to Autumns that, like festal dresses,
the memories of so many poets hide,
and winters too, like lands that none possesses,
seem to be quietly nestling to your side.
Venice, Kasan, and Rome shall come to you,
Florence be yours and Pisa's minster too,
Troisk's convent, and that cloister whose sunk ways
beneath Kiev's hanging gardens in a maze
of darkling corridors go winding round, –
Moscow, with bells like memories, – for sound
shall be yours also: fiddles, horns and voices,
and every song that deep enough rejoices
shall shine upon you like a precious stone.

Only for your sake poets live unknown
and gather rich and rustling images,
and go out and mature through similes
and spend entire life-times so alone . . .
And painters only paint with the intent
that Nature you created transient
may be restored to you immortalised:
all grows eternal. Woman realised
in Monna Lisa her maturity;

no need for one more woman: novelty
can never add new womanhood thereto.
And those who sculpture are like you.
They want eternity. Their hand implores
the stone to be eternal – to be yours!

And it's for you that lovers lay in stores:
they are the poets of a single hour,
they kiss upon a mouth that lacks the power
of language a transforming kiss: devisers
of new voluptuousness; familiarisers
with pain, that source of all developing.
For in their laughter sorrows too they bring,
yearnings, now sleeping, now awakening
to weep within the unfamiliar breast.
They gather up mysteriousness and die
uncomprehendingly, like dying brutes, –
from them, though, some may be at last engendered
in whom their green will turn to ripened fruits;
and you'll inherit all that love thereby
which they with blind instinctiveness surrendered.

Thus every superabundance flows to you.
And as a fountain's upper basin stands
for ever overstreaming, as with strands
of loosened hair, into the lowest bowl,
into your valleys will their fullness roll
whenever things and thoughts are overflowing.

II

I'm only one of your least fashionings,
who watches life from his encloistering,
and, more remote from people than from things,
dares not assess what's happening.
If, though, I've got to face your countenance
and those dark glances which I cannot shun,
do not impute it to sheer arrogance
if I maintain: their lives are lived by none.
Men are but chances, voices, brokennesses,
everydays, worries, many small successes;
even as children muffled and disguised,
mature as mask, as face unexercised.

I often think there must be some unknown
storehouse where all these lives are to be seen
like armours, litters, cradles, in whose clean
interiors no real being's ever been,
and like attires which cannot on their own
stand upright and must languishingly lean
against the massive walls of vaulted stone.

And roaming far afield some evenings,
tired of my garden, I become aware
that every path and every thoroughfare
leads to that arsenal of unlived things.
No tree uprises there, as though the land
had gone to bed, and windowlessly stand,
as round a prison, the high wall's seven rings.
And that wall's iron-fastened gates, prevailing
against all wanters-in, and ranks of railing,
have been constructed by a human hand.

12

And yet, though each is trying to get out
of that gaol self of his that hates and holds,
a mighty marvel in the world unfolds:
all life is being lived, without a doubt.

Who lives it, then? Is it those things, maybe,
lying, like some unextracted melody
a harp's withholding, in the afterglow?
Is it the winds that from the waters blow,
is it the boughs that hail each other so,
is it the flowers from which such perfumes flow,
is it the long, the ageing avenues?
Is it the slow, warm beasts whose toil we use,
is it the birds that soar beyond our view?

Who's living it, this life? God, is it you?

13

You are that veteran whose hair
the sooty flames have singed and tanned;
the inconspicuous giant there,
holding your hammer in your hand.
You are that smith whom songs declare
shall ever at his anvil stand.

You're one that keeps no day of rest,
one concentrated on his labour,
who'd toil to death about a sabre
that did not yet outshine the best.
When mills and saws have ceased their clamour
and tipsy idlers stare and stammer,
the perseverance of your hammer
in every belfry's manifest.

You are the master no survivor
saw serving his apprenticeship;
a here from none knows whence arriver,
of whom now faintlier, now aliver
the rumours go from lip to lip.

14

Rumours surmising you have grown
and doubts that are effacing you.
The idlers and the dreamers too
mistrust those ardours of their own
and want the blood of mountains shown
before they'll pay you reverence.

You, though, bow down your countenance.

You could cut the veins of mountains through
for a judgment sign at a single blow;
the Heathen though
are nothing to you.

You'll neither contend with the crafty crew
nor seek for the light's love in any way;
for the Christians, they
are nothing to you.

With enquirers you've nothing to do.
Gently you view
those that simply endure.

15

All who attempt to find you, tempt you.
And those who find you bind you
to image and gesture.

I, though, want to be knowing
you in the way Earth knows;
ripe with my growing
grows
your realm.

I'll beg from you no idle show
to prove your claim.
Time, I know,
is not the same
as you.

Vouchsafe me no miracle.
Be just to your own decrees,
which grow through the centuries
more visible.

16

When from my window something falls
(however tiny it may be),
how then the law of gravity
leaps like a whirlwind from the sea
on ball or berry instantly
and to the cosmic centre hauls.

Some kindness, ready poised for flight,
guards every thing at every hour,
guards every stone and every flower
and every little child at night.
We only, in our pride, keep straining
out of our well-devised retaining
into some empty liberty,
instead of bowing to wiser power
and climbing upwards like a tree.
Instead of trying to find some station
in that great circuit we are shown,
we join in many a complication, –
and one rejecting all relation
is now unspeakably alone.

He'll have to learn from things more clearly,
and, like a child, begin again,
for they, whom God has loved so dearly,
have never strayed from his domain.

He must re-learn, through constant trying,
to fall and rest in heaviness,
he who had visions of out-flying
the birds in his presumptuousness.

(For even the angels fly no more.
Like ponderous birds are the seraphim
that thoughtfully sit surrounding Him;
no more than ruins of birds, they seem
like penguins as they pine there . . .)

17

You like humility. Those faces
bowed in calm cognisance-of-you.
It's thus a youthful poet paces
the lonely evening avenue.
Thus peasants gravely take their places
around some child whose life has gone, –
it's all the same in all these cases:
something transcendent's going on.

One whose awareness you've just entered
from neighbours and from clocks will flee;
with gaze upon your traces centred
he'll wander bowed and burdenedly;
and only later breathe the air
of Nature, where all things unfold you,
hear meadows whispering you there,
within the singing stars behold you,
till everywhere his heart can hold you
and all is but the cloak you wear.

So new and near and kind you seem
and like a voyage beyond all telling
he takes in silently propelling
vessels along some mighty stream.
The land is spacious, windy, even,
abandoned to a mighty heaven,
and ancient forests domineer.
Small villages keep drawing near,
to fade like pealing bells away,
like yesterday and like to-day
and like all else we've gazed on here.

But on the course this vessel plies
cities continually arise
and, as on beating pinions, wing
towards this festive voyaging.

Sometimes the vessel nears a strand
that, townless, villageless, would seem
to wait for something by the stream, –
for one who has no fatherland . . .
For such men there are waiting there
some little three-horsed carriages
that out into the evening tear
along a road that vanishes.

18

The last, lone dwelling in this hamlet might
well be the last house that the world possessed.

The road, which this small hamlet can't arrest,
goes slowly farther on into the night.

The little hamlet's just a traversing
between two opennesses, shuddering,
a path that leads past houses momently.

Men leave this hamlet for long wandering,
and many perish on the way, maybe.

19

Sometimes at supper one will rise unfed
and go outside and ever onward fare, –
because a church is in the East somewhere.

And all his children hallow him as dead.

And one who dies in his own dwelling-place
dwells on there, dwells in table and in pot,
so that his children leave their home, to trace
throughout the world that church which he forgot.

20

Madness is a watchman just because
he stays awake.
At every hour he laughs and laughs again,
and name on name for Night he tries to make
and calls her 'seven', 'eight-and-twenty', 'ten' . . .

And carries in his hand a triangle,
and, since he's trembling, beats it for a spell
upon the horn he cannot blow, and sings
that same song which to every house he brings.

Their deep sleep-thirstiness the children slake
and hear in dreams that Madness is awake.
The dogs, though, break away from chain and ring
and wander bigly up and down the floors,
and even when he's passed are quivering,
and dread his re-appearance at their doors.

21

Those saints, Lord – something of them you must know?

They felt the thickest of monastic walling
was still too close to laughter and to bawling
and dug themselves into the earth below.

Each with his breathing and his light consumed
the little air his trench had got to give,
forgot the age and features he'd assumed
and like an all-unwindowed house would live
and died no more, as though he'd long been dead.

They read but seldom; all was dry and thin,
as though a frost had bitten every book,
and like their bone-suspended cowls would look
the meaning hanging from each word therein.
They did not greet each other any more
when brushing-by in those black passages;
their unkempt hair was reaching to their knees,
and none could tell whether the one next door
was not dying upright.

In a chamber round,
by fragrant silver lamps illuminated,
those lone companions sometimes congregated
in front of golden doors and contemplated
the dream before them with mistrust profound,
and murmurously their long beards undulated.

Millennial spaciousness had been assumed
by lives which day and night no more divided;
backwards as on a billow they had glided
and been once more maternally enwombed.
Bent in that embryo's posture they'd resumed,
large-headed and small handed, they were sitting,
and did not eat, as though some food befitting
came from the clasping earth wherein they gloomed.

They're shown to thousands now from town and plain,
who come on pilgrimage to this foundation.
Their bodies for three centuries have lain
without experiencing disintegration.
Like soot from smoking light the dark piles high
upon their shrouded forms, so long reposing
and so mysteriously undecomposing,
and their clasped hands, for evermore unclosing,
like mountain ranges on their bosoms lie.

Great Lord, have you forgetfully deferred
to send at last to these insepulchred
the death that should consume them beyond trace
because they dived into the earth's embrace?
Are these, though they resemble those departed,
likest to that which does not pass away?
Is this the life your corpses are imparted,
that life which shall the death of Time outstay?

Have they in your designs some value still?
Are they untransient vessels that you treasure
and, O Immeasurable by any measure,
intend one day with your own blood to fill?

22

You are the future, the great crimson sky
above the plains of everlastingness.

You cockcrow after Time's benightingness,
as dew of morning, mattins, maidenness,
as stranger, mother, death you're passing by.

You're that self-changing shape that's ever stood
in high aloneness out of destiny,
unuttered by lament or jubilee
and all-uncharted as a wildering wood.

You are of everything the innermost
meaning, and keep your final secret sealed;
to others ever otherwise revealed:
to coast as ship and to the ship as coast.

23

You are the Convent of the Stigmata,
with old cathedrals, twenty-two in number,
and fifty churches, having walls of amber
and opal in mosaic patina.
On all that cloister-garth encloses
a stanza of your sound reposes,
right from the *Porta Maxima.*

And seven hundred black-clad nuns
live there in long, low dwelling-places.
One sometimes to the well-head runs,
one stands as though in-spun, and one's
slim figure, as in westering suns,
within the silent alleys paces.

Most never are encountered, though,
and in those silent dwellings rest
as in the fiddle's ailing breast
the tune that no one can out-bow . . .

And round the churches in a ring,
by jasmin yearningly encurled,
are burial places, murmuring,
like quiet stones, about the world.
About that world that's ceased to be,
although against these walls it dashes
and, trimmed in transience and trash, is
ripe for delight or trickery.

It's gone: you *are* eternally.

It flows on, like displayed illumining,
over the inattentive year;
for you, though, for the poet, for evening,
while faces more and more are vanishing,
things in their darksomeness grow clear.

24

The world's kings have grown old, and henceforth heirs to them will be denied.
Their sons in infancy have died,
and their pale daughters have supplied
their sickly crowns to Violence.

These crowns the mob breaks up and spends them,
the world's progressive lord extends them
with fire into machines, until
they grumblingly perform his will,
but little happiness attends them.

The ore is sick for home. And hankers
to quit the coins and wheels that train
it up in all their pettiness.
And out of factories and bankers'
tills it will yet return again
into the opened veininess
of mountains that will close behind it.

25

Grandeur in all things shall be reinstated,
the lands outsmoothed, the waters corrugated,
walls inconspicuous and trees tremendous;
and in the valleys, strong and variegated,
a race of shepherds and of crop-attenders.

No churches, which first capture God and gaol him
like some absconder, and which then bewail him
like some trapped creature panting woundedly, –
houses to every knocker hospitable
and sense of sacrifice immeasurable
in all transactions and in you and me.

No waiting for, no gaze at, things celestial,
just longing to give even Death his due
and humbly train ourselves on the terrestrial
so that his hands shan't find us wholly new.

26

You shall be vast too. Vast beyond the telling
of one who can't postpone his living-span.
In rarity and strangeness far excelling,
as in antiquity, the oldest man.

They'll feel you: as though fragrant exhalations
were rising from some garden's presentness;
and, as an invalid his prized possessions,
will love you with divining tenderness.

All congregating prayer shall discontinue
when that day comes. You're not in company;
and one who's felt you and delighted in you
shall be as though on Earth were only he:
shall be at once cast-out and re-united,
gathered and squandered simultaneously;
a smiler and yet one with tears half-blighted,
small as a house, strong as an empery.

27

There's no peace in the houses, be the cause
that men are bearing onwards someone dying,
or else that one obeying some inner law's
command is taking staff and cloak and hieing
to ask in foreign lands for that outlying
path where he knows you've made a pause.

The roads are never empty of their feet
who youwards as towards that rose are bending
that once in each millennium will expand:
darkly and near-anonymously wending,
and when they reach you they can scarcely stand.

But I have stood and gazed at their procession;
and since then cannot doubt that all winds blow
out of the cloaks that flutter as they go,
and, when these too are lying down, lie low:
so mighty in the plains was their progression.

28

I too would reach you thus: at thresholds strange
gathering, to feed me, a reluctant penny.
And if the ways were wilderingly many,
on with the oldest pilgrims I would range.
With tiny elders I would take my station,
and, when they walked, as in a dream would see
their knees emerging from the undulation
of beards like islands bare of bush and tree.

We'd overtake blind travellers, gazing through
their children as through eyes, and some who tarried
to drink beside the stream, and women wearied,
and women near to childbirth not a few.
I'd feel with all such strange affinity, –
as though in me the women had detected
a friend, the men someone by blood connected,
and all the dogs I saw would come to me.

29

A band of pilgrims, God, I'd like to be,
and thus in long procession go to you,
and be a large part of your deity,
you garth with many a living avenue.
But when I go like this, quite solitary,
who notices? Who sees me going to you?
Who is transported? Who is roused? And who
is turned towards you?
As if nothing new
had happened, they keep laughing on. And I
am glad I'm going in this way; for thereby
I 'scape all notice of the laughing crew.

30

By day you're just a dimly founded
rumour upon the lips of men:
the silence after clocks have sounded
that slowly closes up again.

The more day's ever-faintlier fending
gestures let evening overwhelm,
the more, God, you exist. Your realm
like smoke from every roof's ascending.

31

Morning on pilgrimage. From that hard lying
whereon each like a poisoned victim fell
arise at ringing of the earliest bell
a haggard folk for morning psalmodying
beneath the waxing sunshine's hot descent:

full-bearded men inclining reverently,
children that climb from furs so seriously,
and, wrapped in cloaks and taciturnity,
brown women out of Tiflis and Taschkent.
Christians with gestures which the Moslem taught
are holding out their hands beneath the rills
of fountain-spouts like bowls, like utensils,
in which the water like a soul is caught.

They bow their faces into them and sup,
snatch with the other hand their raiment up
and hold the water close against their breasts,
as though it were a cool and weeping face,
telling of sorrows that on Earth have place.

And all those sorrows now are standing there
with faded eyes; and who they are or were
you know not. Peasants, men of servile station,
merchants, perhaps, who've seen prosperity,
half-hearted monks soon found without vocation,
and thieves that lie in wait for some temptation,
embittered daughters of solicitation,
strayers in forests of insanity: –
like princes, all, who in deep tribulation
have rid themselves of superfluity.
Like sages, all, on whom much knowledge presses,
elect, who've sojourned in the wildernesses,
where God through some strange beast their food supplied;
deep solitaries who through the plains were going,
with many a wind on their dark faces blowing,
constrained by some desire beyond their knowing,
yet thereby marvellously magnified.
Beings transposed from all that they of old did
to mighty organing and choral song,
and kneelers like redeemed ascenders moulded;
banners with portraiture, which long
have lain encabineted and upfolded:

Now they are slowly hanging smooth and new.

And many stand and keep a house in view
where ailing pilgrims are accommodated;
for, but a moment since, a monk came through
its door with habit all askew,
his shadowy face all sickly blue,
and all by demons obfuscated.

As though he'd split in two, with deep prostration
he fell in two bits to the earth below,
which now seemed an extorted exclamation
adhering to his mouth, and just as though
it were but his outsplayed arms' prolongation.

And slowly past his falling seemed to go.

He darted upwards, as if wings secured him,
and his new lightness of sensation lured him
into belief he was a bird in air.
Thinly between his meagre arms suspended,
like some obliquely shifted puppet there,
he was convinced he'd got a mighty pair
of wings, and that the world had long extended
like a far valley down below his feet.
Then all at once he found that he'd descended
and that his journey at the strange retreat
and green sea-bottom of his torment ended.
And was a fish and swam most nimblesome
through waters deep, silent and silver-grey,
saw jelly-fish on coral stems at home,
and saw the tresses of a mermaid sway
through which the water rustled like a comb.
And came ashore and was betrothed to some
dead maid, being chosen for her out of dread
that by the alien pace of maid unwed
the Paradisal meadows should be swept.

He followed her, and carefully he stepped
in circling dance, while in the midst she kept,
and his own arms danced round about him too.
And then his hearing seemed to sense there'd crept
a third unnoticed form into the play,
which seemed to feel this dancing was untrue.
And then he realised: now you must pray,

for this indeed is He the prophets grey,
like a great crown, were given title to.
We hold him now, for whom we've begged each day,
we harvest him who once was sown in clay,
and now, with resting tools, our homeward way,
in long files, as in tunes, we all pursue.
And deeply moved, he made obeisance deep.

That Ancient, though, appeared to be asleep,
and saw it not – and yet his eyes weren't sleeping.

And then he bowed again, with such a sweep
that a great tremor through his limbs went leaping.
That Ancient, though, remained still unaware.

The Monk then seized his sick self by the hair
and beat himself like clothes against a tree.
Still, though, the Ancient scarcely seemed to see.

Then with his own hands on himself he falls,
grasps himself like a sword, and furiously
lashes and hacks therewith, wounds all the walls,
lunging at last into the ground. But He,
that Ancient, still glanced undecidedly.

And then the monk peeled off his habit wildly,
knelt, and outheld it to that form so grey.

And, lo, he came: as to a child, saying mildly:
Do you know *who I am*? And he straightway
did know. And like a fiddle reconciledly
outstretched beneath the Ancient's chin he lay.

32

In riper red the barberries are dressing,
the ageing asters breathe less fragrantly.
One not rich now, at summer's end, will be
for ever waiting, never self-possessing.

One who at this stage cannot close his eyes
sure that a plenitude of imagery
is only waiting nightfall to arise
within his own profound obscurity,
is more extinct than he can realise.

No more awaits him, no more shall be shown,
and all that happens to him is a lie;
even you, my God. And you are like a stone
he's being every day dragged under by.

33

You mustn't be afraid, God. They say *mine*
to all those things whose patience does not fail.
They're like a gale against the branches blowing
and saying '*My* tree'.

They scarcely see
how everything their hands can seize is glowing
so hot that even by its extremity
they could not hold it without getting burnt.

They say *mine*, as with peasants one will dare
to say 'My friend the Prince' in conversation,
when that impressive prince is otherwhere.
They say *mine* of their alien habitation,
while knowing nothing of the master there.
They say *mine* and they speak of properties,
when everything upcloses which they near:
just as a mountebank might have no fear
of calling even sun and lightning his.
That's how they talk: 'My life', they say, 'My wife',
'My dog', 'My child', although they know that life
and wife and dog and child are all alike
remote configurings on which they strike
with outstretched hands in blind obscurity.
True, only great men know this certainly,
and long for eyes. The rest refuse to hear
that all their wretched wandering career
is with no single thing in harmony,
and that, rejected by their property,
owners disowned, they no more have the power
to own a woman than to own a flower,
which leads a life that's foreign to us all.

Ah, God, don't lose your balance. Even he
who loves you and in darkness still can see
and know your face, when like a wavering light
he feels your breath, does not possess you quite.

And if at night by some one you are guessed,
so that you're forced to come into his prayer:
    you're still the guest
    that onwardly will fare.

God, who can hold you? You are just your own,
whom no possessor's hand can be upsetting,
even as the still-maturing, sweeter-getting
vintage belongs but to itself alone.

34

I dig for you, you treasure, in deep night.
For all abundances that I have seen
are poverty, and substitutions slight
for your own beauty, which has not yet *been.*

The way to you's a long one, none the less,
and, since so long untrod, bewildering.
Oh, you are lonely. You are loneliness,
you heart to far-off valleys journeying.

And my two hands, all bloody and unskinned
with digging, I uplift into the wind,
with fingers interbranching like a tree.
I suck you with them out of space to me,
as though you'd been dispersed through that domain
by some self-shattering gesture of impatience,
and now, a vapoured world, fell back again
to this our earth from distant constellations
with all the gentleness of vernal rain.

THIRD BOOK
THE BOOK OF POVERTY AND OF DEATH

Written at Viareggio, 13-20 April 1903. Fair copy for Lou Andreas-Salomé made in Paris, early summer 1903. Revised for the press at Worpswede, 24 April – 16 May 1905. The order of the poems in the book is that of their composition. The numbering of the poems has been introduced by the translator.

Despite the birth of a daughter, Rilke and his wife had soon given up their plan of living the simple life in the cottage at Westerwede, and had resolved that each should seek for conditions more favourable to their artistic developments. In June 1902 Rilke had received a publisher's commission to write a monograph on Rodin, and in the following August he had gone to Paris (which was to remain his headquarters until 1914) in order to study the Master and his works at first hand. The first overwhelming impression made upon him by the grandeurs and miseries of Paris is vividly described in his letters. After a continuous stay of six months he had been compelled to escape for a while to Viareggio, and it was there that he wrote this last part of *The Book of Hours.*

I

Maybe through heavy mountains I am wending,
in hard enveinings, like an ore, alone;
and am so deep that I can see no ending
and no horizon: all in nearness blending,
and all that nearness turned to stone.

Anguish I'm still so far from comprehending,
and that's why this great darkness makes me small;
if, though, it's *You*, get heavy, smash the wall,
that your whole hand on me may be descending,
and you with my whole cry I may befall.

2

You mount that stayed when mountain ranges came, –
slope without shelters, summit without name,
eternal snow in which the stars go lame,
bearer of vales with cyclamen aflame
whence all the fragrances of earth outset;
you, of all mountains mouth and minaret
(whence never yet the evening call has sounded):

Is it in you I'm wending? Am I grounded
in basalt, like some metal still unfound?
I fill your rock-fold, awestruck and astounded,
and feel the hardness of you all around.

Or is it anguish that I now am in,
anguish profound of cities grown too greatly,
in which you've planted me up to the chin?

Would that someone had told you accurately
the madness and the stubbornness therein.
You would arise, you storm of Origin,
and, chaff-like, their dispersal would begin . . .

And if you want to leave me now, speak out –
no mastery in my own mouth I'll retain,
which, wound-like, only wants to close again,
and my hands, like a pair of hounds, remain
crouched at my sides, unstirred by any shout.

Lord, to an hour not mine you now constrain.

3

Make me a watchman of your spaces,
make me a hearkener at stone,
give me a prospect that embraces
the vastness of your oceans lone;
let me accompany your rivers
beyond the cries of bankside-livers
far into night's concording tone.

Send me into your sparsely-peopled
countries, where spacious winds expand,
and where great convents, lofty-steepled,
round unlived lives like garments stand.
There I'll join pilgrims, never leaving,
through any subsequent deceiving,
their forms and voices any more,
and tread, to some blind ancient cleaving,
the way that none has gone before.

4

For, Lord, the great towns, without doubt,
are lost and broken; and the chief's[1]
like flight from flames, – and no relief's
awaiting to relieve her griefs,
and her brief time is running out.

There men are living lives of cark and care
in deep rooms, shy in gesture and in word,
more terror-stricken than a yearling herd;
and outside wakes the Earth your breath has stirred
to life of which these now live unaware.

Children grow up at window-ledges where
at every hour the self-same shadow's falling,
and do not know that outside flowers are calling
to days all full of distance, joy and air,
and must be children, but sad children, there.

Girls are upgrowing there for something distant
and yearning for their childhood's lost repose;
there, though, the thing they've burned for 's non-existent,
and tremblingly their opened petals close.

[1] Paris. It was after his first six months in that city that Rilke escaped to Viareggio and wrote this last part of *The Book of Hours*.

They spend that motherhood they've so awaited
in endless days of back-roomed hiddenness;
to nights of will-less whimpering are fated
and years of uncontending powerlessness.
And somewhere in the dark death-beds are lying,
and thither all their yearnings slowly tend,
and long, as though in fetters, they're a-dying,
and like some beggar-woman's is their end.

5

And people live there, pallid, blooming whitely,
and die of this hard world in dark amaze,
and no one sees the gaping-wide grimace
to which the smiling of a gentle race
is unbelievably distorted nightly.

They grow degraded through the toilsomeness
of spiritlessly serving senseless things,
and withered on them grow their coverings,
and their fine hands soon lose their youthfulness.

The crowd thrusts on, with no consideration
for these that travel less assuredly, –
only shy dogs, that have no habitation,
follow them for a moment, silently.

To hundreds of tormenting hands submitted,
and screamed at by the strokes of every hour,
they anxiously await to be admitted
into the hospitals round which they cower.

In there is Death. Not that which so serenely
they sometimes felt in childhood so akin, –
the little death, as understood therein;
their own is hanging sourly and greenly
like fruit in them whose ripening won't begin.

6

O Lord, grant each his own, his death indeed,
the dying which out of that same life evolves
in which he once had meaning, love, and need.

7

For we are just the leaf and just the skin.
But that great death which each one has within,
that is the fruit around which all revolves.

For its sake girls begin their loveliness,
emerging like a tree out of a lyre,
and boys for its sake long for manliness;
and women from upgrowing youths inspire
telling of else unsharable distress.
For its sake all beheld remains entire,
and transience seems like everlastingness, –
and every fashioner and edifier
grew world around this fruit, and its supplier
with frost and dew and wind and shiningness.
And into it all warmth has percolated,
all ardour that in hearts and brains has been: –
When, though, like birds, your angel flocks migrated,
they soon discovered all the fruits were green.

8

Lord, we are poorer than poor beasts, for they
can die their deaths, if but instinctively,
while we are all going on undyingly.
Send us someone who'll learn devotedly
to train life on espaliers which May
will then begin around more seasonably.

For what in dying so alienly shakes us
is that it's not our death, but one that takes us
only because we've not matured our own;
therefore there comes a storm and down we're blown.

We stand within your garden year by year
as trees from which sweet death's desiderated;
by harvest, though, we're superannuated,
and, like those women you have castigated,
closed, useless and unfruitful we appear.

Or is this arrogance of mine unjust?
Are the trees better? Are we merely lust
and sex and womb of women without caution?

We with Eternity have played the whore,
and, when our time has come, the dead abortion
of our own death is all we labour for;
that twisted, miserable embryo
which (as in terror of some dread surprise)
has covered with its hands its budding eyes,
and on whose bulging brow even now protrude
its fears of all the suffering still to be, –
and all of us, like prostitutes, conclude
in child-bed spasms and hysterotomy.

9

Make someone glorious, Lord, make someone great,
build a fine womb for him, and, like a gate
within a flaxen forest of young hair,
erect its entrance, and, yourself advancing
through the unmentioned member, lead those prancing
cavalry in, those hosts all whitely glancing,
those myriad seeds that are assembled there.

And grant a night that to mankind here brings
more than all human depths have quivered at;
make it a night all full of flowering things,
and sweeter than syringa's perfumings,
and more sleep-rocking than your wind's own wings,
and more rejoicing than Jehosaphat.

And grant him a long period of gestation,
set him, in growing garments, out of range,
bestow upon him a star's isolation,
lest any eye bewitch with admiration
when meltingly his features start to change.

Renew him with some purer sustenance,
with dew, with dishes for which nothing dies,
with that same life which, soft as suppliance
and warm as breathing, from the fields will rise.

Make him re-know his childhood, make him see
the mystery and the marvel, till he hears
the saga of those first divining years
in all its vastly rich obscurity.

And thus command him wait his hour and bear,
when it shall come upon him, Death the Lord:
lone-murmuring like some great garden there
and one convened from far abroad.

10

Let the last sign for *us* be now availing,
come in the crown of all your kinglihood,
and grant us (after woman's long travailing)
mankind's more real motherhood.
Not for that dream's fulfilment to betide us
of a god-bearing woman is our prayer, –
that needed, that death-bearing man, provide us,
and on to him through all the legions guide us
of persecutors that will gather there.
For, oh, to me his enemies grow clear,
and they exceed all time's mendaciousness, –
and in the land of laughers he'll appear
and shall be called a dreamer; for a seer
seems among drunkards lost in dreaminess.

Establish him within your favour, though,
implant him in your ancient splendidness;
and as this covenant's dancer let me go,
make me the new *Messiad*'s mouth, the so
loud cryer in the wilderness.

11

I'll praise him. Like the trumpets going before
an army, I'll uplift those cries of mine.
Louder than all the seas my blood shall roar,
my words be sweet and make men long therefor,
and yet not cause bewilderment like wine.

And in those vernal nights, when something brings
some few companions to remain with me,
I'll blossom then within my lyre-strings
as softly as oncoming Northern Springs,
around each leaf so late and anxiously.

For in my growing voice there's been a fission
into a crying and a fragrantness:

the one for him far-off would make provision,
the other must continue as the vision
and bliss and angel of my loneliness.

12

Make both those voices my companions still,
should you re-scatter me to towns and care.
With them the fury of the years I'll bear,
and out of my interior sound prepare
a bed for you at every place you will.

13

They're false, are those great cities; stultifying
both day and night, both animal and child;
their silence lies, with noises they are lying
and with those things that are so reconciled.

Nothing of all that spacious, real on-going
that round you, Great Becomer, is astir
goes on in them. Those winds of yours, their blowing
falls into alleys that reverse its flowing,
their roaring, through continual to-and-froing,
gets ever angrier and exciteder.

They come to walks and beds where flowers are growing: -

14

For there are gardens too, – by monarchs planted,
who took their pleasure for some fleeting hours
there with young women, who would gather flowers
to match their laughter's sound that so enchanted.
They kept those weary parks in wakefulness;
they whispered like soft breezes in the bushes,
they glistened in their furs and in their plushes,
and like a streamlet's were the silken rushes
on gravel pathways of their morning dress.

And now all gardens carry their impress –
and, with no end in view, will silently
take in these unfamiliar Springs their share,
and slowly burn, with Autumn flames aflare,
upon their branches' mighty gridiron there,

that seems, with myriad monograms, some rare
design of black wrought-iron artistry.

And, dazzlingly from all points manifest
(like pale sky with diffused illumination),
by weight of fading portraiture possessed
as by some deep interior contemplation,
the palace, in unfestal resignation,
stands taciturn and patient as a guest.

15

Live palaces would also meet my eye,
flaunting themselves like those fine birds from which
no sound emerges but a hideous cry.
Many are rich and want to sit on high, –
these rich, though, are not really rich.

Not like the rulers of your shepherd-trains,
those old beclouders of the clear, green plains,
who with their fleecy multitudes would ply
through those expanses like a morning sky.
And when they had encamped, and every pealing
order had died into night's youthfulness,
it seemed as though another soul were feeling
in their flat nomad-land for consciousness: –
the dusky ridges of humped camels kneeling
surrounded it with mountain splendidness.

And far behind their line of march would hang
for ten days long their herded cattle's tang,
heavy and warm and wind-resistingly.
And as at bright-lit bridals flowingly
rich vintages throughout the night regale,
milk came from their she-asses pail on pail.

Not like those desert sheikhs who spent the night in
sleep on a faded carpet and who yet
were always having silver combs inset
with rubies for the mares they took delight in.

Not like those princes whom such gold as could
invent no perfume never fascinated,
and whose proud lives were so consociated
with amber, almond-oil and sandalwood.

Not like that Eastern Gossudar,[1] with share
of godlike honour by whole kingdoms shown,
who none the less with desolated hair
beat his old brow against the flooring stone
and wept, because not one hour for his own
those regal paradises had to spare.

Not like old harbour-cities' signory,
trying to surpass their own reality
with portraits unsurpassably sublime,
and then those portraits too with their own time;
those figures that like parchment-sheets would fold
into their civic robes of silk and gold
and breathe with their white temples, silently . . .

Those were the rich who forced life to attain
such breadth and warmth and full maturity.
Gone, though, for ever is such rich men's reign,
and none will beg it back from you again:
let but the poor regain their poverty.

16

They are not poor. They're only not-rich, living
without a will, without a world achieved;
marked with the marks of ultimate misgiving
and utterly disfigured and disleaved.

On them the cities' dust has all collected,
they are the dump all refuse settles on.
They're shunned with loathing like a bed infected;
like broken pots, like skeletons, rejected,
like calendars whose year's already gone, –
and yet, were this your Earth enough dejected,
all these upon a rosary chain collected
it would be wearing for a talisman.

For they are purer than the purest stone
and like blind beasts in earliest infancy
and simple and so endlessly your own
and wish for nothing and need this alone:

leave to be poor as they have come to be.

[1] Gossudar: the Russian word for 'ruler'.

17

For poverty's a great shine from within . . .

18

You're the poor man, the utterly denuded,
you are the stone for which no place was found,
you are that leper whom the town excluded
before whose gates he rattles on his round.

For, like the wind, you're wholly unpossessive,
and all your fame scarce hides your nakedness;
an orphan's week-day wear is more impressive
and something he seems really to possess.

You're poor as that seed's strength but recently
sprung in a girl who'd not be seen a mother
and, pressing in her thighs, attempts to smother
the earliest breathing of her pregnancy.

And you're as poor as is the vernal rain
that falls on city roofs so blissfully,
and as some wish that prisoners retain
within their cells, unrealisably.
And as the sick, who, turning yet again,
are happy; as the flowers in railroad gravel,
so sadly poor in passing gusts of travel;
and poor as is the hand we weep into . . .

And how can even freezing birds compare
with you, or dogs unfed the livelong day,
and what, compared with you, is the despair
of sad dumb creatures fastened in somewhere
by some forgetter who has gone away?

And what are all the paupers, nightly filling
the shelters, when we think what you survive?
They're only little stones, not mills, though milling
a little bread to keep themselves alive.

You've reached a deeper depth of desolation,
the beggar with the hidden countenance;
you're poverty's great consummation,
the everlasting transmutation
of gold into the sun's own radiance.

Beyond this world's accommodation,
in silent homelessness you stand:
too great and hard for all that men require.
You howl in storms. You're like a lyre
on which is shattered every playing hand.

19

You that know all things with a knowledge founded
in poverty and poverty's excess,
oh, let the poor no longer be outhounded
and trampled down into vexatiousness.
The others look as though they'd been unplanted,
but these are flower-like in their rootedness;
fragrance like lemon-thyme they have been granted,
and tender is their leaves' serratedness.

20

Consider them and see what they resemble:
they'll stir as though exposed to wind, and then,
like something held in hands, repose again.
And in their eyes those shadows will assemble
with which the sunny meadows gravely tremble
beneath a sudden shower of summer rain.

21

They almost look like things, so quiet they are.
And if they're asked to come into the room,
they seem like friends returning from afar,
and merge into the small particular,
and like some peaceful implement will loom.

They're like custodians guarding shrouded cases
of treasure which they own eyes never knew,
they're carried by the depths like a canoe,
and not the linen on the bleaching-places
is so unfolded and exposed to view.

22

And look, now, at the life their footing leads:
like that of beasts, in endless intrication
with every path; full of association
with stone and snow and gentle suspiration
of cooling breezes over youthful meads.

They suffer pain from that immense provision
of pain whence men have fallen to petty woe;
the grass's balsam and the stone's incision
they take as destiny, without misprision,
and move as on your dearest field of vision
and as a player's hands through strings will go.

23

And their hands are like women's hands, and such
as serve for every sort of mothering;
as cheerful as the building birds in Spring, –
warm in their clasp and tranquil in their cling,
and like a drinking-vessel to the touch.

24

Their mouths are like a statue's mouth, which, though
it never spoke, breathed, kissed, yet long ago,
from some existence briefly tarrying,
received all that through sage infashioning:
we feel there's nothing that it doesn't know,
and yet it's only symbol, stone, and thing . . .

25

And their voice comes to us so distantly,
and before sunrise has been wont to waken,
and in great forests has been long forsaken,
has talked in sleep with Daniel, and has taken
vibrations from the contemplated sea.

26

And sleeping, they seem given back to all
that loans them out so inconspicuously:
bestowed, like bread in famines, far and wide
on many a mid-night and red morning-tide,
and like a gentle rain, all full of fall
into some youthful dark's fertility.

There's not one scar of name in evidence
upon their bodies, germinatingly
bedded like seeds of that same seed from whence
you shall upspring through all eternity.

27

And now their bodies are like bridegrooms: look,
they flow in their recumbence like a brook,
and live as lovely as the loveliest thing,
so passionate and so astonishing.
Within their slimness there is concentrating
much female weakness and timidity;
their sex is strong, though, like a dragon, waiting
asleep there in the vale of privacy.

28

For, look: they're meant for living and increasing,
and shall elude all time's imperiousness
and grow like woodland berries without ceasing,
hiding the ground with their deliciousness.

For blest are those that never have retreated,
but stood there still and roofless in the rain;
by all the final harvests they'll be greeted,
and myriad fullness shall their fruit contain.

Their term shall last beyond all termination,
beyond the realms whose meaning has expired;
like rested hands shall be their exaltation
when all the hands of every other station
and every nation shall be tired.

29

Only redeem them from the guiltiness
of towns, where all is angry and confused,
and where, in days of mere tumultuousness,
they wither, with their patientness abused.

Has, then, the Earth for them no vacancy?
Whom will the wind seek? Who shall drink the stream?
Can no reflection in the landscape-dream
of ponds for door and threshold still find place?
They need no more than such a little space,
on which they're all-sufficient like a tree.

30

The poor man's house is like an altar-shrine,
wherein the Everlasting turns to food,
and, when the evening comes, will re-conclude
its spacious orbit and retire to brood,
long-echoingly, in its own self divine.

The poor man's house is like an altar-shrine.

The poor man's house is like the childish hand,
which, leaving all that grown-ups love so well,
takes but a beetle with quaint mandible,
the round stone that has felt the streamlet's swell,
the trickling sand, the sounding mussel-shell:
hand like a mounted balance, that will tell
the weight of what is scarce perceptible
with scales that come, long-swaying, to a stand.

The poor man's house is like the childish hand.

And, oh, the poor man's house is like the Earth:
that splinter from some future crystal ball,
now light, now sombre in its fleeing fall;
poor as warm poverty of cattle-stall, –
and yet ther're certain evenings when it's all
and from it all the stars will take their birth.

31

The cities, though, want only what will speed them,
and drag all with them on their headlong course.
They smash the beasts like rotten wood to feed them
and use whole nations up without remorse.

Their people serve some culture's domination
and fall afar from measure and from poise,
and give the name of progress to gyration,
and travel with a growing acceleration,
and have a harlot's soul and scintillation,
and louder rings their glass and metal noise.

Some phantom seems to lure them every hour,
they can no longer be themselves at all;
their money grows, engrosses all their power,
and swells to east wind size, and they are small
and vacuous and wait there for the call
of wine and every poisonous distillation
to rouse them to some transient occupation.

32

And your own poor groan under these devices,
and bear the weight of all that they survey,
and hotly shiver as in fever-crises,
and, flung from every dwelling that entices,
like ghosts of strangers through the night will stray;
they're burdened with the whole abomination,
like something rotting in the sun bespat, –
by anything, a harlot's titivation,
a vehicle, a street-lamp, shouted at.

And if some mouth can bring them mitigation,
oh, set it working with your might thereat!

33

Oh, where is he who could with one strong stride
from ownership to poverty repair,
and doffed his clothing in the market-square
and went unclad before the bishop's pride?

He, passing all in love and fervency,
who came and sojourned like a youthful year;
your nightingales' brown-vestured brother, he
in whom such wonder and such ecstasy
and such content to be on earth were clear.

For he was quite unlike those weary others
who keep on growing ever joylesser;
with little flowers as with little brothers
he paced along the meadows to confer.
Spoke of himself and of his application
of that self to provide a joy for each;
and his heart's brightness knew no limitation,
that heart which nothing was too small to reach.
From light to ever more illumination
he passed; his cell was bathed in cheerfulness.
That smile of his began its germination
and had its childhood and initiation
and ripened like a young girl's youthfulness.

And when he sang, the long-relinquished yester
and all-forgotten came and re-occurred;
and silence grew and grew in every nester,
save that the crying hearts were manifester
in sisters whom his bridegroom-touch bestirred.

Then, though, the pollen of his song was lifted
out of his red mouth inconspicuously,
and dreamingly to those that loved him drifted,
and through their open calyxes was sifted
in slow descendance to the ovary.

And him, the all-unblemished, each encloses,
like her own soul, within her body there.
And their closed eyelids were like leaves of roses,
and filled with nights of loving was their hair.

And him both great and little were receiving.
To many creatures there came cherubim,
as butterflies of brilliance past believing,
to tell them that their mates would be conceiving:
for he was clear to all perceiving,
and all had fruitfulness from him.

And when, so nameless-lightly, he lay dying,
he was distributed; his seed ran free

in brooks; in trees his seed was psalmodying
and gazed at him from flowers tranquilly.
He lay and sang. And left the sisters crying
round their beloved consort bitterly.

34

Oh, where has the clear sound of him departed?
Why do they not, the poor, the patient-hearted,
feel from afar his youth and joyancy?

Why in their twilight has he not outstarted,
    great evening star of poverty?

FROM

THE BOOK OF IMAGES

First Edition published July 1902, containing poems written between 1898 and 1901
Second Edition published December 1906, containing additional poems written between 1902 and 1906

GIRLS

I

Others on lengthy wanderings
to the darksome poets are forced to fare;
must always be asking a traveller
if he's not seen one singing there
or laying his hands on strings.
Only girls will never ask
what bridge leads to images;
will smile merely, brightlier than necklaces
of pearl against silver bowls unfurled.

All doors from their lives are entrances
into a poet
and into the world.

Worpswede, 29 September 1900

II

What you are within your lone-existent
selves, you teach some poets to express;
and they learn to live through you, so distant,
as the evenings, through the great persistent
stars, get used to everlastingness.

None may ever lawfully surrender,
should he seek the woman in the maid;
for his mind can only read or render
you as maids: the feeling in your tender
wrists would snap beneath brocade.

Leave him in his garden, so secluded,
where like angels he would welcome you
on those paths he daily wandered through,
by those waiting seats where shadows brooded;
in there where the lute hung leave him too.

Go . . . it's getting dark. His feeling reaches
for your voices and your forms no more.
Empty pathways stretching far before
he loves, and no white under sombre beeches,
and the room with the excluding door.
. . . Now your voices mingle from afar
with the voices he'd be fain forgetting,
and his tender memories with regretting
that so many see you where you are.

Worpswede, 9 or 10 September 1900

The 'girls' who inspired these two poems were the painter Paula Becker, later to be commemorated in the Requiem *For a Friend*, and the sculptress Clara Westhoff, whom Rilke married in April 1901.

WOMAN IN LOVE

Yes, I'm longing for you. Self-succumbing,
to outslip my own hand I begin,
with no hope of ever overcoming
what to me, as from your side, is coming,
grave and undeterred and unakin.

. . . in those days: I was so undistracted,
untold, undivulged by anything;
like a stone's my silence was protracted
over which a brook runs murmuring.

Now, though, in these weeks when Spring has woken,
by a something I've been slowly broken
from the dark unconscious year away.
Through some power my poor warm life is going
into hands of one not even knowing
what I still was only yesterday.

Undated, first printed 1906

THE SILENCE

Listen, I'm lifting them, I, your lover,
my hands – hark: a russeling . . .
What solitary gestures might not discover
themselves overheard by many a thing?

Listen, beloved, my eyes I'm closing,
and that too's a rustle that you can hear;
listen, beloved, now they're unclosing . . .
. . . Why, though, are you not here?

The imprint of all my tiniest motions
stays visible within this silken silentness;
indestructibly even the slightest emotions
into the outstretched curtain of distance press.
Stars on the breaths I draw are setting and rising
incessantly.
Up-stealing fragrances at my lips are drinking,
and the wrists I am recognising
of angels, distantly.
You only, of whom I'm thinking,
I do not see.

c. 1900-1901

MUSIC

What are you playing, boy? Through the gardens there,
like footsteps, whispering commands were going.
What are you playing? Your soul, look, all unknowing,
is now in reeds of Syrinx prisoner.

Why lure her thus? That sound is like a prison,
where yearningly she pines herself away.
Strong is your life, but stronger what you play,
to clasp your longing sobbingly uprisen.

Give her, poor soul, a pause, till she's regained her
place in the fluctuant and many-sided,
where waxing, widely, wisely she abided
before that tender playing of yours constrained her.

Her flutterings are already showing some sign
of weariness: you'll squander her elation,
dreamer, till song-sawn pinions will decline
to carry her across these walls of mine
when I shall summon her to delectation.

Berlin-Schmargendorf, 24 July 1899

THE ANGELS

They all have mouths so tired, tired
and lucent souls without a seam.
And something guiltily desired
goes sometimes fluttering through their dream.

All so resemblingly reposing
there in God's gardens silently,
like many pauses interposing
within his might and melody.

Save that when each with wings engages
the waiting air, a wind begins
as strong as though beyond the ages
God's sculptor-fingers turned the pages
in the dark book of origins.

Berlin-Schmargendorf, 22 July 1899

CHILDHOOD

The school's long stream of time and tediousness
winds slowly on, through torpor, through dismay.
O loneliness, O time that creeps away . . .
Then out at last: the streets ring loud and gay,
and in the big white squares the fountains play,
and in the parks the world seems measureless. –
And to pass through it all in children's dress,
with others, but quite otherwise than they: –
O wondrous time, O time that fleets away,
O loneliness!

And out into it all to gaze and gaze:
men, women, women, men in blacks and greys,
and children, brightly dressed, but differently;
and here a house, and there a dog, maybe,
and fear and trust changing in subtle ways: –
O grief uncaused, O dream, O dark amaze,
O still-unsounded sea!

And then with bat and ball and hoop to playing
in parks where the bright colours softly fade,

brushing against the grown-ups without staying
when ball or hoop their alien walks invade;
but when the twilight comes, with little, swaying
footsteps going home with unrejected aid: –
O thoughts that fade into the darkness, straying
alone, afraid!

And hours on end by the grey pond-side kneeling
with little sailing-boat and elbows bare;
forgetting it, because one like it's stealing
below the ripples, but with sails more fair;
and, having still to spare, to share some feeling
with the small sinking face caught sight of there: –
Childhood! Winged likenesses half-guessed at, wheeling,
oh, where, oh, where?

Meudon-Val Fleury, winter 1905-6

FROM A CHILDHOOD

Rich darkness round the room was streaming
where the boy sat, quite hidden in himself.
His mother came, a dream within his dreaming,
and a glass quivered on a silent shelf.
Feeling the room had given her away,
she kissed him – 'So it's you' – and let him be . . .
Then both glanced at the piano timidly,
for often of an evening she would play,
and had a song that drew him deep and clung.

He sat there very still. His large gaze hung
upon her hand which, under bright rings bowing,
as though with labour through a snow-drift ploughing,
over the white keys softly swung.

Berlin-Schmargendorf, 21 March 1900

THE BOY

I'd like, above all, to be one of those
who drive with wild black horses through the night,
torches like hair uplifted in affright
when the great wind of their wild hunting blows.

I'd like to stand in front as in a boat,
tall, like a long floating flag unrolled.
And dark, but with a helmet made of gold,
restlessly flashing. And behind to ride
ten other looming figures side by side,
with helmets matching mine for changefulness,
now clear as glass, now old and lustreless.
And one to stand by me and blow us space
with the brass trumpet that can blaze and blare,
blowing a black solitude through which we tear
like dreams that speed too fast to leave a trace.
Houses behind us fall upon their knees,
alleys cringe crookedly before our train,
squares break in flight: we summon and we seize:
we ride, and our great horses rush like rain.

(Probably) Paris, winter 1902-3

KNIGHT

The knight arrayed in his steel-dark mail
rides out to the rustling world.

And without are all things: day and dale,
friend and foe and the hall-mates' hail,
May and the maid and the grove and the grail,
and banners of God, who cannot fail,
in every street unfurled.

But the knight is riding in armour whereunder,
behind the darkest enringing,
crouches Death, who must wonder and wonder:
When will the sword be springing
open this iron embrace,
strange sword enfranchising
me from the hiding-place
where dolefully day by day
I am buckled by cramp and sting,
that at last I may have some space
and play
and sing.

Berlin-Schmargendorf, shortly before 14 July 1899

THE LAST SUPPER

Amazed, bewildered, they are gathered round him,
whose pondered resolution comes to rest,
withdrawing him from all the ties that bound him –
a stranger gliding by with thoughts unguessed.
He feels that former loneliness draw near
in which the deep command was comprehended;
again the olive slope shall be ascended,
and those that love him shall depart in fear.

To the last meal of all they've been invited;
and (as a shot will scare some new-alighted
flock from the wheat) their feeding hands, affrighted
from the dealt portions by his prophecy,
fly up to him and flutter in despair
round the round table to escape. But he,
like the still twilight hour, is everywhere.

Paris, 19 June 1903

Inspired by Leonardo da Vinci's famous fresco in the refectory of Santa Maria delle Grazie at Milan.

TO BE SAID FOR FALLING ASLEEP

I'd like to sing someone asleep now,
be with someone and sitting by.
I'd like to rock you asleep now,
and at sleeping and waking be nigh.
I'd like next day to be solely aware
in the house that the night was cold;
and within and without to be hearkening there,
to you, to the world, to the wold.
The clocks are calling each other with blows,
to the bottom of time one can see.
And below there an unknown man still goes,
and a dog barks wakefully.
Then all grows silent. I've laid them so
wide-open on you, these eyes;
and they hold you gently and let you go
when sounds in the dark arise.

Berlin-Schmargendorf, 14 November 1900

PEOPLE AT NIGHT

Nights were not made with the many in view.
Night from your neighbour divorces you,
and his absence you should not refuse.
And if at night you illumine a place
in order to gaze at a human face,
you need to consider: whose.

It disfigures them fearfully, that light
that from peoples' faces drips;
and, if they have gathered together at night,
a wavering world assails your sight
without any relationships.
Upon their foreheads the yellow shine
has driven all thoughts away;
within their glasses flares the wine,
and from their hands will sway
the ponderous gesturing whereby
they help their speeches through;
and they keep on saying *I* and *I*,
and mean they know not who.

Berlin-Schmargendorf, 25 November 1899

THE NEIGHBOUR

Unknown violin, are you following me?
In how many far cities your solitary
night must have talked to my own!
Do hundreds play you? Does one alone?

Are there in all great cities livers
who, had it not been for you,
would already have ended themselves in the rivers?
And why must I always be there too?

Why am I evermore the neighbour
of those that timidly force you to sing
and to say: This life is a heavier labour
than the heaviness of everything?

(Probably) Paris, 1902-3

PONT DU CARROUSEL

That blind man standing by the parapet,
grey as some nameless empire's boundary stone,
he is perhaps that something unbeknown
to which the planetary clock is set,
the silent centre of the starry ways;
for all around him strives and struts and strays.

He keeps his movelessly inerrant station
where manifold perplexing crossways go;
the sombre entrance to the world below
among a superficial generation.

(Probably) Paris, 1902-3

THE SOLITARY

Like one who's sailed an unfamiliar sea
I move among these all so much at home;
upon their tables stands their day's whole sum,
but my horizon's full of fantasy.

A world may reach into my gaze, revealing
cold planetary space on every side;
they hate to see a solitary feeling,
and all their words have long been occupied.

The things I brought with me from where I came
look strange indeed compared with what these own: –
in their great homeland they are beasts full-grown,
here, though, they have to hold their breath for shame.

Viareggio, 2 April 1903

THE ASHANTIS

JARDIN D'ACCLIMATATION

No caught glimpse into untroddennesses,
no sensation of brown women, all
dancing out of their descending dresses.

No wild foreign music to recall.
No songs which the blood had liberated,
and no blood upcrying prophetical.

No brown maidens who luxuriated
velvetly in tropic weariness;
no eyes that like weapons scintillated,

only mouths relaxed in laughingness.
And a singular accommodation
to the white men's overweeningness.

And I gazed there in such desolation.

Oh, the animals are so much truer,
pacing in a cage from end to end,
unconforming to the drift of newer,
foreign things they do not comprehend;
burning quietly out like silent fire
into their own embers, they disown
all the new adventure and retire
into their own mighty blood, alone.

(Probably) Paris, 1902-3

AUTUMN DAY

Lord, it is time. The summer was so great.
Impose upon the sundials now your shadows
and round the meadows let the winds rotate.

Command the last fruits to incarnadine;
vouchsafe, to urge them on into completeness,
yet two more south-like days; and that last sweetness,
inveigle it into the heavy vine.

He'll not build now, who has no house awaiting.
Who's now alone, for long will so remain:
sit late, read, write long letters, and again
return to restlessly perambulating
the avenues of parks when leaves downrain.

Paris, 21 September 1902

AUTUMN

The leaves are falling, falling as from far,
as though above were withering farthest gardens;
they fall with a denying attitude.

And night by night, down into solitude,
the heavy earth falls far from every star.

We are all falling. This hand's falling too –
all have this falling-sickness none withstands.

And yet there's One whose gently-holding hands
this universal falling can't fall through.

Paris, 11 September 1902

PROGRESS

Again my deep life's murmuring more clearly,
as though in broader banks it now were flowing.
More and more kin to me all things are growing
and every image gazed upon more nearly.
I feel the Never-Namable more dearly:
with bird-like senses from the trees upspringing,
into the windy skies I keep emerging,
and down to broken day of ponds, submerging
as though on fishes' backs, my feeling goes.

Worpswede, 27 September 1900

PRESENTIMENT

I'm like a flag surrounded by distance.
Divining the coming winds, I must share their existence,
whereof things below reveal as yet no traces:
doors are still closing softly and quiet are the fire-places;
windows are not yet shaking, and dust lies heavily.

But I can already sense the storm, and surge like the sea.
And spread myself out and into myself downfall
and hurtle myself away and am all
alone in the great storm.

(Perhaps) Sweden, autumn 1904; first printed 1906

EVENING IN SKÅNE

The park stands high. And from its glimmering,
as from a house, I now am wandering
out into plain and evening. Into wind,

that self-same wind the clouds are also feeling,
the shining rivers, and the slowly wheeling
sails of those mills that on the sky-line stand.
I too am now a thing within His hand,
smallest beneath this sky. – But, looked into,

Is that *one* sky?
That blissfully light blue,
to which throng ever-purer cloud-formations;
and, down below, whiteness in all gradations;
and, up above, that thin grand grey outspun,
warmly, as painted over crimson, gleaming;
and, over all, this quiet outstreaming
of setting sun.

Amazing edifice,
self-moved and by itself preserved from falling,
what shapes, what giant wings, what peaks it's calling,
before the firstling stars, into existence!
Then, suddenly: A gate into such distance
as maybe only birds know what it is . . .

Jonsered near Göteborg, c. 1 November 1904

EVENING

The evening's slowly changing the attire
to which a line of ancient trees attends;
and from your gaze the regions both retire,
one faring heavenwards while one descends;

and leave you there, to neither quite pertaining,
not quite so dark as silent house, nor quite
so sure a witness to the never-waning
as what becomes a climbing star each night –

and leave you (to unravel what you are)
your timorous, giant-like, maturing being,
which, now incircumscribed and now inseeing,
is varyingly within you stone and star.

(Perhaps) Sweden, autumn 1904; first printed 1906

ANNUNCIATION

(WORDS OF THE ANGEL)

You are not nearer God than we;
he's far from everyone.
And yet your hands most wonderfully
reveal his benison.
From woman's sleeves none ever grew
so ripe, so shimmeringly:
I am the day, I am the dew,
you, Lady, are the Tree.

Pardon, now my long journey's done,
I had forgot to say
what he who sat as in the sun,
grand in his gold array,
told me to tell you, pensive one
(space has bewildered me).
I am the start of what's begun,
you, Lady, are the Tree.

I spread my wings out wide and rose,
the space around grew less;
your little house quite overflows
with my abundant dress.
But still you keep your solitude
and hardly notice me:
I'm but a breeze within the wood,
you, Lady, are the Tree.

The angels tremble in their choir,
grow pale, and separate:
never were longing and desire
so vague and yet so great.
Something perhaps is going to be
that you perceived in dream.
Hail to you! for my soul can see
that you are ripe and teem.
You lofty gate, that any day
may open for our good:
you ear my longing songs assay,
my word – I know now – lost its way
in you as in a wood.

And thus your last dream was designed
to be fulfilled by me.
God looked at me: he made me blind . . .

You, Lady, are the Tree.

Berlin-Schmargendorf, 21 July 1899

CHARLES THE TWELFTH OF SWEDEN RIDING IN THE UKRAINE

Kings whom legends praise
are like mountains at evening. Daze
eyes that gaze thitherward.
Their girdles and golden chains
and burdensome mantle-trains
with lands and lives they afford.
With their rich-gloved hands remains,
naked and slim, the sword.

A young king out of the North was there
in the Ukraine defeated.
He hated Spring-time and women's hair
and harps and what they repeated.
The horse he rode upon was grey,
and greyly gazed his eyes,
that never had wished with brighter ray
from a woman's feet to rise.
Not one found favour in his sight,
to kiss him none had gained the right;
and, when his anger flared,
he'd rend a pearl-comb in despite
from even the loveliest-haired.
And, when some sadness overcame,
he'd sometimes make a maiden tame,
and search out, by whose ring she came,
and whom she'd given hers,
and hunted to death the man she'd name
with a hundred harriers.

And he forsook his grey, grey land,
where reigned such silentness,
and rode against what made a stand,
and fought for perilousness,
till marvel conquered him instead:
his hand, as it were dreaming, sped

from corsleted to corsleted
without a sword to guide;
he'd been awakened into sight:
it wheedled him, the lovely fight,
out of his stubborn pride.
He sat his horse; no gesture flung
escaped his noticing.
Now link to link in silver sung,
and voice from everything outrung,
and as in many bells was hung
the soul of every thing.
The very wind appeared more vast
that spread the banners wide –
slim as a panther, breathing fast,
and reeling with the trumpet-blast
that laughingly defied.
Downwards at times that wind would roar:
there went a boy, one bleeding sore,
who beat incessantly
the rallying drum, as though he bore
his own heart to the grave before
his perished company.
There many a mountain was uprolled,
as though the earth were not yet old,
but forming all the while;
now basalt-like the iron stood,
now swayed there like an evening wood,
in broad-ascending amplitude,
the grandly-motioned pile.
The darkness steamed round clammily,
not time's was that obscurity, –
and everything turned grey,
until another log took light
and once again the flame was bright
and festivally gay.
They charged in – a fantastic crowd
of provinces in strange array:
how all the iron laughed aloud!
Some prince's armour, silver-proud,
went shimmering through the dimmed mêlée.
Flags fluttered there like jubilations,
and some royal prodigality
appeared in all gesticulations, –
the stars at distant conflagrations
were kindled into brilliancy . . .

Night fell. The battle more and more
ebbed like a tired sea that had sped
uncounted unknown dead ashore,
and felt the weight of all those dead.
Attentively the grey horse wended
(by many a mighty fist forfended)
through men that lay unknownly dying,
and trod on shallow blackened grass.
And he on the grey horse saw pass
below, on the damp colours lying,
much silver, like fragmented glass.
Saw helmets drinking, iron unlustred,
and swords in coats of mail upstand,
saw, with some shred of lace, the mustered
motion of many a dying hand . . .
And saw it not.

And after-rode that loud confusion
of battle as in some illusion,
upon his cheeks a warm suffusion,
and with the eyes of one in love . . .

Worpswede, 2 October 1900

THE CZARS

A POETIC SEQUENCE (1899 AND 1906)

I

That was in days when mountains were appearing:
unsubjugated trees were wildly rearing,
and into shining armour rivers roared.
Two foreign pilgrims called a name, and, hearing,
out of his age-long palsy came careering
Ilya, the giant of Murom, restored.

His aged parents laboured on their acres
at clearing stones and undergrowth away,
when came their giant son from his awakers
and forced the furrows to the ploughshare's sway.
He lifted up the trunks, the fighter-fisted,
and at their tottering burden laughed outright,
and roots, upstartled like black serpents, twisted,
they that in darkness only had existed,
within the widely stretching grasp of light.

The dew of early morning fortified her,
the mare in whom slept strength and nobleness;
she grew beneath the burden of her rider,
her neighing had a voice's ringfulness, –
and both felt how some unimagined Wider
was calling them with dangerous promises.

And rode and rode . . . perhaps a thousand years.
Who counts the time, when someone simply *will*?
(Perhaps he sat a thousand years quite still.)
The real is like the wonderful: will measure
the world with measurement that domineers,
find in millennia too much youthfulness.

Far shall they stride who long have sat at leisure
within their own deep twilightness.

II

Great birds are still dismayingly overfaring
and dragons glow and guard with lashing tail
the forest's marvels and the narrow dale;
and boys are growing up and men preparing
themselves for battle with the nightingale,

which, in the tops of nine far-upward reaching
oaks, like some myriad-seeming monster lies,
and out of it an unimagined screeching,
an outscreamed to-the-very-end-outreaching,
from evening onwards through the night will rise;
that night of spring-time, that was more appalling
and harder than all else to labour through:
no sign of sudden enmity on-falling,
yet all so full of passing-on-into,
casting itself away, in pieces shedding,
even, despite the terror it was in,
invoking that invisible outspreading
and, like a shipwreck, going down therein.

Surpassing strong were those that still outlasted,
by that gigantic something all unblasted
that out of throats as out of craters rolled:
they lasted, and, growing gradually old,
young April consciousness they comprehended,
and peaceful hands to many they extended

and led through fears and troubles manifold
to days wherein, grown joyfuller and sounder,
they built the walls round many a city-founder
who over all sat kind and wittingly.

And down the earliest streets came finally,
from caverns and all-odious recesses,
the beasts accounted perilous to meet.
They climbed in silence out of their excesses
(ashamed and antiquated violentnesses)
and lay obedient at the elders' feet.

III[1]

His servants are feeding continually
with ever more and with ever more
a herd of wild tales that are all still he.

Out of his range his favourites flee.
And his mistresses whisper together and found
confederacies. And he hears them debating,
deep in their lodgings, of poison with waiting-
women, who furtively glance around.

Panels in hollow walls are sliding,
murderers under the roofs are hiding
and playing the monk most skilfully.

And nothing else but a glimpse has he
now and then; nothing else but the light
step on the circling flight
of stairs; nothing else but his staff's iron barb.

Nothing else but the thin penitential garb
(through which, as though with claws, comes creeping
up and about him the flagstones' chill),
nothing on which he dares to call,
nothing but anxiousness unsleeping,
nothing but fear of one and all,
which hounds him on through those onhounded
countenances, past dark, unsounded,
and, maybe, guilty hands each day.

Sometimes he's just in time to stay
one gliding past with a sudden twitch,

[1] The subject of this poem is Ivan the Terrible.

and drags him in furiously;
at the window, though, wonders uncertainly:
holder and holden, which is which?
Who am I and who is he?

IV[1]

It is the hour when the vain realm assembles
to gaze upon its mirrored majesty.

The pale Czar, last of all his family,
dreams on his throne before the pageantry,
and just perceptibly his shamed head trembles,
as do his hands, that flee, as from the spurning
of those impurpled arm-rests, with vague yearning
into confused uncertainty.

And all around his silentness extending,
bright-mailed and panther-skinned, from many nations,
boyars like strange royal perils are low-bending,
perils encircling him with dumb impatience.
Far through the hall their awe excites vibrations.

And to another Czar their thoughts are tending,
one who, with words insanity was sending,
would often thrust their brows against the stone.
And when that Czar was seated on the throne
he did not leave, as further they recall,
so much room on the faded silk below.

He was the obscure scale of all,
and the boyars had long since ceased to know
that the throne's seat was red, his robes lay so
ponderously there in outspread goldenness.

And go on thinking: the imperial dress
slumbers upon those shoulders infantine.
Although throughout the hall the torches flare,
pale are the pearls that in seven rows incline,
like pallid children, round his neck, and where
the sleeve-enclasping rubies used to glare
like crystal goblets filled with wine,
they're now as black as cinders there –

[1] The subject of these last three poems is Feodor, son of Ivan the Terrible, the last of the Ruriks.

And their thinking swells.

And presses on that pallid monarch tighter,
for whom the crown he carries ever lighter,
and willing ever more remote will seem;
he smiles. The appraisers' cautiousness grows slighter,
their bows draw near, their flattery rings unrighter, –
and now a sword has rattled in his dream.

V

Made sacrosanct, though, by his strange obsessions,
the pale Czar will not perish by the sword,
but will inherit all those wide possessions
with which his gentle soul is so abroad.

Already, from a Kremlin window gazing,
he sees a Moscow whiter, more amazing,
wrapt in its night so long a-fashioning:
such as it is in wakening Spring's first lurches,
when in the streets the fragrance of the birches
with many bells is quivering.

The mighty bells, that sound so dominating,
are those primeval Czars, his ancestry,
who, even before the Tartar cavalry,
through sagas, perils, rage, humility
have hesitantly been inculminating.

And who they were, he fathoms suddenly,
and that, to find their own dark meaning, they
had often dived into those depths of his,
and him, the mildest of the majesties,
had used in great and pious purposes
long before he himself saw day.

And a great gratitude comes over him
that they were so extravagantly giving
him to all being's thirst and stress.
He was the strength for their unboundedness,
the golden ground before which their large living
mysteriously seemed to dim.

He sees himself in all they could avail,
like silver in fine jewelry intertwisted;

there's not one deed of which their doing consisted
that has not once in his quiet states existed
wherein all action's redness has grown pale.

VI

Sapphires like women's eyes are contemplating
in the surrounding panels' argentine.
Creepers of golden filigree entwine
like beasts in splendour of their hotness mating,
and silent faces of soft pearls are waiting
within the shade of many a wild design
the brief attention of some passing shine.
And all that's mantle, crown, and dwelling-place;
and to and from each border motions race –
like corn in wind, like river in a valley,
shimmer the changeful splendours that encase.

Within their sun three darker ovals rally;
the Mother from the larger one looks down,
and right and left, as thin as almonds, sally
two virgin hands out of the silver gown.
Those two hands, singularly quiet and brown,
announce that in the costly ikon's dwelling,
as in a convent, that royal, all-excelling
she, who with him will soon be overwelling,
that son, that drop, wherein, past all foretelling,
Heaven shall appear without a frown.

The hands are witnesses therefor;
the countenance appears, though, like a door
into warm twilightnesses opened wide,
wherein the smile of this celestial bride,
straying with its light, has vanished long before.

The Czar asks, bending with deep reverence:
With feeling, fearing, longing, all we do,
can you not feel how deep we've entered you?
We're waiting for your loving countenance,
that has departed from us – whither to?

For the great saints it's never out of view.

He trembled deeply in his rigid dress
that stood so radiantly. He did not guess

how far he was from all and to her blessing
blissfully near in his loneliness.

And still the pale Czar ponders through the night.
And now his face, which, under sickly hair,
has long been sunk and ready to forth-fare,
like that which from the golden oval glimmered
passed in his mighty golden robe from sight.

(On to behold her countenance progressing.)

Two golden garments in the chamber shimmered
and in the glow of hanging lamps grew bright.

Meiningen, August-September 1899 and Paris, beginning of February 1906

THE SINGER SINGS BEFORE A PRINCE'S CHILD

In memory of
Paula Becker-Modersohn

You pale child, every evening there shall stand,
darkly among those things of yours, one singing;
to you across his voice's causeway bringing
the sagas that within his blood are ringing
and a harp crowded with his playing hand.

And what he tells he does not take from time,
it's lifted as from weaving on a screen;
such forms no living eye has ever seen, –
and he calls life that which has never been.
And this is what to-day shall be his rhyme:

Pale child of princes, and of those princesses
lone-waiting in the drawing-room hung with white, –
all, almost, were consumed with anxiousnesses
to bring you up and from their gilt recesses
be gazing on your eyes' deep earnestnesses
and on your hands, so small and white.

From them you've many a pearl and turkey-stone,
those pictured women standing there as steady
as though they stood in evening fields alone, –
from them you've many a pearl and turkey-stone, –
and rings with mottoed meanings hardly known,
and silks whence withered fragrances will eddy.

With jewels from their sashes you retire
to the tall window where the beams rebound,
and in the silk of softest bride-attire
your little books are delicately bound, –
and therein, hailed by many lands as sire,
inscribed majestically you have found
that name of yours in letters rich and round.

And all's as though it had occurred already.

As it were no more likely that you came,
they've set their mouths to every cup,
to every pleasure whipped their feelings up,
and every suffering sufferingly seen;
so that with shame
you steal upon the scene.

. . . You pale child, your life too is more than seeming, –
the singer comes to say that you exist.
And that you're more than any woodland's dreaming,
more than the happiness of suns whose streaming
many a grey day's never missed.
Your life's so wholly yours because so teeming
with multitudes of lives that still persist.

Can you not feel the weight of generations,
after you've lived a little, lighter grown? –
How softly they prepare for revelations,
afford you images for all sensations, –
and how whole ages seem but preparations
for some consummate gesture of your own?

The end of all that once has been is thus
not to remain with all its heaviness,
but to return to our existentness,
inwoven deep and wondrously in us:

Women were ivory-like for this alone,
and had the redness of the rose imparted;
for this the mien of monarchs weary-hearted
sombred, and princely mouths became as stone,
unmoved by widow's or by orphan's moan;
for this to sound like viols boys have started
and perished for a woman's heavy hair,
for this have world-bewildered maids departed

to serve the Virgin with a life of prayer.
For this by hands unknown some greater-arted
music on lute and mandolin was played, –
into warm velvet slid the polished blade, –
destinies rose from joyance and believing,
in evening arbours mounted sobs of leaving,
and, over hundreds of black helmets heaving,
the stubborn battle like a vessel swayed.
For this towns slowly grandeured and subsided
into themselves again like waves of sea,
for this to high-rewarded goals was guided
the iron spear's bird-powered celerity,
and children for their garden games were tidied, –
and seriousness and triviality
have happened just in order to provide you
great similes for all that may betide you,
so that in growing you may still continue.

Past generations are implanted in you
to rise again, like gardens, from inside you.

You pale child, how immensely rich you make
the singer, with that destiny to sing!
Like some great garden-party's mirroring,
with all its lights, in the astonished lake.
Each single thing in the dark poet's soul –
star, dwelling, wood – is silently reflected.
And many of the things he would extol
around your moving figure are collected.

Worpswede, 3 October 1900

THE VOICES

NINE LEAVES WITH A TITLE-LEAF

TITLE-LEAF

The rich and fortunate need no mention,
what they are troubles no one's mind.
The needy, though, have to attract attention,
have to be saying: I am blind,
or else: that's what I soon shall be;
or: everything here goes wrong with me;
or: I've left an ailing child behind;
or: that's the place where I've been spliced . . .

And perhaps this hasn't at all sufficed.

And, since otherwise everyone just goes flinging
past them like things, they have to be singing.

And there one still can hear good song.

People are odd; they'll travel farther
and hear a choir of *castrati* rather.

When tired of such choirs, though, to listen for long
to these voices comes God the Father.

THE BEGGAR'S SONG

From door to door in shower and shine
I pass continually;
into my right hand I consign
my right ear suddenly.
Then as something I never knew was mine
my voice will seem to me.

Then who is crying, whether it's I
or another, I'm not quite sure.
It's only a trifle for which I cry.
The poets cry for more.

And finally I can shut my face
with both my eyes up tight;
as it lies with its weight in my hand's embrace
it's quite a restful sight.
Lest any should think I'd got no place
to lay my head at night.

THE BLIND MAN'S SONG

I'm blind, you outsiders, and that's an affliction,
that's an abhorrence, a contradiction,
something that daily exceeds me.
My hand upon my wife's arm I lay,
grey hand of mine upon her grey grey,
and through a sheer void she leads me.

You touch and push and imagine your own
sound differs from that of stone upon stone,
and yet you're mistaken: I alone
am living and suffering and sighing.

In me there's a never-ending cry –
it may be my heart or my bowels, but I
don't know which of them's crying.

If ever you sang these songs, no trace
was there of this inflection.
Warmly each day to your dwelling-place
comes a new sun's reflection.
And you've got a feeling of face-to-face,
and that makes for self-protection.

THE DRINKER'S SONG

It wasn't in me. In and out it would go.
I wanted to hold it. The wine held it, though.
(What it was, I no longer can say.)
Then the wine held this and the other thing out,
till I came to trust it beyond all doubt.
In my imbecile way.

Now I'm in its power, and it flings me at will
about and about and is losing me still
to Death, that son of a bitch.
If he wins me, dirty card that I am,
he'll use me to scratch his grisly ham
and toss me into the ditch.

THE SUICIDE'S SONG

Another moment to live through, then.
How the rope I fasten, again and again
someone cuts.
I'd got prepared so wonderfully,
and already a little eternity
was in my guts.

They bring me now, as they've done before,
this spoonful of life to sup.
No, I won't, I won't have any more,
let me bring it up.

Life's an excellent thing, I know,
through all the world outspread;
I simply can't digest it, though,
it only goes to my head.

It nourishes others, it makes me ill;
one *can* dislike the thing.
What for a thousand years I'll still
require is dieting.

THE WIDOW'S SONG

Life was kind to me at the start.
It kept me warm, it put me in heart.
That with all who are young it has that art,
how could I then be aware?
I didn't know what life could be, –
it was nothing but years quite suddenly,
with no kindness or wonder or novelty,
as though torn in two pieces there.

That was neither its fault nor my own;
we both were left with patience alone,
but Death has not a whit.
I saw him coming (in what a way!),
and watched him taking and taking away:
I had no claim to it.

What was my own, mine really?
Was not even my misery
only a loan from Fate?
Fate doesn't merely want happiness,
but pain back as well and outscreamed distress,
and buys ruin at a second-hand rate.

Fate was there and obtained for a sou
every expression that came into
my face or away would glide.
A clearance sale was held each day,
and when I was empty it went away
and left me unoccupied.

THE IDIOT'S SONG

They don't interfere. They let me be.
They say that nothing can happen to me.
How good!
Nothing can happen. All comes to soar
round the Holy Spirit for evermore,
round that Spirit for ever sure, –
how good!

No, one mustn't suppose there could ever begin
to be any kind of danger therein.
There is, to be sure, the blood.
The blood's the hardest, without a doubt.
I sometimes think I shall have to fall out. –
(How good!)

Oh, what a lovely ball up there;
red and round as an everywhere.
Good, that you caused it to be.
Would it come if I called it to me?

All's behaving in such a remarkable way,
now drifting together, now swimming away:
friendly, a little hard to survey.
How good!

THE ORPHAN GIRL'S SONG

I'm no one, and no one is what I shall be.
I'm still too small to exist, I agree;
but I'll always be so.

Mothers and fathers, oh,
have pity on me.

Bringing up's not worth the pains, I'll allow:
I shan't escape my fate.
No one can need me: it's too soon now,
and to-morrow it's too late.

I've only got this dress you see,
growing thin and colourless;
but perhaps it'll last an eternity
before God none the less.

I've only got this bit of hair
(the same as it was before),
which used to be someone's dearest care.

Nothing's dear to him any more.

THE DWARF'S SONG

My soul is straight and good maybe;
my heart, though, my blood flowing crookedly,

all that which so distresses me,
just can't hold it upright here.
It has no garden, it has no bed,
it clings to my sharp bones instead
and beats its wings with fright here.

My hands too will always be failing me.
How hopelessly stunted they are you can see:
damp, heavy, hopping constrictedly
like little toads in wet weather.
And everything else about me too
is old and worn and sad to view;
why does God delay to do
away with it altogether?

Is he angry with me for my face
with the mouth that seems to rue it?
It was often so ready to grow in grace
and let a light shine through it.
But of all that moved about the place
big dogs came closest to it.
And of that dogs have no trace.

THE LEPER'S SONG

Look, I am forsaken by everything.
Of me not one in the town knows anything,
I have become a leper.
And I rattle about with this rattle of mine,
knocking my melancholy sign
into the ears, to their dismay,
of every too-near-stepper.
And those that hear its woodenness, they
take good care not to look this way,
and won't learn what has happened here.

As far as my rattle's sound reaches, I
am at home; but perhaps the reason why
you make my rattle so loud is just
that my distance too may provoke mistrust
in those my nearness can terrify.
And thus for years on end I can,
without discovering maid or man,
woman or child, be faring.

Brutes I'll refrain from scaring.

Paris, 7-12 June 1906 (all except *The Leper's Song*, which is undated)

THE READER

I'd long been reading. Since with rush of rain
this afternoon first dimmed the window-pane.
The wind outside had passed from my regard:
my book was hard.
And, as I turned its pages, I would con them
like features darkened by reflectiveness;
time's flow was stemmed around my studiousness.
Then of a sudden something overshone them,
and, ousting anxious verbal maziness,
stood: Evening, Evening . . . everywhere upon them.
I do not yet look out, but the long lines
have split in two, and words from their combining
threads roll away wherever they're inclining . . .
And then I know: above the serpentining,
glittering gardens there's a spaciousness;
yes, once again the sun must have been shining.
Now summer-night is all encompassing:
small groups are formed by what lay scatteredly,
people on long walks wander darksomely,
and strangely far, as though more meaningly,
is heard the little that's still happening.

And when I gaze up now from what I've read,
everything's great and nothing's unakin.
Out there exists what I live here within,
and here and there it's all unlimited;
save that I weave myself still more therein
when on to outward things my glances fly
and gravely simple masses formed thereby, –
there far beyond itself the earth's outswelling.
It seems to be embracing all the sky,
and the first star is like the farthest dwelling.

Westerwede, September 1901

THE SPECTATOR

I watch the storms in the trees above:
after days of mild decaying
my windows shrink from their assaying,
and the things I hear the distance saying,
without a friend I find dismaying,
without a sister cannot love.

There goes the storm to urge and alter,
through forest trees and through time's tree;
and nothing seems to age or falter:
the landscape, like an open psalter,
speaks gravely of eternity.

How small the strife that's occupied us,
how great is all that strives with us!
We might, if, like the things outside us,
we let the great storm over-ride us,
grow spacious and anonymous.

We conquer littleness, obtaining
success that only makes us small,
while, unconstrained and unconstraining,
the permanent eludes us all:
that angel who, though loath, yet lingers
to wrestle with mortality,
and, when opponents' sinews settle
in strife and stretch themselves to metal,
can feel them move beneath his fingers
like strings in some deep melody.

The challenger who failed to stand
that trial so constantly rejected
goes forth upright and resurrected
and great from that hard, forming hand
that clasped about him and completed.
Conquests no longer fascinate.
His growth consists in being defeated
by something ever-grandlier great.

Berlin-Schmargendorf, mid-January 1901

THE BLIND WOMAN

The Stranger:

You're not afraid to talk about it?

The Blind Woman:

No.
It's such a long way off. She was another.
Who used to see, who lived aloud and looking,
who died.

The Stranger:

And was the death she died a hard one?

The Blind Woman:

Dying's a cruelty to the unsuspecting.
One needs strength even for deaths of those unknown.

The Stranger:

She was unknown to you?

The Blind Woman:

– Or: she's become so.
Death can estrange the mother from the child. –
But it was dreadful during those first days.
All of my body was one wound. The world,
that in things blooms and ripens,
had been torn out of me with all its roots,
with my heart too (it seemed), and there I lay
open as excavated earth and drank
the cold rain of my tears,
which out of my dead eyes incessantly
and softly streamed, as out of empty skies,
when God is dead, the clouds will start to fall.
My hearing, though, was vast and all-receptive.
I heard things that are quite inaudible:
time, as it flowed away across my hair,
the silence that in fragile glasses tinkled, –
and felt how very close beside my hands
the breathing of a large white rose was passing.
And I was always thinking: Night and: Night,
and thought I saw a strip of brightness showing
that into daylight would expand;
and thought that to that morning I was going
which long had lain within my hand.
I woke my mother when sleep heavily
had tumbled down from my dark sight,
I shouted to my mother: 'Come to me!
Give me a light!'
And listened. All was silent, all;
my pillows' softness turned to stoniness, –
and then I seemed to see a shiningness:
my mother's tears in her distress
which I'm unwilling to recall.
Light! Light! in dreams I'd often cry:
space has collapsed. Oh, come and try
to take it away from my face and my breast.
You'll have to lift it, lift it high,
give it back to the stars in the sky;

I can't live like this, with the sky upon me.
Am I speaking to you, though, mother?
If not, to whom? Is there another
behind the curtain? – Winter? Mother:
Storm? Mother: Night? Oh, say!
Or: day? . . . Day!
Without me! But how *can* there be day without me?
Am I missing from nowhere?
Is no one asking about me?
Are we then quite forgotten?
We? . . . But you're still there;
still have everything, haven't you?
For your sight everything's still busily
doing its best.
When your eyes rest,
however tired they may have been,
they can rise when they will.
. . . Mine must lie still.
From my flowers the colours will steal.
My mirrors will all congeal.
In my books the lines will grow into each other.
My birds will be fluttering
in the streets and be hurt on strange window-panes.
Nothing united with me remains.
I'm forsaken by everything. –
I'm an island.

The Stranger:

And I've come here across the sea.

The Blind Woman:

What? On to the island? . . . Come here?

The Stranger:

I'm still in the boat.
I've brought it gently alongside –
of you. It moves with the tide:
landwards its flag is blown.

The Blind Woman:

I am an island and alone.
I am rich. –
At first, while the old tracks still were there
within my nerves, by much wayfare
well hollowed-out,
I suffered, no doubt.

All went from my heart beyond recall,
where to, I just didn't know;
all of a sudden I found them, though,
all feelings, all I amount to, all
gathered there, crowding and crying,
at my walled-up eyes that never moved.
All of my misled feelings . . .
They may have been standing there year after year;
those weeks, though, are with me still
when they all came back so ill
and recognised no one here.

Then the way to my eyes became overgrown.
I've forgotten it utterly.
Now everything's moving about in me,
secure and carefree; my feelings proceed
like convalescents, enjoying their motion,
in my body's dark house about and about.
Some bendingly read
of things long ago;
the younger, though,
are all looking out.
For when one of them comes to my verge and stands,
in glass I am garmented.
My forehead sees, poems in other hands
my hand has read.
My foot can talk to the stones it has stirred,
out of these daily walls with each bird
my voice has sped.
There's nothing now that I have to lack,
all colours are rendered back
as sound and fragrancy.
And, lovely beyond imagining,
as notes they ring.
What's a book to me?
Leaves of trees are being turned by the air;
and I know what wonderful words are there,
and sometimes repeat them, murmuring low.
And Death, who snaps eyes like flower-stalks,
will not find mine where he walks . . .

The Stranger (softly):

I know.

Berlin-Schmargendorf, 25 November 1900

FROM
NEW POEMS

New Poems published December 1907, containing poems written between 1903 and 1907.

New Poems, Second Part published November 1908, containing poems written between 31 July 1907 and 17 August 1908.

These poems were the result of a new conception of the possibilities of the short poem, which Rilke had formed under the influence of Rodin and, later, of Cezanne's paintings. The emphasis is much more upon the 'subject' which has inspired the poet, or, rather, which he has *compelled* to inspire him, and much less upon the 'feelings' it has excited in him. His 'feelings' are still present, but they have been to a much greater extent objectified, intellectualised and transmuted. Many of the poems included in the second edition (1906) of the *Book of Images* and in the First Part of *New Poems* were written concurrently, but Rilke recognised between them a distinction of kind, and was never in any doubt as to which poem was appropriate to which collection. He proposed, he wrote in February 1906, to include in the *Book of Images* all those poems 'which cannot yet be numbered among those belonging to the next stage, those co-equal with *The Panther*, – even *The Last Supper*'. And he wrote to his wife of the First Part of *New Poems*: 'It's a book: work, the transition from inspiration that comes to that which is summoned and seized.'

ARCHAIC TORSO OF APOLLO

Though we've not known his unimagined head
and what divinity his eyes were showing,
his torso like a branching street-lamp's glowing,[1]
wherein his gaze, only turned down, can shed

light still. Or else the breast's insurgency
could not be dazzling you, or you discerning
in that slight twist of loins a smile returning
to where was centred his virility.

Or else this stone would not stand so intact
beneath the shoulders' through-seen cataract
and would not glisten like a wild beast's skin;

and would not keep from all its contours giving
light like a star: for there's no place therein
that does not see you. You must change your living.

Paris, early summer 1908

CRETAN ARTEMIS

Promontory wind: was not her meeting
brow like some bright obstacle for you?
Counter-wind through which lithe beasts were fleeting,
did you form her, moulding to

those unconscious breasts of hers that flowing
garment like a wild presentiment?
While herself, as though she were all-knowing,
cool and kirtled, all-intent

on the farthest, stormed with nymph and hound,
testing what her bow could do, inbound
into that hard, high upgirth:

[1] *Wie ein Kandelaber*. In Germany and Austria *Kandelaber* was the usual word for a street-lamp: not for the comparatively short post with a single square lantern, but for the much taller and more elegant sort with two globes, each suspended from either end of a wide semi-circular cross-piece. Gas-lighting had not yet been replaced by electricity. Rilke had already used the word in the poem *Night Drive* (p. 181).

sometimes only hailed from isolated
huts and, to her fury, dominated
by some woman's cry for birth.

Paris, early summer 1908

LEDA

When first the god set foot there in his need,
the swan's great beauty almost frightened him;
he vanished into it with wits a-swim.
But his deceit onswept him to his deed

before the feelings of that life untried
could be experienced. And, all-robeless, she
knew who that comer in the swan must be,
and knew already that he eyed

what her confused endeavour to withstand
no longer could conceal. The god alighted,
and, necking through the ever-weaker hand,

loosed himself into her he doted on.
Then really felt his plumage and, delighted,
became within her lap entirely swan.

Paris, autumn 1907 or Capri, spring 1908

SAPPHO TO ALCAEUS

FRAGMENT

What, though, would you have to tell me really,
what are you to my soul anyway,
when your eyes sink down before that nearly
uttered something that you never say?

Look, man, these are just the things whose saying,
till we're famed, has so enraptured us.
When I think: with you would be decaying
that sweet maidenhood which now we've thus, –

I the seer and all those who've been illumined by me, to a god's delight, –

borne inviolate, till Mytilene,
like an apple-orchard in the night,
with the ripening of our breasts is fragrant. –

Yes, with these breasts too that you have passed
over for your fruit-wreaths, wooer there,
standing with the countenance downcast.
Leave me, so that what you will not spare,
to my lyre may come: all's unbegun.

This god's no assistance to a pair;
when, though, he shall deign to pass through one

. . . . . .

Paris, 24 July 1907

A letter to his wife on the day after he had written this poem reveals that it was inspired by an ancient vase-painting – almost certainly that of the fifth century B.C. in the Glyptothek at Munich – which represents Sappho and Alcaeus, with lyres in their hands, confronting each other, Alcaeus with bowed head. This may perhaps be regarded as an illustration of some verses attributed to Alcaeus and Sappho by Aristotle and quoted by him in the *Rhetoric* (I, ix, 20) as an example of the kind of things that make us feel ashamed. Alcaeus says: 'I want to tell you something, but shame restrains me'; to which Sappho replies (I translate that version of the text which had reached Rilke): 'If your wish had been for things good or noble and your tongue had not been concocting for its utterance something base, shame would not have cast down your eyes, but you would have rightly spoken of it.' For a full discussion of the fragment see Denys Page, *Sappho and Alcaeus*, 1955, pp. 104ff.

A SIBYL

Once, long, long ago, they'd called her old.
She, though, went on living there and ranging
daily through the self-same street. Till, changing
measure, like a forest's now they told

her age by centuries. But she returned
every evening to her wonted station,
black as some primeval castellation,
high and hollow and outburned;

ever circled by the screaming flight
of words that, all unwatched for and unwilled,
lodged within her breast and propagated,

while the home-returningly fulfilled
sombrely beneath her eyebrows waited,
ready for the coming night.

Paris, 22 August - 5 September 1907

LOVE-SONG

How shall I hold my soul, that it may not
be touching yours? How shall I lift it then
above you to where other things are waiting?
Ah, gladly would I lodge it, all-forgot,
with some lost thing the dark is isolating
on some remote and silent spot that, when
your depths vibrate, is not itself vibrating.
You and me – all that lights upon us, though,
brings us together like a fiddle-bow
drawing *one* voice from two strings it glides along.
Across what instrument have we been spanned?
And what violinist holds us in his hand?
O sweetest song.

Capri, mid-March 1907

FUNERAL MONUMENT OF A YOUNG GIRL

We recall it still. As though once more
all of it must sometime come to be.
Like a tree along the lemon-shore,
those small lightsome breasts of yours you bore
out towards his blood's insurgency

– that divinity's.
That slim, appealing
fugitive, so spoiling womenkind.
Sweet and glowing, warm as your own feeling,
overshadowing your unconcealing
flanks and, like those brows of yours, inclined.

Meudon, winter 1905-6

SACRIFICE

How my body flowers with ever-greater
fragrance since you came into my ken;
look, my walk is slimmer now and straighter,
and you merely wait: – Who are you, then?

Look: I feel how far I am already,
shedding, leaf on leaf, what used to be.
Your smile only like a star hangs steady
over you and soon will over me.

What through childish years I can but claim to
see like nameless water glittering,
on that altar I will give your name to,
altar which your hair has set a flame to
and your breasts are lightly garlanding.

Meudon, winter 1905-6

EASTERN AUBADE

Does it not, though, like a coast appear,
a strip of coast, this bed on which we're lying?
Those lofty breasts of yours alone are clear
to my grown-dizzy feeling's dim descrying.

For, oh, this night in which so much was screaming,
in which beasts called and rent themselves in prey,
is it not grimly strange to us? And, gleaming
outside so slowly there and called the day,
is that too really more familiar-seeming?

One needs to be as much within another
as anthers are in petals: so unending
around us things immeasurably transcending
accumulate until they almost smother.

While, though, with these embraces we are keeping
unnoticed that in-closing enmity,
from you, from me, it still can be outleaping:
for, oh, our spirits live by treachery.

Paris, May-June 1906

JOSHUA'S COUNCIL

As some outflowing river breaks its tether,
pouring in pomp of waters from afar,
so broke upon the elders met together
for the last time the voice of Joshua.

How those who had been laughing were discounted,
how hearts and hands were checked by every man,
as though the din of thirty battles mounted
within one mouth, and that one mouth began.

And once again the thousands were astounded
as on the great day before Jericho,
though now it was in him the trumpets sounded
and their own lives the walls that tottered so

that not till rolling in the pangs of fear,
defencelessly, they seemed to understand
that this was he who, born to domineer,
had shouted to the sun in Gideon: Stand!

And God had gone off in humiliation,
and held the sun, until his hands were tired,
above that immolating generation,
only because one man had so required.

And this was he – whose blood, though they had ceased
to care about him in their calculations,
his five score years and ten had not decreased.
He rose and broke upon their habitations.

Like hail on standing harvests he descended.
What would ye promise God? On every side
uncounted gods await what ye decide.
Choose, and be crushed by Him ye have offended.

And then, with arrogance till then unspoken:
I and my house have been and are his bride.

Whereat they all cried: Help us, give some token,
that this hard choice may not bring punishment.

But they saw him, silent, without pity,
reascending to his mountain city;
then no more. It was the last descent.

Paris, shortly before 9 July 1906

DAVID SINGS BEFORE SAUL

I

Can you hear, King, how my instrument
flings out distances through which we're wending?
Stars encounter us uncomprehending,
and at last like rain we are descending,
and a flowering follows that descent.

Girls you still were able to possess
flower from women tempting my defences;
scent of virgins re-assails your senses;
slender boys stand, all excitedness,
panting where some hidden stair commences.

Would my strings could bring back everything!
But my music's reeling drunkenly.
Ah, those nights of yours, those nights, my King, –
and, grown heavier from your handselling,
how superb those bodies all could be!

I can match you their remembered splendour,
since I can divine it. How, though, render
for you their dark groans of ecstasy?

II

King, who had such blessings here below,
and who now with life that never ceases
overshadow me and overthrow:
come down from your throne and break in pieces
this my harp you are exhausting so.

Look, it's like an amputated tree:
through its boughs, where fruits for you were growing,
depths now, as of days to come, are showing, –
scarcely recognisable by me.

Let me by its side no more be sleeping;
look, King, at this boyish hand: do you
really think it cannot yet be leaping
through the octaves of a body too?

III

Though you're hiding in the dark somewhere,
King, I have you still within my hold.
Look, my firm-spun song's without a tear,
and the space around us both grows cold.
My deserted heart and your untended
in your anger's clouds are both suspended,
madly bit into each other there
and into a single heart uprolled.

How we change each other, can you clearly
feel now? Burden's being inspirited.
If we hold to one another merely,
you to youth, King, I to age, we're nearly
like a star that's circling overhead.

Meudon, winter 1905-6

SAMUEL'S APPEARANCE TO SAUL

And then the Witch of Endor cried: I see –
The monarch seized her by the shoulder: Who?
And even before she was describing, he
already felt that he'd been seeing too:
Him, by whose voice he was once more addressed:
Why do you rouse me? I'm at rest.
Will you, now Heaven's curses press you,
now that to all your prayers the Lord is dumb,
seek in my mouth how victory may bless you?
Shall I tell every tooth that I can trace there?
They're all that's left to me . . . It vanished. She
then screamed and flung her hands before her face there,
as though she'd been compelled to see: Succumb –

And he, who in the days he prospered so
had towered above his people like a crest,
collapsed before he'd ventured to protest:
so certain was his overthrow.
She, though, who'd struck him down unwillingly,
hoped he'd forgot and was himself again;
and when she heard he'd ceased to eat, she then
went out and killed and plied her cookery
and came to him herself and got him seated;

he sat like one with too much to forget:
all that had been and what had now completed.
Then, as a serf at evening eats, he ate.

Paris, 22 August - 5 September 1907

LAMENT FOR JONATHAN

Are even kings unable to withstand?
Can they too pass away like common things,
although their pressure, like a signet ring's,
imprints itself into the yielding land?

How could you all at once, though, so begun here
with your heart's initial letter,
stop, you warmer of these cheeks of mine?
Would it were possible some one here
could become your re-begetter
when his seed within him came to shine!

Some unknown hand's accomplished our dividing,
and your own second self is nothing there,
and must contain himself and hear the tiding;
as wounded animals outroar in hiding,
I'd like to lie and scream somewhere:

for here and here, at all my shyest places,
you've been torn from me like the hair that grows
within my arm-pits and like that which laces
the spot whence sport for women rose,

before you skeined up all my therein centred
senses as one unpicks a tangled clew;
my eyes looked up then and your image entered: –
Now, though, they nevermore shall gaze on you.

Paris, early summer 1908

JEREMIAH

Tender as the wheat upspringing greenly
I began, but, rager, you knew how
to provoke my proffered heart so keenly
that it's boiling like a lion's now.

What a mouth it was that you were needing,
almost since my boyish days, from me:
it became a wound, and now there's bleeding
from it year on year of misery.

Daily I re-echoed new distresses
you would so insatiably devise,
and this mouth of mine survived their stresses;
see if you can still it anywise,
when those we've been cursing and confounding
all shall be dispersed and disappear
in catastrophe that shall not fail:
for it's then I hope again to hear
in the ruins my own voice resounding
that from the beginning was a wail.

Paris, mid-August 1907

ESTHER

The chamber women combed for seven days
the ashes of her grief and her dismay's
lees and precipitation from her hair,
and carried it and sunned it like a fleece
and fed it with the purest spiceries
for two days longer: then the hour was there

when she must cross, unbidden, unobeying,
unlooked for, like a ghost from graveyard straying,
the doorless threshold of that house of fear,
and, leaning on her women, through the dim
yet shining distance of its halls, see him
by whom men die when they draw near.

He shone so, she could feel the incandescence
of those imperial rubies that she wore;
she took a swift upfilling of his presence
and, like a vessel that could hold no more,

was overflowing already with his might
before she'd passed the third of those great halls
that poured the greenness of its green-stone walls
all over her. She had not guessed aright

that length of way, and all those stones and rings
grown heavier from this shining of the king's,
cold from her fear. She went on traversing. –

And when she felt the shining shafts combine
and centre on the throne of tourmaline,
and saw him towering, real as a thing:

the right-hand maid, whose arms she fainted in,
upheld her to that throne that shone so brightly.
He touched her with his golden sceptre, lightly:
. . . and, senseless there, she understood, within.

Paris, early summer 1908

THE DEPARTURE OF THE PRODIGAL SON

Now to depart from all this incoherence
that's ours, but which we can't appropriate,
and, like old well-springs, mirrors our appearance
in trembling outlines that disintegrate;
from all this, that with bramble-like adherence
is once more clinging to us – to depart,
and then to start
bestowing on this and that you'd ceased to see
(so took for granted was their ministration)
a sudden gaze: all reconciliation,
tender and close and new-beginningly;
and to divine the whelming desolation,
the inexorable impersonality,
of all that childhood needed to withstand: –
And even then depart, hand out of hand,
as though you tore a wound that had been healing,
and to depart: whither? To unrevealing
distance, to some warm, unrelated land,
that, back-clothwise, will stay, without all feeling,
behind all action: garden, sea or sand;
and to depart: why? Impulse, generation,
impatience, obscure hope, and desperation
not to be understood or understand:

To take on all this, and, in vain persistence,
let fall, perhaps, what you have held, to die
alone and destitute, not knowing why –

Is this the way into some new existence?

Paris, June 1906

THE OLIVE GARDEN

And still he climbed, and through the grey leaves thrust,
quite grey and lost in the grey olive lands,
and laid his burning forehead full of dust
deep in the dustiness of burning hands.

After all, this. And, this, then, was the end.
Now I'm to go, while I am going blind,
and, oh, why wilt Thou have me still contend
Thou art, whom I myself no longer find.

No more I find Thee. In myself no tone
of Thee; nor in the rest; nor in this stone.
I can find Thee no more. I am alone.

I am alone with all that human fate
I undertook through Thee to mitigate,
Thou who art not. Oh, shame too consummate . . .

An angel came, those afterwards relate.

Wherefore an angel? Oh, there came the night,
and turned the leaves of trees indifferently,
and the disciples stirred uneasily.
Wherefore an angel? Oh, there came the night.

The night that came requires no specifying;
just so a hundred nights go by,
while dogs are sleeping and while stones are lying –
just any melancholy night that, sighing,
lingers till morning mount the sky.

For angels never come to such men's prayers,
nor nights for them mix glory with their gloom.
Forsakenness is the self-loser's doom,
and such are absent from their father's cares
and disincluded from their mother's womb.

Paris, May-June 1906

PIETÀ

So, Jesus, once again I am beholding
those feet that seemed so youthful to me there
when I unshod and washed them, greatly fearing;
oh, how they stood entangled in my hair,
like some white wild thing from a thorn-bush peering.

Those limbs, from every lover so withholding,
for the first time in this love-night I view.
We've never felt each other's arms enfolding,
and now I only weep and watch for you.

But, look, how torn your hands have come to be: –
not from my bites, beloved, not by me.
Your heart stands open now for all to share:
I only should have had the entry there.

Now you are tired, and your tired mouth is urged
by no desire for my sad mouth, alas! –
O Jesus, Jesus, when did our time pass?
How strangely both of us are being submerged.

Paris, May-June 1906

THE ARISEN

He had never brought himself as yet
to forbid and chide those subtle tones
that betrayed her love as self-admired;
and she sank before the cross attired
in a sorrow that was all beset
with her love's most precious stones.

When she came, though, on her ministration,
to the sepulchre in bitter woe,
he had risen, just for her salvation,
saying with final benediction: No –

Only in her cave she comprehended
how at last, grown stronger through his death,
proffered oil's relief he had forfended
and presentiment of touch and breath,

that from her he might create the lover
whom a loved one can no longer bind,
since, upswept by forces far above her,
she has left his voice so far behind.

Paris, autumn 1907 or Capri, spring 1908

THE EGYPTIAN MARY

Since her fleeing, bed-hotly, as the whore,
over Jordan, when she yielded up
all her pure heart's undiluted store,
grave-like, for Eternity to sup,

former givingness had ceaselessly
grandeured into such unselfawareness,
she at last, like all creation's bareness,
nothing but time-yellowed ivory,

lay there in her brittle hair's persistence.
And a lion circled, and there sought her
one grown old who called for his assistance:

(and they dug in unison.)

And the ancient laid her there alone.
And the lion, like a shield-supporter,
sat near by and held the stone.

Paris, early summer 1908

THE CALLING OF MOHAMMED

When, though, into his hiding-place the towering,
the not to be mistaken angel came,
erect, illustrious and overpowering:
he then implored, renouncing every claim,

permission to remain that over-journeyed,
distracted merchant he was really;
he'd never been a reader – and to see
a word like that, too much for the most learned.

The angel, though, imperious, paid no heed,
but showed and kept on showing to the pleader
the writing on his scroll and willed him: *Read.*

He then so read, the angel's self saluted.
And was already one who'd *been* a reader
and could and lent his ear and executed.

Paris, 22 August - 5 September 1907

GOD IN THE MIDDLE AGES

And they'd got him in themselves upstored,
and they wanted him to reign forever,
and they hung on him (a last endeavour
to withhold his journey heavenward

and to have him near them in their slumbers)
their cathedrals' massive weights. He must
merely wheel across his boundless numbers
pointingly and, like a clock, adjust

what they daily toiled at or transacted.
But he suddenly got into gear,
and the people of the stricken town

left him – for his voice inspired such fear –
running with his striking-works extracted,
and absconded from his dial's frown.

Paris, 19-23 July 1907

LEGEND OF THE THREE LIVING AND THE THREE DEAD

Three lords had hawked by a forest side,
and now it was feast they would.
But the hermit seized them and turned them aside,
and the riders halted, each astride,
where the three-fold sarcophagus stood,

and stank at them in a three-fold way,
in the mouth, in the nose, in the eyes;
and they knew at once: for many a day
three dead therein had been wasting away
their substance in hideous wise.

And they'd only their hunters' ears so keen
behind their hat-straps still left clean;
but their guide hissed thereinto:
The needle's eye they have never been,
and never will be, through.

They still retained their sense of touch,
strong and hot from their exercise;
but a frost from behind had that in its clutch
and was turning its sweat to ice.

Paris, early summer 1908

Partly inspired, it would seem, by recollections of one of the frescoes in the Campo Santo at Pisa.

FROM THE LIFE OF A SAINT

He knew of terrors that encompassed one
swiftly and unsurvivably as death.
His heart toiled slowly through with labouring breath,
the heart he nurtured like a son.

Ineffable extremities he knew,
dawnless as dungeons hidden from the sky;
obediently he gave his soul up too,
when she reached womanhood, that she might lie

beside her bridegroom and her lord; while he
remained behind without her, in a place
where loneliness surpassed reality,
and shunned all speech and never showed his face.

But as some recompense, before the sands
had quite run out, he knew the happiness
of holding, when he yearned for tenderness,
himself, like all creation, in his hands.

Paris, 22 August - 5 September 1907

SAINT SEBASTIAN

Like one lying down he stands there, all
target-proffered by his mighty will.
Far-removed, like mothers when they still,
self-inwoven like a coronal.

And the arrows come, and, as if straight
out of his own loins originating,
cluster with their feathered ends vibrating.
But he darkly smiles, inviolate.

Only once his eyes show deep distress,
gazing in a painful nakedness;
then, as though ashamed of noticing,
seem to let go with disdainfulness
those destroyers of a lovely thing.

Meudon, winter 1905-6

There are many representations of the martyrdom of St. Sebastian by Renaissance artists, but Rilke would seem to have had more particularly in mind that by Botticelli in the Kaiser Friedrich Museum at Berlin.

THE DONOR

The painters' guild was given this commission.
His Lord, perhaps, he did not really see;
perhaps, as he was kneeling in submission,
no saintly bishop stood in this position
and laid his hand upon him silently.

To kneel like this was everything, maybe
(just as it's all that we ourselves have known):
to kneel: and hold with choking breath one's own
contracted contours, trying to expand,
tight in one's heart like horses in one's hand.

So that, if something awesome should appear,
something unpromised and unprophesied,
we might dare hope it would not see nor hear,
and might approach, until it came quite near,
deep in itself and self-preoccupied.

Paris, mid-July 1906

L'ANGE DU MÉRIDIEN

CHARTRES

In storm, that round thc strong cathedral rages
like a denier thinking through and through,
your tender smiling suddenly engages
our hearts and lifts them up to you:

O smiling angel, sympathetic stone,
with mouth as from a hundred mouths distilled:
do you not mark how, from your ever-filled
sundial, our hours are gliding one by one –

that so impartial sundial, upon which
the day's whole sum is balanced equally,
as though all hours alike were ripe and rich?

What do you know, stone-nurtured, of our plight?
With face that's even blissfuller, maybe,
you hold your tables out into the night.

Paris, May-June 1906

THE CATHEDRAL

In those small towns, where clustered round about
old houses squat and jostle like a fair
that's just caught sight of it, and then and there
shut up its stalls, and, silenced every shout,

the criers still, the drum-sticks all suspended,
stands gazing up at it with straining ears:
while it, as calm as ever, in the splendid
wrinkled buttress-mantle rears
itself above the homes it never knew:

in those small towns you come to realise
how the cathedrals utterly outgrew
their whole environment. Their birth and rise,
as our own life's too great proximity
will mount beyond our vision and our sense
of other happenings, took precedence
of all things; as though that were history,
piled up in their immeasurable masses
in petrification safe from circumstance,
not that, which down among the dark streets passes
and takes whatever name is given by chance
and goes in that, as children green or red,
or what the dealer has, wear in rotation.
For birth was here, within this deep foundation,
and strength and purpose in this aspiration,
and love, like bread and wine, was all around,

and porches full of lovers' lamentation.
In the tolled hours was heard life's hestitation,
and in those towers that, full of resignation,
ceased all at once from climbing, death was found.

Paris, c. 1 July 1906

THE PORCH

I

They've lingered there, as though it had receded,
that tide which once so thunderously surged
against these massive stones till they emerged;
and with it many an emblem's ebbed unheeded

out of their hands, so much too liberal
and kindly to retain their grasp of things.
They've lingered, from a cliff's ensculpturings
distinguished only by vestigial

nimbus or mitre or, at times, a smile,
for which a face, to serve as silent dial,
has saved up all the peace its hours once brought.

Rapt now into their porch's emptiness,
they used to be an ear's wide-openedness
wherewith this city's every groan was caught.

II

Therewith great distantness is signified:
as with some stage-set we are looking at
the world is signified, and as through that
the hero, mantled in his act, will stride,

the tragic stage of its profundity
by this great door's enacting dark is trod,
as boundless and as fluctuant as God,
and, like him, self-transforming wondrously

into a Son, disseminated there
in multitudes of small parts, almost mute,
taken from misery's repertoire of woes.

For now it's only thus (we're well aware)
that out of those blind, mad and destitute
the Saviour, like a single actor, grows.

III

And thus they tower with arrested hearts
(they'll stand for ever and for ever stay);
though sometimes from the fall of folds outstarts
a sudden gesture, upright, steep as they,

and, after half a step, will stop, until
it's overtaken by the centuries.
They're poised on brackets whose interstices
a world they do not see enlivens still,

that wildering world they have not trodden out,
where shape and beast, as though imperilling,
writhe and upsurge and yet uphold them all:

because, like acrobats, that monstrous rout
only indulge in such wild gesturing
so that the brow-supported staff shan't fall.

Paris, 8-11 July 1906

THE ANGEL

Bowing his head a little, he absolves
himself from things that limit and direct,
for through his heart moves, mightily erect,
the eternal future, that revolves.

Before him full of shapes deep heaven stands,
and each can call to him with pleading claim.
Put nothing into his unburdened hands
from your encumbrancy. Unless they came

by night for wrestlinger investigating,
and crossed like raging furies your threshold
and seized on you as though they were creating
and breaking you from your retaining mould.

Paris, early summer 1906

THE UNICORN

And then the saint looked up, and in surprise
the prayer fell like a helmet from his head:
for softly neared that never-credited
white creature, which, like some unparented,
some helpless hind, beseeches with its eyes.

The ivory framework of the limbs so light
moved like a pair of balances deflected,
there glided through the coat a gleam of white,
and on the forehead, where the beams collected,
stood, like a moon-lit tower, the horn so bright,
at every footstep proudly re-erected.

Its mouth was slightly open, and a trace
of white through the soft down of grey and rose
(whitest of whites) came from the gleaming teeth;
its nostrils panted gently for repose.
Its gaze, though, checked by nothing here beneath,
projecting pictures into space,
brought a blue saga-cycle to a close.

Meudon, winter 1905-6

THE LAST COUNT OF BREDERODE ESCAPES FROM TURKISH CAPTIVITY

They followed fearsomely; from distantness
hurling their motley death at him, while he
fled lost, with nothing but his threatenedness.
It seemed the farness of his ancestry

for him had ceased to count; for so to flee
needs but a hunted animal. Until
the stream roared near and bright. An act of will
raised him and his distress and suddenly

made him again a boy of princely race.
A smile of noble women gone before him
once more poured sweetness into that young face

too soon complete. He forced his horse to pace
as grandly as his blood-glowing heart. It bore him
into the stream as into his own place.

Capri, mid-March 1907

THE ENSIGN

The others feel in all they are arrayed
no touch of sympathy: iron, cloth and leather.
There is at times the flattery of a feather,
but each is lone and loveless altogether;
he carries though – as if it were a maid –
the precious ensign in her gala dress.
Sometimes he feels her heavy silk's caress
flowing along his fingers fold on fold.

Shutting his eyes, he only can behold
a smile, a smile; never must he forsake her. –

And if a flashing of cuirasses shake her
and grasp at her and strive and try to take her: –

then he may tear her boldly from the lance,
as though he tore her from her virgin name,
to hold beneath his tunic in a trance.

The others call that bravery and fame.

Paris, 11-19 July 1906

LAST EVENING

BY PERMISSION OF FRAU NONNA

And night and distant travel; for the train
of the whole army swept along the park.
He looked up from the harpsichord again
and played and glanced at her without remark,

almost like looking in a mirror's round:
so filled with his young features was that face,
features that bore his sadness with a grace
suing more seductively at every sound.

Then all at once that seemed to disappear:
she stood, as though with a great effort, near
the window-seat, and clasped her beating breast.

His playing stopped. Outside a fresh wind blew.
And on the mirror-table, strange and new,
stood the black shako with the death's head crest.

Paris, June 1906

'Frau Nonna' was Rilke's friend Julie Freifrau von Nordeck zur Rabenau, whose first husband had fallen in the battle of Königgrätz, 3 July 1866.

BEFORE SUMMER RAIN

Quite suddenly, from all the green around,
something – you hardly know just what – has gone;
you feel the park itself drawing in upon
the windows and growing silent. The last sound

is the rain-piping dotterel in the wood,
reminding you of somebody's *Jerome* –
there rises so much zeal and solitude
from that one voice the downpour soon will come

responding to. The lofty walls, arrayed
with ancient portraits, as though recollecting
they should not listen to our talk, withdraw.

The faded tapestries are now reflecting
the uncertain light we in our childhood saw
those afternoons when we were so afraid.

Paris, beginning of July 1906

Written after a visit to the château at Chantilly.

PARTING

How I have felt that thing that's called 'to part',
and feel it still: a dark, invincible
cruel something by which what was joined so well
is once more shown, held out, and torn apart.

In what defenceless gaze at that I've stood,
which, as it, calling to me, let me go,
stayed there, as though it were all womanhood,
yet small and white and nothing more than, oh,

a waving, now already unrelated
to me, a slight, continuous wave, – scarce now
explainable: perhaps a plum-tree bough
some perching cuckoo's hastily vacated.

Early 1906

DEATH EXPERIENCED

We know just nothing of this going hence
that so excludes us. We've no grounds at all
to greet with plaudits or malevolence
the Death whom that mask-mouth of tragical

lament disfigures so incredibly.
The world's still full of parts being acted by us.
Till pleasing in them cease to occupy us,
Death will act too, although unpleasingly.

When, though, you went, there broke upon this scene
a shining segment of realities
in at the crack you disappeared through: green
of real green, real sunshine, real trees.

We go on acting. Uttering what exacted
such painful learning, gesturing now and then;
but your existence and the part you acted,
withdrawn now from our play and from our ken,

sometimes recur to us like intimations
of that reality and of its laws,
and we transcend awhile our limitations
and act our lives unthinking of applause.

Capri, 24 January 1907

In memory of Countess Luise Schwerin, who had died 24 January 1906.

MORGUE

Here they lie ready, as though what were still
needful were that some action be invented
whereby with one another and this chill
they might become united and contented;

for all is still as though without conclusion.
What names, we'd like to know, may have been found
inside their pockets? All the disillusion
about their mouths has been washed round and round:

it didn't go; it merely came quite clean.
Their beards are left them, just a bit less pendant,
but tidier, as it seems to the attendant,

so that the starers shan't be disconcerted.
The eyes beneath their eyelids have averted
their gaze from outwardness to that within.

Paris, beginning of July 1906

THE DEATH OF THE BELOVED

He only knew of death what all men may:
that those it takes it thrusts into dumb night.
When she herself, though, – no, not snatched away,
but tenderly unloosened from his sight,

had glided over to the unknown shades,
and when he felt that he had now resigned
the moonlight of her laughter to their glades,
and all her ways of being kind:

then all at once he came to understand
the dead through her, and joined them in their walk,
kin to them all; he let the others talk,

and paid no heed to them, and called that land
the fortunately-placed, the ever-sweet. –
And groped out all its pathways for her feet.

Paris, 22 August - 5 September 1907

THE LACE

I

Humanness: name for wavering possession,
still undetermined term of happiness:
is it inhuman that there went to fashion
this piece of lace-work's fine enwovenness
two eyes? – Do you regret their absentness?

You long-departed and at last benighted,
is all your bliss within this thing, where went,
as between trunk and bark, your lofty-flighted
feeling in magical diminishment?

Through some small chink in destiny, some gaping,
you drew your soul from temporality;
and it's so present in this airy shaping,
I have to smile at the expediency.

Paris, early summer 1906

II

And if one day our doing and our ado's
and all that happens to us should appear
trivial and strange, and it were far from clear
why we should struggle out of children's shoes
merely for that – would not, perhaps this run
of yellowed lace, this finely woven length
of flowery lace, then have sufficient strength
to keep us here? For look, it all got done.

A life perhaps was slighted, who can know?
A chance of happiness let slip – yet, spite
of all, there still emerged, however slow,
this thing, not easier than life, but quite
perfect, and, oh, so beautiful – as though
now were no more too soon for smiles and flight.

Capri, c. 10 February 1907

GOING BLIND

She'd sat just like the others there at tea.
And then I'd seemed to notice that her cup
was being a little differently picked up.
She'd smiled once. It had almost hurt to see.

And when eventually they rose and talked
and slowly, and as chance led, were dispersing
through several rooms there, laughing and conversing,
I noticed her. Behind the rest she walked

subduedly, like someone who presently
will have to sing, and with so many listening;
on those bright eyes of hers, with pleasure glistening,
played, as on pools, an outer radiancy.

She followed slowly and she needed time,
as though some long ascent were not yet by;
and yet: as though, when she had ceased to climb,
she would no longer merely walk, but fly.

Paris, end of June 1906

THE GROWN-UP

All that was standing on her and composed
the world, and all its dread and graciousness,
standing like trees in straight upshootingness,
all image, like God's ark, yet imageless,
and solemn, as upon a race imposed.

And she could bear it; bore high over her
the flying, fleeing, far away extended,
the unimagined, still unapprehended
as calmly as a water-carrier
her jar. Till midst of that activity,
transforming and for something else disposing,
the first white veil, scarce-feelably enclosing,
over that opened face fell suddenly,

almost opaque and lifting nevermore,
and somehow to all questioning anew
giving the same vague answer as before:
In you yourself, you once a child, in you.

Paris, 19 July 1907

PIANO PRACTICE

The summer hums. The hot noon stupefies.
She breathed her fresh white dress distractedly,
and laid into the cogent exercise
impatience after some reality

might come to-morrow, or to-night – was there,
perhaps, already, though they kept it dark;
and then she all at once became aware,
through the tall windows, of the pampered park.

Thereupon stopped her playing; gazed out, clasped her
two hands together; longed for a long book –
and in a sudden fit of anger shook
the jasmin scent away. She found it rasped her.

Paris, autumn 1907 or Capri, spring 1908

WOMAN IN LOVE

That is my window. Ending
softly the dream I was in
of being on wings ascending.
How far is my life extending,
and where does the night begin?

Everything, I'm inclining
to think, is me all round;
a crystal's deep through-shining,
dark and without a sound.

I could still let stars be filling
the spaces in me; my heart
seems so immense, so willing
to let him again depart

whom I perhaps have started
to love – to hold, maybe.
Strange and all-uncharted
seems my destiny.

How among what surpasses
I have been lightly laid,
fragrant as flowering grasses,
hither and thither swayed,

calling and full of fear
lest someone should hear my call,
and fated to disappear
in another for good and all.

Paris, 5-9 August 1907

SONG OF WOMEN TO THE POET

Look, how all's now unfolding: we are too,
for we are nothing but such blissfulness.
What in the brutes was blood and darkness grew
in us to soul, and its outcryingness

as soul continues. And it's crying for you.
You, though, ingaze it in a mild repose,

uncravingly, as if it were a view.
And therefore it's not you, we must suppose,

it's crying for. And yet, are you not he
on whom we could be utterly expended?
And more than that in whom else shall we be?

With us the Infinite keeps going again.
You, though, you mouth, that we may apprehend it,
you, though, you us-expresser, must remain.

Capri, mid-March 1907

THE POET'S DEATH

He lies. His pillowed features now appear
pale and denying above the silent cover,
since the whole world and all this knowledge of her,
torn from the senses of her lover,
fell back again to the unfeeling year.

Those who had seen him living saw no trace
of his deep unity with all that passes;
for these, these valleys here, these meadow-grasses,
these streams of running water, *were* his face.

Oh yes, his face was this remotest distance,
that seeks him still and woos him in despair;
and his mere mask, timidly dying there,
tender and open, has no more consistence
than broken fruit corrupting in the air.

Paris, May-June 1906

BUDDHA

As though he listened. Stillness: something far . . .
We hold our breath, but it has ceased to be.
And he is star. And great star on great star
stands round about him, though we cannot see.

Oh, he is all. Lingering, have we the least
hope that he'll notice? Could he ever need?
And if we fell before him here to plead,
he'd still sit deep and idle as a beast.

For that in him which drags us to his feet
has circled in him for a million years.
He who forgets our hopes and fears
in thoughts from which our thoughts retreat.

Meudon, end of 1905

On a little mound in Rodin's garden at Meudon stood an image of Buddha, which Rilke could see from his window and to which he often refers in his letters.

PORTRAIT

Lest there fall from her renouncing face
even one of those great sorrows there,
slowly through the tragedy she'll bear
all her beauty's withering bouquet,
wildly tied and almost loose already;
sometimes, like a tuberose, will eddy
some lost smile outweariedly away.

And she tiredly passes, with those thin
beautiful blind hands that have resigned it,
hands aware that they would never find it, –

and she speaks fictitiousness, wherein
some too common lot is made to moan,
and she makes it with her soul akin,
till it sounds like something all its own:
like the crying of a stone –

and she lets those words, with high-held chin,
all those words she's given, once more fall,
doing without them; for not one of all
answers to that sad reality
which, sole thing that she can claim,
like some foot-less vessel she
has to hold out high above her fame
and the passage of her evenings.

Paris, 1-2 August 1907

The subject is Eleonora Duse.

PORTRAIT OF A LADY OF THE EIGHTIES

Waiting there against the heavy-weighing
sombre satin drapery,
that above her seems to be displaying
shows of false intensity;

since her scarce-outdistanced girlishnesses
changed with someone else, it might appear:
weary underneath her high-heaped tresses,
inexperienced in her ruche-trimmed dresses,
and as if those folds could overhear

all her homesickness and hesitating
plans for what life now is going to be:
realer, as in novels, scintillating,
full of rapture and fatality, –

to have something safe from all detection
in one's escritoire and, when inclined,
lull oneself in fragrant recollection;
for one's diary at last to find

some beginning that no longer grows,
while one writes, mendacious and unmeaning,
and to wear a petal from a rose
in that heavy, empty locket, leaning

on each indrawn breath. To have at some
time just waved out of the window there –
that would be sufficient and to spare
for this new-ringed hand for months to come.

Paris, 22 August - 5 September 1907

DON JUAN'S CHILDHOOD

Already in his slimness it was clear,
that bow which, bent on women, does not split;
and, now no longer failing to appear,
an inclination through his face would flit

to one who passed him by, to one whose deeper
secrets some ancient foreign portrait kept:
he smiled. He was no longer now the weeper,
who stole away into the dark and wept.

And while a wholly novel self-assurance
oftener consoled him almost spoilingly,
he now confronted with a grave endurance
what gazed from women so disturbingly.

Paris, autumn 1907 or Capri, spring 1908

DON JUAN'S ELECTION

And the Angel came to him: Be given
wholly up to me. That's my behest:
For, till someone be surpassing even
those by whom the sweetest partner's driven
into bitterness, I cannot rest.
You're not much more capable of love
(do not interrupt, you're wrong),
still, you're ardent. And it's written above
that you'll lead a goodly throng
to that loneness you'll supply
entrance to. Let in thereby
those whom I into your way may
send, that Heloisa they may
overtop and overcry.

Paris, beginning of August 1908

THE LUTE

I am the lute. To make my body rise
out of your words, its strips' fine curvature,
speak of me as you would of some mature
upcurving fig. And overemphasise

the dark you see in me. That darkness there
was Tullia's own. Not in her shyest nook
was there so much, and her illumined hair
was like a lighted hall. At times she took

a little sound from the outside of me
into her face and sang. Then I'd bestir
and stretch myself against her frailty,
till all I had within me was in her.

Paris, autumn 1907 or Capri, spring 1908

'Tullia' is probably the celebrated Roman courtesan and poetess, Tullia d'Aragona (c. 1510-56), who is said to have been an excellent musician.

LULLABY

If I lose you and your love,
will you still slumber as before
without my murmuring any more
like lofty linden leaves above?

Without my watching every sign
here beside you and reposing
on your breasts, limbs, lips, like closing
eyelids almost, words of mine?

Without my having finally
locked you with your self alone,
like a garden thickly-sown
with balm-mint and the anise tree?

Paris, early summer 1908

THE ABDUCTION

As a child she'd often eluded the care
of attendants to see the wind and the night
(because inside they are different quite)
at their very beginnings out there;

but no storm-night had so known how
to rend the gigantic park in pieces
as her conscience rent it now,

when down from the silken ladder he caught her
in his arms and further and further brought her . . . :
till the carriage was everything.

And she smelt the black carriage, round which there lay
peril and hot pursuit
ready to spring.
And she found it covered with cold like spray;
and the blackness and coldness were in her too.
Into her hood she crept away
and felt her hair like a friend still true,
and heard estrangedly a stranger say:
I'm here with you.

Paris, summer 1908

THE BALCONY

NAPLES

Up there, by their balcony's inhemming
caused, as by a painter, to cohere,
bound as into a bouquet, comprised
of old and youthful faces, they appear
more ideal, more touching, in the clear
evening, and as though eternalised.

Those two sisters, each on each inclining,
as if out of some great distantness
hopelessly for one another pining,
loneliness supporting loneliness;

and their gravely silence-keeping brother,
unconfiding, full of destiny,
none the less, though, all unnoticedly
matched by one soft moment with his mother;

and between, outlived and elongated,
long now unrelated to them all,
mask of an old woman, insulated,
stayed, as in the middle of a fall,

by one hand, whose fellow, shrivelleder,
like a leaf downspinning, as it were,
hangs adheringly in front of her

by that child-face, thereinto
last inserted, contoured without shading,
quickly crossed out by the balustrading,
as if still unsettled, still to do.

Paris, 17 August 1907

BLACK CAT

Glances even at an apparition
still seem somehow to reverberate;
here on this black fell, though, the emission
of your strongest gaze will dissipate:

as a maniac, precipitated
into the surrounding black, will be
halted headlong and evaporated
by his padded cell's absorbency.

All the glances she was ever swept with
on herself she seems to be concealing,
where, with lowering and peevish mind, they're
being downlooked upon by her and slept with.
As if wakened, though, she turns her face
full upon your own quite suddenly,
and in the yellow amber of those sealing
eyes of hers you unexpectedly
meet the glance you've given her, enshrined there
like an insect of some vanished race.

Paris, summer 1908

THE FLAMINGOS

PARIS, JARDIN DES PLANTES

In Fragonard-like mirrorings no more
of all their white and red is proffered to you
than would have been conveyed if one who knew you
had said of her he'd chosen to adore:

'She was still soft with sleep'. For if, forsaking
pool for green grass, they stand together there,
rose-stalked, as in some blossoming parterre,
they're taken by themselves with lures more taking

than Phryne's; till they've necked that pallidness
of eye deep into their own downiness,
where black and ripe-fruit-ruddiness are hiding.

A screech of envy rends the aviary;
they, though, in stretched astonishment, are striding,
each singly, into the imaginary.

Paris, autumn 1907 or Capri, spring 1908

THE PANTHER

JARDIN DES PLANTES, PARIS

His gaze, going past those bars, has got so misted
with tiredness, it can take in nothing more.
He feels as though a thousand bars existed,
and no more world beyond them than before.

Those supply powerful paddings, turning there
in tiniest of circles, well might be
the dance of forces round a centre where
some mighty will stands paralyticly.

Just now and then the pupils' noiseless shutter
is lifted. – Then an image will indart,
down through the limbs' intensive stillness flutter,
and end its being in the heart.

Paris, 1903 or (possibly) end of 1902

First published September 1903. The earliest of *New Poems*.

THE MERRY-GO-ROUND

JARDIN DU LUXEMBOURG

With roof and shadow for a while careers
the stud of horses, variously bright,
all from that land that hesitates for quite
a length of time before it disappears.
Several indeed pull carriages, with tight-
held rein, but all have boldness in their bearing;
with them a wicked scarlet lion's faring
and now and then an elephant all white.

Just as in woods, a stag comes into view,
save that it has a saddle and tied fast
thereon a little maiden all in blue.

And on the lion a little boy is going,
whose small hot hands hold on with all his might,
while raging lion's tongue and teeth are showing.

And now and then an elephant all white.

And on the horses they come riding past,
girls too, bright-skirted, whom the horse-jumps here
scarce now preoccupy: in full career
elsewhither, hitherwards, a glance they cast –

And now and then an elephant all white.

And this keeps passing by until it's ended,
and hastens aimlessly until it's done.
A red, a green, a grey is apprehended,
a little profile, scarcely yet begun. –
And now and then a smile, for us intended,
blissfully happy, dazzlingly expended
upon this breathless, blindly followed fun . . .

Paris, June 1906

PERSIAN HELIOTROPE

The rose's praise might seem to you to ring
too loud for your beloved friend, so try
this herb so finely broidered and outvie
with heliotrope's insistent whispering

the bulbul, that among her favourite trees
outcries in ignorance her celebration.
For look: as sweet words, nights, in sentences
stay close together, with no separation,
from the vowels' wakeful violet fragrantly
circling beneath the silent canopy: –

before the arbour thus clear starry shapes
are now consorting with the silken grapes
and mingling, till it almost vanishes,
vanilla and cassia with the silentness.

Paris, early summer 1908

LANDSCAPE

How, at last, all instantaneously,
one piled heap of houses and of ridges,
bits of ancient sky and broken bridges,
lighted on, as though by destiny,

by the blazing sunset over there,
criminated, broken open, bare,
that small place would have a tragic ending:

fell there not into its woundedness
from the next hour's sudden presentness
that cool drop of blue which now is blending
night already with the evening,
so that what the sunset fired acquires
soft, redemption-like extinguishing.

Gate and arch in rest are now arrayed,
translucent clouds parade
above pale rows of houses, so
absorbed already into gathering shade;
yet a sudden moon-cast gleam will go
brightly gliding through it all, as though
some archangel had unsheathed his blade.

Capri, end of March, and Paris, 2 August 1907

SONG OF THE SEA

CAPRI, PICCOLA MARINA

Primeval breath from sea,
sea-wind by night;
   you come unseekingly;
one lying till light
must seek and find what he
may interpose:
   primeval breath from sea,
that only blows
as for primeval stone,
pure space
rushing from realms unknown . . .

How felt by a high-sown
fig-tree that clings for place
in the moonlight alone.

Capri, end of January 1907

LATE AUTUMN IN VENICE

The city drifts no longer like a bait now,
upcatching all the days as they emerge.
Brittlier the glassy palaces vibrate now
beneath your gaze. And from each garden verge

the summer like a bunch of puppets dangles,
headforemost, weary, made away.
Out of the ground, though, from dead forest tangles
volition mounts: as though before next day

the sea-commander must have rigged and ready
the galleys in the sleepless Arsenal,
and earliest morning air be tarred already

by an armada, oaringly outpressing,
and suddenly, with flare of flags, possessing
the great wind, radiant and invincible.

Paris, early summer 1908

NIGHT DRIVE

ST PETERSBURG

When, with that black, smoothly trotting pair
(fathered by some Orloff stallion), –
while behind the lofty street-lamps there
city night-fronts lay, dawn-greyed upon,
dumb, responsive to no hour's decrees, –
we were driving – no, were flying or surging,
and round burdening palaces emerging
out into the Neva breeze,

whirled on through that wakefully extended
nightfall that has neither earth nor sky, –
as the pressure of unsuperintended
gardens mounted bubblingly on high
from the Ljetnij-Ssad,[1] whose stone-upreared
forms with swooning contours disappeared
fadingly behind as we careered: –

[1] Ljetnij-Ssad: lit. 'Summer Garden', a private domain of the Czars, eventually opened to the public.

then this city with a sigh
stopped existing. All at once confessed
it had never been, imploring rest:
as when suddenly one long insane
finds his twist untwisted and outgrown,
and can feel a morbid, deep-enwrought,
utterly unalterable thought
he need nevermore be thinking: Stone –
falling from his empty, reeling brain
down and down into the unbeknown.

Paris, 9-17 August 1907

THE ISLAND

NORTH SEA

I

Across the mud-flat track the next tide sweeps,
and everything on all sides grows alike;
the little island over there, though, keeps
its eyes shut; dizzy-makingly its dyke

circles the dwellers there, born into dreams
where quietly universe with universe
will get confused; for seldom they converse,
and like an epitaph each sentence seems

for something unfamiliar, inundated,
that comes to them mysteriously and stays.
And such is everything that meets their gaze

from childhood on: something all-unrelated
to them, too big, regardless, transmigrated,
making still lonelier their lonely days.

Paris, 23 July 1906

II

As though it lay within some lunar crater's
outthrust, each farm's surrounded by a dyke,
and garths are costumed by their cultivators
the same way and, like orphans, combed alike

by that storm-wind, so roughly educating
and cowing for days on end with perishings.
One sits inside the house then, contemplating
in mirrors hung aslant what far-fetched things

stand on the dresser. And when day is done
one son will draw from his accordion
before the door a sound that seems to weep –

such, in some foreign port, it reached his ears. –
And huge and almost threateningly appears
on that surrounding dyke one of the sheep.

Paris, 24 July 1906

III

Only within is near; all else is far.
And this within crowded and day by day
too filled with all and what no words can say.
The island's like a too exiguous star

which unperceiving space, without a word,
has shattered in unconscious savagery,
so that it, unillumined and unheard,
tries solitarily,

hoping all this may somewhere find an end,
to move along its self-discovered line
in darkness, blindly, out of the design
wherein the planets, suns and systems wend.

Paris, 23-4 July 1906 (ll. 1-5) and 20 August 1907 (the rest)

THE APPLE ORCHARD

BORGEBY-GÅRD

Come just after sunset and inspect it,
evening greenness of the new-mown sward:
is it not like something long collected
by ourselves and inwardly upstored,

that we now, from feeling and reviewing,
new hope, jubilation half-forgot,
mixed with inner darkness still, are strewing
out in thoughts before us on this spot,

under trees like Dürer's, that to-day
bear the weight of work-days uncomputed
in their ripe abundancy enfruited,
serving, patient, finding out the way

that which overtops all measure so
yet may be ingathered and outgiven,
when a long life willingly has striven
to will only that and quietly grow.

Paris, 2 August 1907

Borgeby-gård was a country-house in Sweden where Rilke had stayed with Hanna Larsson and the painter Ernst Norlind in 1904.

THE STRANGER

Now as ever careless to unravel
what might be the view his nearest took,
once more he departed; lost, forsook. –
For he clung to them, these nights of travel,

closelier than to any lover's night.
How he'd watched in slumberless delight
out beneath the shining stars all yonder
circumscribed horizons roll asunder,
ever-changing like a changing fight;

others, with their moon-bright hamlets tendered
like some booty they had seized, surrendered
peacefully, or through tall trees would shed
glimpses of far-stretching parks, containing
grey ancestral houses that with craning
head a moment he inhabited,
knowing more deeply one could never bide;
then, already round the next curve speeding,
other highways, bridges, landscapes, leading
on to cities darkness magnified.

And to let all this, without all craving,
slip behind him meant beyond compare
more to him than pleasure, goods, or fame.
Though the well-steps in some foreign square,
daily hollowed by the drawers there,
seemed at times like something he could claim.

Paris, early summer 1908

THE PRISONER

Suppose that what's now sky and wind for you,
air for your mouth and brightness for your vision,
turned into stone all round that small provision
of space your heart and hands were welcome to.

And what's *to-morrow* in you now and *then*
and *later* and *next year* and *something waiting*
became all sore in you and suppurating
and festered on and never dawned again.

And what had been became insane and raged
within you, and your mouth, so disengaged
from laughter, were now laughing long and hard.

And what had once been God were just your guard,
attempting with a dirty eye to fill
the last hole up. And yet you lived on still.

Probably first half of 1906

THE BLIND MAN

PARIS

Look, his progress interrupts the scene,
absent from his dark perambulation,
like a dark crack's interpenetration
of a bright cup. And, as on a screen,

all reflections things around are making
get depicted on him outwardly.
Just his feeling stirs, as if intaking
little waves of world invisibly:

here a stillness, there a counter-stand, –
as if pondering whom to choose, he'll tarry:
then surrenderingly he'll lift his hand,
almost ritually, as if to marry.

Paris, 21 August 1907

THE SOLITARY

No, my heart shall be a tower, and there,
beneath the topmost cornice, I'll remain:
still, where nothing else is, with a share
of world, ineffability, and pain.

Only, in the Incommensurable,
one lone thing, now glooming, now a-glance,
only one last, longing countenance
thrust into the never-silenceable.

One extreme stone face, with steadfastness
mirroring some inward equipoise;
urged by that which silently destroys
on to ever-greater blissfulness.

Paris, mid-August 1907

THE CHILD

Long they watch it playing in its place,
half-aware; at moments it's emerging
from its profile, that round, real face,
clear and whole as some full hour upsurging

into sound and striking to an end.
They, though, fail to count the strokes it's giving,
dulled with toil and indolent with living;
yet it's bearing, could they comprehend,

even now, with effort never-ending,
all things, while, as in some wearisome
waiting-room, it sits by them, intending
just to wait until its time has come.

Paris, 31 July - 1 August 1907

BUDDHA IN GLORY

Cores' core, centre of all circulations,
almond self-enclosed and sweetening, –
all from here to all the constellations
is your fruit-pulp: you I sing.

How released you feel from all belonging!
In the Infinite expands your rind,
and within it your strong juice is thronging;
and a radiance from without is kind,

for those glowing suns of yours are spinning
on their ways high overhead.
But in you has had beginning
what shall live when they are dead.

Paris, summer 1908

TOMBS OF THE HETÆRÆ

They lie in their long hair, and their brown faces
have now withdrawn deep, deep into themselves.
Eyes closed, as though confronting too much distance.
Skeletons, mouths, and flowers. Within the mouths
the smooth teeth like a set of pocket-chessmen
marshalled together in two ivory rows.
And flowers, yellow pearls, and slender bones,
and hands, and tunics – withering warp and woof
above the inward-fallen heart. But there,
beneath those rings, beneath the talismans
and eye-blue stones (those cherished souvenirs),
there still remains the silent crypt of sex,
filled to its vaulted roof with flower petals.
And once more yellow pearls, rolled far asunder, –
dishes of hard-burnt clay, whose rondure once
her image decorated, – green remains
of unguent vases that once smelt like flowers, –
figures of little gods, too: household altars,
Hetæræ-heavens with ecstatic gods!
The unsprung girdle, the flat scarabæus,
and little figures of gigantic sex;
a mouth that laughs, and dancing girls, and runners,
and golden clasps that might be little bows
for hunting beast- and bird-shaped amulets;
and long pins, quaintly fashioned crockery,
and a round potsherd with a reddish ground
whereon, like dark inscriptions over entries,
appear the taut legs of a team of horses.
And flowers again, pearls that have rolled apart,
the shining loins of a tiny lyre,

and then, between the veils that fall like vapours,
crept, as it were, from chrysalidal shoe,
the ankle, like an airy butterfly.

And thus they lie, filled to the brim with things,
with precious things, with jewels, toys, bric-à-brac,
with broken trash (all that fell into them),
and sombre as the bottom of a river.

Yes, they were river beds:
over and over them in short, swift waves
(all pressing onwards to some life that waited)
bodies of many youths would hurtle headlong,
and manly rivers, too, would roar within them.
And sometimes boys, emerging from the mountains
of Childhood, would descend in timid torrents,
and play with what they found upon the bottom,
till all at once the falling gradient gripped them:

And then they'd fill with shallow crystal water
the whole expanse of these broad watercourses,
and set up eddies in the deeper places;
and mirror, for the first time, the wide-spreading
banks and far cries of birds, while, high above them,
the starry nights of a sweet country blossomed
into a heaven that could nowhere close.

Rome, beginning of 1904

ORPHEUS. EURYDICE. HERMES

That was the strange unfathomed mine of souls.
And they, like silent veins of silver ore,
were winding through its darkness. Between roots
welled up the blood that flows on to mankind,
like blocks of heavy porphyry in the darkness.
Else there was nothing red.

But there were rocks
and ghostly forests. Bridges over voidness
and that immense, grey, unreflecting pool
that hung above its so far distant bed
like a grey rainy sky above a landscape.
And between meadows, soft and full of patience,
appeared the pale strip of the single pathway
like a long line of linen laid to bleach.

And on this single pathway they approached.

In front the slender man in the blue mantle,
gazing in dumb impatience straight before him.
His steps devoured the way in mighty chunks
they did not pause to chew; his hands were hanging,
heavy and clenched, out of the falling folds,
no longer conscious of the lightsome lyre,
the lyre which had grown into his left
like twines of rose into a branch of olive.
It seemed as though his senses were divided:
for, while his sight ran like a dog before him,
turned round, came back, and stood, time and again,
distant and waiting, at the path's next turn,
his hearing lagged behind him like a smell.
It seemed to him at times as though it stretched
back to the progress of those other two
who should be following up this whole ascent.
Then once more there was nothing else behind him
but his climb's echo and his mantle's wind.
He, though, assured himself they still were coming;
said it aloud and heard it die away.
They still were coming, only they were two
that trod with fearful lightness. If he durst
but once look back (if only looking back
were not undoing of this whole enterprise
still to be done), he could not fail to see them,
the two light-footers, following him in silence:

The god of faring and of distant message,
the travelling-hood over his shining eyes,
the slender wand held out before his body,
the wings around his ankles lightly beating,
and in his left hand, as entrusted, *her*.

She, so belov'd, that from a single lyre
more mourning rose than from all women-mourners, –
that a whole world of mourning rose, wherein
all things were once more present: wood and vale
and road and hamlet, field and stream and beast, –
and that around this world of mourning turned,
even as around the other earth, a sun
and a whole silent heaven full of stars,
a heaven of mourning with disfigured stars: –
she, so beloved.

But hand in hand now with that god she walked,
her paces circumscribed by lengthy shroudings,
uncertain, gentle, and without impatience.
Wrapt in herself, like one whose time is near,
she thought not of the man who went before them,
nor of the road ascending into life.
Wrapt in herself she wandered. And her deadness
was filling her like fullness.
Full as a fruit with sweetness and with darkness
was she with her great death, which was so new
that for the time she could take nothing in.

She had attained a new virginity
and was intangible; her sex had closed
like a young flower at the approach of evening,
and her pale hands had grown so disaccustomed
to being a wife, that even the slim god's
endlessly gentle contact as he led her
disturbed her like a too great intimacy.

Even now she was no longer that blonde woman
who'd sometimes echoed in the poet's poems,
no longer the broad couch's scent and island,
nor yonder man's possession any longer.

She was already loosened like long hair,
and given far and wide like fallen rain,
and dealt out like a manifold supply.

She was already root.

And when abruptly,
the god had halted her and, with an anguished
outcry, outspoke the words: He has turned round! –
she took in nothing, and said softly: Who?

But in the distance, dark in the bright exit,
someone or other stood, whose countenance
was indistinguishable. Stood and saw
how, on a strip of pathway between meadows,
with sorrow in his look, the god of message
turned silently to go behind the figure
already going back by that same pathway,
its paces circumscribed by lengthy shroudings,
uncertain, gentle, and without impatience.

Rome, beginning of 1904; revised Sweden, autumn 1904

ALCESTIS

Then all at once the Messenger was there,
flung in among them like a new ingredient
just as the wedding feast was boiling over.
The revellers, they did not feel the god's
secret incoming, for he clasped his godhead
as closely to himself as a wet mantle,
and seemed like one of them, one or another,
as he passed through the hall. But suddenly
one of the guests, talking away there, saw
the hall's young master at the upper table
snatched, as it were, aloft, no more reclining,
and everywhere and with his whole existence
mirroring some strange and terrible demand.
And thereupon, as though the mixture cleared,
was silence: with some dregs, right at the bottom,
of cloudy hubbub, and a sediment
of falling babble, giving off already
the smell of hollow laughter that's gone flat.
And then they recognised the slender god,
and, as he stood there, full of inward mission
and unentreatable, they almost knew.
And yet, when it was uttered, it was far
beyond all knowledge, past all comprehension.
Admetus dies. When? In this very hour.

He, though, had started breaking, piece by piece,
his shell of fright, and was already stretching
his hands therefrom to bargain with the god.
For years, for yet one single year of youth,
for months, for weeks, for a few days – alas!
not days, – for nights, just for a single one,
for one night, just for this one: just for this.
The god refused, and then he screamed aloud
and screamed it out, withheld it not, and screamed
as his own mother screamed when he was born.

And she came up to him, an aged woman,
and then his father came, his aged father,
and both stood, aged, antiquated, helpless,
beside the screamer, who suddenly, never yet
so closely, looked at them, stopped, gulped, and said:

Father,
does it mean much to you, this residue,
this sediment, that hinders you in swallowing?
Go, pour it out. And you, old woman, you,
Mother,
why are you here still? You have given birth.
And held them both, like sacrificial beasts,
in one hard grip. Then suddenly let go,
pushed the old folk away, radiant, inspired,
and breathing hard, and shouting: Creon, Creon!
and nothing else, and nothing but that name.
But in his face appeared that something else
he did not utter, longing for the moment
when, glowingly, across the tangled table,
he'd proffer it the young friend, the beloved.
Look, the old folk (appeared there) are no ransom,
they are worn out and poor and almost worthless,
but you – it's different, you in all your beauty –

Now, though, he could no longer see his friend.
He stayed behind, and it was she that came,
almost a little smaller than he'd known her,
and light and sad in her pale bridal dress.
The others are all nothing but her street,
down which she comes and comes (she'll soon be there
within his arms, so painfully extended).

But while he waits, she speaks, though not to him.
Speaks to the god, and the god listens to her,
and all hear, as it were, within the god:

None can be substitute for him. I'm that.
I'm substitute. For no one's reached the end
of everything as I have. What remains
of all I used to be? What's this but dying?
Did she not tell you, she who sent you hither,
that yonder couch waiting in there for me
belongs to the underworld? I said farewell.
Farewell upon farewell.
None dying could say more. And why I went,
was that all this, buried beneath the man
who's now my husband, might dissolve and fade. –
Lead me away: I'm dying for him already.

And, like a veering wind on the high seas,
the god approached her almost as one dead,

and all at once was far off from her husband,
to whom, concealed within a little token,
he tossed the hundred lives of mortal men.
He stumbled dizzily towards the pair
and grasped at them as in a dream. Already
they'd nearly reached the entrance, where the women
were crowding tearfully. But yet once more
he saw the maiden's face, that turned to him,
smiling a smile as radiant as a hope,
that was almost a promise: to return,
grown up, out of the depths of death again,
to him, the liver –

Thereupon he flung
his hands, as he knelt there, before his face,
so as to see no more after that smile.

Capri, 7-10 February 1907

BIRTH OF VENUS

The morning following that fearful night
that passed with shouting, restlessness, and uproar,
the sea burst open yet again and screamed.
And, as the scream ebbed slowly to its close,
and, from the sky's pale daybreak and beginning,
was falling back to the dumb fishes' darkness –
the sea gave birth.

The first rays shimmered on the foaming hair
of the wide wave-vagina, on whose rim
the maiden rose, white and confused and wet.
And, as a young green leaf bestirs itself,
stretches and slowly opens out encurlment,
her body was unfolded into coolness
and into the unfingered wind of dawn.

Like moons the knees went climbing clearly upwards
to dive into the cloud-brims of the thighs;
the narrow shadow of the calves retreated,
the feet extended and grew luminous,
and all the joints became as much alive
as drinkers' throats.

And in the pelvis-chalice lay the belly,
like a young fruit within a childish hand.
And there, within its navel's narrow goblet,
was all this limpid life contained of darkness.
Thereunder lightly rose the little swell
and lapped continually towards the loins
where now and then a silent trickle glistened.
Translucent, though, and still without a shadow,
lay, like a group of silver birch in April,
warm, empty, all unhidden, the vagina.

And now the shoulders' mobile balance hung
in equipoise upon the wand-straight body,
which mounted from the pelvis like a fountain,
and in the long arms lingeringly descended,
and swiftlier in the hair's abundant fall.

Then, very slowly came the face's progress,
from the fore-shortened dimness of its drooping
into clear horizontal exaltation,
brought to abrupt conclusion by the chin.

Now, when the neck was stretched out like a jet
and like a flower-stalk where sap is mounting,
the arms began to stretch out too, like necks
of swans, when they are making for the shore.

Then entered the dim dawning of this body,
like matutinal wind, the first deep breath.
Within the tenderest branches of the vein-trees
a whispering arose, and then the blood
began to rustle over deeper places.
And this wind grew and grew, until it hurtled
with all its power of breath at the new breasts
and filled them up and forced itself within them,
and they, like filled sails full of the horizon,
impelled the lightsome maiden to the shore.

And thus the goddess landed.

And behind her,
who swiftly left behind the youthful shores,
kept springing up throughout the whole forenoon
the flowers and the grasses, warm, confused,
as from embracing. And she walked and ran.

At noontide, though, in that most heavy hour,
the sea rose up yet once again and flung
a dolphin out upon that self-same spot.
Dead, red, and open.

Rome, beginning of 1904 (first draft); Sweden, autumn 1904 (final version)

THE BOWL OF ROSES

You've seen the flare of anger, seen two boys
bunch themselves up into a ball of something
that was mere hate and roll upon the ground
like a dumb animal attacked by bees;
actors, sky-towering exaggerators,
the crashing downfall of careering horses,
casting away their sight, flashing their teeth
as though the skull were peeling from the mouth.

But now you know how such things are forgotten;
for now before you stands the bowl of roses,
the unforgettable, entirely filled
with that extremity of being and bending,
proffer beyond all power of giving, presence,
that might be ours: that might be our extreme.

Living in silence, endless opening out,
space being used, but without space being taken
from that space which the things around diminish;
absence of outline, like untinted groundwork
and mere Within; so much so strangely tender
and self-illumined – to the very verge: –
where do we know of anything like this?

And this: a feeling able to arise
through petals being touched by other petals?
And this: that one should open like an eyelid,
and lying there beneath it simply eyelids,
all of them closed, as though they had to slumber
ten-fold to quench some inward power of vision.
And this, above all: that through all these petals
light has to penetrate. From thousand heavens
they slowly filter out that drop of darkness
within whose fiery glow the mazy bundle
of stamens stirs itself and reaches upwards.

And then the movement in the roses, look:
gestures deflected through such tiny angles,
they'd all remain invisible unless
their rays ran streaming out into the cosmos.

Look at that white one, blissfully unfolded
and standing in the great big open petals
like Venus upright in her mussel shell;
look how that blusher there, as in confusion,
has turned towards a cooler bloom, and how
the cool one is unfeelingly withdrawing;
and how the cold one stands, wrapped in herself,
among those open roses doffing all.
And *what* they doff – the way it can appear
now light, now heavy – like a cloak, a burden,
a wing, a domino – it all depends –
and *how* they doff it: as before the loved one.

What can they *not* be: was that yellow one
that lies there hollow, open, not the rind
upon a fruit, in which that self-same yellow
was the intenser, orange-ruddier juice?
And did her blowing prove too much for this one,
since, touched by air, her nameless rosiness
assumed the bitter after-taste of lilac?
And is not yonder cambric one a dress,
wherein, still soft and breath-warm, clings the vest
flung off along with it among the shadows
of early morning by the woodland pool?
And what's this opalescent porcelain,
so fragile, but a shallow china cup,
and full of little shining butterflies?
And that, containing nothing but herself?

And are not all just that, just self-containing,
if self-containing means: to take the world
and wind and rain and patience of the spring-time
and guilt and restlessness and muffled fate
and sombreness of evening earth and even
the melting, fleeing, forming of the clouds
and the vague influence of distant stars,
and change it to a handful of Within?

It now lies heedless in those open roses.

Capri, c. New Year 1907

REQUIEM

Written in Paris between 31 October and 5 November 1908, published May 1909.

NOTE ON THE REQUIEM FOR A FRIEND

The friend was Paula Modersohn-Becker (1876-1907), perhaps the only painter of real genius among those whom Rilke met while staying in the artists' colony of Worpswede in 1900. Shortly after his own marriage to her friend Clara Westhoff in April 1901, Paula Becker married the good-natured but rather mediocre artist Otto Modersohn, another member of the colony. The marriage was not successful, and in February 1906 Paula, who felt that it was strangling her creative powers, left her husband and went to Paris, from where, however, her husband persuaded her to return to him at the end of the year. She died at Worpswede on 21 November 1907, shortly after giving birth to a child.

What made her fate so significant for Rilke was that it seemed to symbolise in an especially poignant and tragic fashion that opposition between the claims of art and the claims of life of which he himself was continually aware. He found the attempt to be a poet and nothing but a poet so difficult that he was sometimes tempted to abandon it for some other profession. The 'help' which he begs of her at the end of the poem may be regarded as help to resist this temptation.

FOR A FRIEND

I have my dead, and I would let them go
and be surprised to see them all so cheerful,
so soon at home in being-dead, so right,
so unlike their repute. You, you alone,
return; brush past me, move about, persist
in knocking something that vibratingly
betrays you. Oh, don't take from me what I
am slowly learning. I'm right; you're mistaken,
if you're disturbed into a home-sick longing
for something here. We transmute it all;
it's not here, we reflect it from ourselves,
from our own being, as soon as we perceive it.
  I thought you'd got much further. It confounds me
that *you* should thus mistake and come, who passed
all other women so in transmutation.
That we were frightened when you died, or, rather,
that your strong death made a dark interruption,
tearing the till-then from the ever-since:
that is our business: to set that in order
will be the work that everything provides us.
But that you too were frightened, even now
are frightened, now, when fright has lost its meaning,
that you are losing some of your eternity,
even a little, to step in here, friend, here,
where nothing yet exists; that in the All,
for the first time distracted and half-hearted,
you did not grasp the infinite ascension
as once you grasped each single thing on earth;
that from the orbit that already held you
the gravitation of some mute unrest
should drag you down to measurable time:
this often wakes me like an entering thief.
If I could say you merely deign to come
from magnanimity, from superabundance,
because you are so sure, so self-possessed,
that you can wander like a child, not frightened
of places where ther're things that happen to one: –
but no, you're asking. And that penetrates
right to the bone and rattles like a saw.
Reproach, such as you might bear as a spirit,

bear against me when I withdraw myself
at night into my lungs, into my bowels,
into the last poor chamber of my heart,
such a reproach would not be half so cruel
as this mute asking. What is it you ask?
Say, shall I travel? Have you left somewhere
a thing behind you, that torments itself
with trying to reach you? Travel to a country
you never saw, although it was as closely
akin to you as one half of your senses?
I'll voyage on its rivers, set my foot
upon its soil and ask about old customs,
stand talking with the women in their doorways
and pay attention when they call their children.
I will observe how they take on the landscape
outside there in the course of the old labour
of field and meadow; will express a wish
to be presented to the king himself,
and work upon the priests with bribery
to leave me lying before the strongest statue
and then withdraw, shutting the temple doors.
But in conclusion, having learnt so much,
I'll simply watch the animals, that something
of their own way of turning may glide over
into my joints; I'll have a brief existence
within their eyes, that solemnly retain me
and slowly loose me, calmly, without judgment.
I'll make the gardeners repeat by heart
the names of many flowers and so bring back
in pots of lovely proper names a remnant,
a little remnant, of the hundred perfumes.
And I will purchase fruits too, fruits, wherein
that country, sky and all, will re-exist.
For that was what you understood: full fruits.
You used to set them out in bowls before you
and counterpoise their heaviness with colours.
And women too appeared to you as fruits,
and children too, both of them from within
impelled into the forms of their existence.
And finally you saw yourself as fruit,
lifted yourself out of your clothes and carried
that self before the mirror, let it in
up to your gaze; which remained, large, in front,
and did not say: that's me; no, but: this is.
So unenquiring was your gaze at last,

so unpossessive and so truly poor,
it wanted even you no longer: holy.
  That's how I would retain you, as you placed
yourself within the mirror, deep within,
and far from all else. Why come differently?
Why thus revoke yourself? Why are you trying
to make me feel that in those amber beads
around your neck there was still something heavy
with such a heaviness as never lurks
in the beyond of tranquil pictures? Why
does something in your bearing bode misfortune?
What makes you read the contours of your body
like lines upon a hand, and me no longer
able to see them but as destiny?
  Come to the candle-light. I'm not afraid
to look upon the dead. When they return
they have a right to hospitality
within our gaze, the same as other things.
  Come; we'll remain a little while in silence.
Look at this rose, here, on my writing-desk:
is not the light around it just as timid
as that round you? It too should not be here.
It ought to have remained or passed away
out in the garden there, unmixed with me, –
it stays, unconscious of my consciousness.

Don't be afraid now if I comprehend:
it's rising in me – oh, I must, I must,
even if it kills me, I must comprehend.
Comprehend, that you're here. I comprehend.
Just as a blind man comprehends a thing,
I feel your fate although I cannot name it.
Let both of us lament that someone took you
out of your mirror. If you still can cry?
No, you can't cry. You long ago transformed
the force and thrust of tears to your ripe gazing,
and were in act of changing every kind
of sap within you to a strong existence
that mounts and circles in blind equipoise.
Then, for the last time, chance got hold of you,
and snatched you back out of your farthest progress,
back to a world where saps will have their way.
Did not snatch all, only a piece at first,
but when reality, from day to day,
so swelled around that piece that it grew heavy,

you needed your whole self; then off you went
and broke yourself in fragments from your law,
laboriously, needing yourself. And then
you took yourself away and from your heart's
warm, night-warm, soil you dug the yet green seeds
your death was going to spring from: your own death,
the death appropriate to your own life.
And then you ate those grains of your own death
like any others, ate them one by one,
and had within yourself an after-taste
of unexpected sweetness, had sweet lips,
you: in your senses sweet within already.
Let us lament. Do you know how unwilling
and hesitatingly your blood returned,
recalled from an incomparable orbit?
With what confusion it took up again
the tiny circulation of the body?
With what mistrust it entered the placenta,
suddenly tired from the long homeward journey?
You drove it on again, you pushed it forward,
you dragged it to the hearth, as people drag
a herd of animals to sacrifice;
and spite of all desired it to be happy.
And finally you forced it: it was happy,
and ran up and surrendered. You supposed,
being so accustomed to the other measures,
that this was only for a little while;
but now you were in time, and time is long.
And time goes by, and time goes on, and time
is like relapsing after some long illness.
How very short your life, when you compare it
with hours you used to sit in silence, bending
the boundless forces of your boundless future
out of their course to the new germination,
that became fate once more. O painful labour.
Labour beyond all strength. And you performed it
day after day, you dragged yourself along to it
and pulled the lovely woof out of the loom
and wove your threads into another pattern.
And still had spirit for a festival.
For when you'd done you looked for some reward,
like children, when they've drunk a nasty drink
of bitter-sweet tea that may make one better.
You gave your own reward, being still so distant,
even then, from all the rest; and no one there

who could have hit on a reward to please you.
You yourself knew it. You sat up in child-bed,
a mirror there before you, that returned
all that you gave. Now everything was you,
and right in front; within was mere deceit,
the sweet deceit of Everywoman, gladly
putting her jewels on and doing her hair.
And so you died like women long ago,
died in the old warm house, old-fashionedly,
the death of those in child-bed, who are trying
to close themselves again but cannot do it,
because that darkness which they also bore
returns and grows importunate and enters.

Ought they not, though, to have gone and hunted up
some mourners for you? Women who will weep
for money, and, if paid sufficiently,
will howl through a whole night when all is still.
Observances! We haven't got enough
observances. All vanishes in talk.
That's why you have to come back, and with me
retrieve omitted mourning. Can you hear me?
I'd like to fling my voice out like a cloth
over the broken fragments of your death
and tug at it till it was all in tatters,
and everything I said was forced to go
clad in the rags of that torn voice and freeze –
if mourning were enough. But I accuse:
not him who thus withdrew you from yourself
(I can't distinguish him, he's like them all),
but in him I accuse all: accuse man.
If somewhere deep within me rises up
a having-once-been-child I don't yet know,
perhaps the purest childness of my childhood:
I will not know it. Without looking at it
or asking, I will make an angel of it,
and hurl that angel to the foremost rank
of crying angels that remembrance God.
For now too long this suffering has lasted,
and none can stand it; it's too hard for us,
this tortuous suffering caused by spurious love,
which, building on prescription like a habit,
calls itself just and battens on injustice.
Where is the man who justly may possess?
Who can possess what cannot hold itself

but only now and then blissfully catches
and flings itself on like a child a ball?
As little as the admiral can retain
the nikê poised upon his vessel's prow
when the mysterious lightness of her godhead
has caught her up into the limpid sea-wind,
can one of us call back to him the woman
who, seeing us no longer, takes her way
along some narrow strip of her existence,
as through a miracle, without mischance –
unless his calling and delight were guilt.
 For this is guilt, if anything be guilt,
not to enlarge the freedom of a love
with all the freedom in one's own possession.
All we can offer where we love is this:
to loose each other; for to hold each other
comes easy to us and requires no learning.

Are you still there? Still hiding in some corner? –
You knew so much of all that I've been saying,
and could so much too, for you passed through life
open to all things, like a breaking day.
Women suffer: loving means being lonely,
and artists feel at times within their work
the need, where most they love, for transmutation.
You began both; and both exist in *that*
which fame, detaching it from you, disfigures.
Oh, you were far beyond all fame. Were inconspicuous; had gently taken in
your beauty as a gala flag's intaken
on the grey morning of a working-day,
and wanted nothing but a lengthy work, –
which is not done; in spite of all, not done.
 If you're still there, if somewhere in this darkness
there's still a spot where your perceptive spirit's
vibrating on the shallow waves of sound
a lonely voice within a lonely night
starts in the air-stream of a lofty room:
hear me and help me. Look, without knowing when,
we keep on slipping backwards from our progress
into some unintended thing, and there
we get ourselves involved as in a dream,
and there at last we die without awakening.
No one's got further. Anyone who's lifted
the level of his blood to some long work

may find he's holding it aloft no longer
and that it's worthlessly obeying its weight.
For somewhere there's an old hostility
between our human life and greatest work.
May I see into it and it say: help me!
  Do not return. If you can bear it, stay
dead with the dead. The dead are occupied.
But help me, as you may without distraction,
as the most distant sometimes helps: in me.

NOTE ON THE REQUIEM FOR WOLF GRAF VON KALCKREUTH

Wolf Graf von Kalckreuth (1887-1906), translator of Baudelaire and Verlaine and author of some original poems of great promise, had shot himself, at the age of nineteen, on 9 October 1906, at the beginning of his period of military service.

Although Rilke had never known the young man personally, his fate had acquired for him a significance complementary, as it were, to that of Paula Modersohn-Becker; for, while Paula had endured until she was destroyed, Kalckreuth had found the task of being a poet too difficult to face and had surrendered almost without a struggle. Rilke does not reproach him, because he too has so often felt the temptation to kill, if not himself, at any rate the poet in himself.

It may perhaps be said that the main subject of both Requiems is the 'endurance' which the life of a wholly dedicated poet or artist demands. Years later (18 November 1920) Rilke wrote to Baladine Klossowska ('Merline'): 'If the idea of sacrifice is that the moment of greatest danger coincides with that in which one is saved, then there is certainly nothing more like sacrifice than this terrible will to art.'

FOR WOLF GRAF VON KALCKREUTH

Can I have never seen you? For my heart
feels you like some too-burdensome beginning
one still defers. Oh, could I but begin
to tell of you, dead that you are, you gladly,
you passionately dead. And was it so
alleviating as you supposed, or was
no-more-alive still far from being-dead?
You thought you could possess things better there
where none care for possessions. You supposed
that over there you'd be inside the landscape
that here closed up before you like a picture,
would enter the beloved from within
and penetrate through all things, strong and wheeling.
Oh, that you may not have too long had cause
to tax your boyish error with deception!
Loosened within that rush of melancholy,
ecstatically and only half-aware,
may you, in motion round the distant stars,
have found the happiness that you transposed
from here into that being-dead you dreamt of.
How near you were to it, dear friend, even here.
How much it was at home here, what you purposed,
the earnest joy of your so strenuous longing.
When, tired of being happy and unhappy,
you mined into yourself and painfully
climbed with an insight, almost breaking down
under the weight of dark discovery:
you carried what you never recognised,
you carried joy, you carried through your blood
your little saviour's burden to the shore.
   Why did you not wait till the difficult
gets quite unbearable: until it turns,
and is so difficult because so real?
That was perhaps your next allotted moment;
it may perhaps have been already trimming
its garland at the door you slammed for ever.
   Oh that percussion, how it penetrates,
when somewhere, through impatience's sharp draught,
something wide open shuts and locks itself!
Who can deny on oath that in the earth

a crack goes springing through the healthy seeds?
Who has investigated if tame beasts
are not convulsed with sudden lust for killing
when that jerk shoots like lightning through their brains?
Who can deduce the influence leaping out
from actions to some near-by terminal?
Who can conduct where everything's conductive?
The fact that you destroyed. That this must be
related of you till the end of time.
Even if a hero's coming, who shall tear
meaning we take to be the face of things
off like a mask and in a restless rage
reveal us faces whose mute eyes have long
been gazing at us through dissembling holes:
this is sheer face and will not be transfigured:
that you destroyed. For blocks were lying there,
and in the air already was the rhythm
of some now scarce repressible construction.
You walked around and did not see their order,
one hid the other from you; each of them
seemed to be rooted, when in passing by
you tried at it, with no real confidence
that you could lift it. And in desperation
you lifted every one of them, but only
to sling them back into the gaping quarry
wherein, being so distended by your heart,
they would no longer fit. Had but a woman
laid her light hand on the still mild beginning
of this dark rage; had someone occupied,
occupied in the inmost of his being,
but quietly met you on your dumb departure
to do this deed; had even something led you
to take your journey past some wakeful workshop
where men were hammering and day achieving
simple reality; had there been room
enough in your full gaze to let the image
even of a toiling beetle find admittance:
then, in a sudden flash of intuition,
you would have read that script whose characters
you'd slowly graved into yourself since childhood,
trying from time to time whether a sentence
might not be formed: alas, it seemed unmeaning.
I know; I know: you lay in front and thumbed
away the grooves, like someone feeling out
the inscription on a grave-stone. Anything

that seemed to give a light you held as lamp
before those letters; but the flame went out
before you'd understood – your breath, perhaps,
perhaps the trembling of your hand; perhaps
just of its own accord, as flames will do.
You never read it. And we do not dare
to read through all the sorrow and the distance.

We only watch the poems that still climb,
still cross, the inclination of your feeling,
carrying the words that you had chosen. No,
you did not choose all; often a beginning
was given you in full, and you'd repeat it
like some commission. And you thought it sad.
Ah, would you had never heard it from yourself!
Your angel sounds on, uttering the same
text with a different accent, and rejoicing
breaks out in me to hear his recitation,
rejoicing over you: for this was yours:
that from you every proffered love fell back,
that you had recognised renunciation
as price of seeing and in death your progress.
This was what you possessed, you artist, these
three open moulds. Look, here is the casting
from the first: space for your feeling; and look, there,
from the second I'll strike out for you the gaze
that craves for nothing, the great artist's gaze;
and in the third, which you yourself broke up
too soon, and which as yet the first outrushing
of quivering feed from the white-heated heart
had scarce had time to reach, a death was moulded,
deepened by genuine labour, that own death
which has such need of us because we live it,
and which we're nowhere nearer to than here.

All this was your possession and your friendship;
as you yourself often divined; but then
the hollowness of those moulds frightened you,
you groped within and drew up emptiness
and mourned your lot. – O ancient curse of poets!
Being sorry for themselves instead of saying,
for ever passing judgment on their feeling
instead of shaping it; for ever thinking
that what is sad or joyful in themselves
is what they know and what in poems may fitly
be mourned or celebrated. Invalids,

using a language full of woefulness
to tell us where it hurts, instead of sternly
transmuting into words those selves of theirs,
as imperturbable cathedral carvers
transposed themselves into the constant stone.
  That would have been salvation. Had you once
perceived how fate may pass into a verse
and not come back, how, once in, it turns image,
nothing but image, but an ancestor,
who sometimes, when you watch him in his frame,
seems to be like you and again not like you: –
you would have persevered.

                                        But this is petty,
thinking of what was not. And some appearance
of undeserved reproach in these comparings.
Whatever happens has had such a start
of our supposing that we never catch it,
never experience what it really looked like.
  Don't be ashamed, when the dead brush against you,
those other dead, who held out to the end.
(What, after all, does end mean?) Exchange glances
peacefully with them, as is customary,
and have no fear of being conspicuous
through carrying the burden of our grief.
The big words from those ages when as yet
happening was visible are not for us.
Who talks of victory? To endure is all.

THE LIFE OF MARY

ζάλην ἔνδοθεν ἔχων

Written at Schloss Duino, 15-23 January 1912, to replace ten much earlier *Songs of Mary* which Rilke had heard that his friend Heinrich Vogeler, the impressionist painter, wished to publish with his own illustrations. Vogeler never carried out his part of the plan, but Rilke published the cycle in June 1913.

Rilke must have taken the Greek motto from the so-called *Mount Athos Painter's Book*, a very ancient but still widely circulated iconographical hand-book of the Greek Orthodox Church, which we know that he used for the background and 'keepings' of these poems. Instructions are there given for illustrating, among other things, each of the twenty-four stanzas of the famous Byzantine Hymn to the Virgin known as the *Hymnos Akathistos*, the Hymn to be sung 'unseated', i.e., standing, of which the sixth stanza describes the angel's reproof of Joseph's suspicions and begins with the three words which Rilke has taken as his motto: 'Storm within having of conflicting thoughts, decent Joseph was confused.' In the 1855 German translation of the hand-book, which was in the library at Duino and which Rilke used, the Greek first lines of each stanza of the hymn are given in foot-notes, but in the text the first word of this stanza, ζάλην, 'storm', is incorrectly rendered (probably as the result of the printer's misreading of the author's handwriting) as *Raum*, 'space'. It is almost certain, therefore, that Rilke took the three words of his motto to mean 'having space within', and regarded them as an expression of his own characteristic conception of 'inner space' and 'inner world-space' – a conception which may well have been developed under the influence of this fruitful misunderstanding, for it first appears in the poem 'Everything beckons to us to perceive it' (p. 312), written in 1914.

The brilliant piece of literary detection of which the results are here summarised will be found *in extenso* in an article by Professor Ernst Zinn, 'Rainer Maria Rilke und die Antike', in *Antike und Abendland*, Bd. III, 1948, pp. 215-17.

TO HEINRICH VOGELER
IN GRATITUDE
FOR OLD AND NEW INDUCEMENT
TO THESE VERSES

THE BIRTH OF MARY

O what it must have cost them, the hosts of Heaven,
not to burst into song, as though into tears,
knowing so well: this night would the mother be given,
be born for the Boy, the One coming before many years.

They hovered in silence, a gesture their sole indication
of where the lone farm lay belonging to Joachim.
Ah, they felt in themselves and in space the pure concentration,
but not one of them dared to go down to him.

For the pair were distraught enough, there was such a to-doing.
A neighbour, a know-all, came and tried to arrange,
and the old man thoughtfully went and hushed the mooing
of a dark cow. For things were never so strange.

THE PRESENTATION OF MARY IN THE TEMPLE

To grasp how she was then, try if you can
to place yourself where pillars mount to ceilings
which are in you; where you can share the feelings
of steps; where arches take great risks to span
the gulf of inward space you could not part with,
since it was made of such huge blocks to start with,
heaving it from you would have meant the fall
of your whole being: if you'd had the strength.
When you are stone-filled, when you've reached the length
of being just vault, vista, entrance, wall, –
seize the great curtain hung before your face,
hiding the gleam of objects so exalted
breathing is checked by them, blind groping halted:
try, with both hands, to pull it back, a trace.
High, low, near, far, palaces fill the place;
banisters stream, as stair from stair emerges,
broaden, then balance on such dizzy verges
you're seized with vertigo. Near things efface
their outlines in the cloud of smoke that surges
from burning censers; but each levelled ray
from those far off makes for you, straight and lancing, –
and if clear light from fire-bowls should be dancing
on robes that very slowly come your way:
could it be borne?

She came though, and she raised
her eyes, and stood there taking it all in.
(A child, a little girl between grown women.)
And went up to the pampered splendour then,
(it swayed a little) calmly, quite undazed:
so far was all that had been built by men
inferior to the voice that praised
within her heart. And the desire
to go by inner signs, by these alone.
Her parents thought they lifted her; the one,
so menacing, whose breast flashed jewels' fire,
seemed to receive her: but she went through all,
the child, out of their hands into her fate,
prepared already, higher than the hall,
pressing more hardly than the building's weight.

ANNUNCIATION TO MARY

The angel's entrance (you must realise)
was not what made her frightened. The surprise
he gave her by his coming was no more
than sun- or moon-beam stirring on the floor
would give another, – she had long since grown
used to the form that angels wear, descending;
never imagining this coming-down
was hard for them. (O it's past comprehending,
how pure she was. Did not, one day, a hind
that rested in a wood, watchfully staring,
feel her deep influence, and did it not
conceive the unicorn, then, without pairing,
the pure beast, beast which light begot. –)
No, not to see him enter, but to find
the youthful angel's countenance inclined
so near to her; that when he looked, and she
looked up at him, their looks so merged in one,
the world outside grew vacant suddenly,
and all things being seen, endured and done
were crowded into them: just she and he;
eye and its pasture, vision and its view,
here at this point and at this point alone: –
see, this arouses fear. Such fear both knew.

Then he sang out and made his tidings known.

MARY'S VISITATION

In those first days she moved lightly still,
though she grew aware from time to time
of her marvellous body on a hill, –
and she rested, breathing, from her climb

to the heights of Juda. But her own,
not the fields', abundance lay around her;
walking on she felt: O a profounder
sense of greatness never has been known.

And it moved her, entering, to laying
her hand on the riper body there.
And the women came together swaying
and they touched each other's robes and hair.

Each, big with the shrine that she was keeping,
soothed her cousin and forgot her fear.
Ah the Saviour was a flower still, sleeping,
but the other felt the Baptist leaping
in her womb, for joy, to have him near.

JOSEPH'S SUSPICION

And the angel, striving to explain,
told the man who stood shut-fisted, surly:
Can't you see that she is pure as early
dawn – does not each fold there make it plain?

But the shadow stayed upon his brow.
What, he growled, has changed her? The reply
then came loudly: Joiner, even now
can't you see the hand of the Most High?

You who work with boards, is your pride such
you would argue with the One who urges
buds to fullness, at whose quiet touch,
and from this same wood, the green emerges?

Then at last he saw. And when he lifted
his scared look to meet the angel's gaze,
found him gone. At that the slowly-shifted
heavy cap came off. Then he sang praise.

ANNUNCIATION TO THE SHEPHERDS FROM ABOVE

Look up, you men. Men at the fire there, you
familiar with the sky's unbounded ways,
star-readers, hither! Look, I am a new
uprising star. My being is one blaze,
so filled with light the firmament is too
small now to hold me and my powerful rays,
for all its depth. Do let my splendour throw
its beams right into you: oh the dark sight,
the gloomy hearts, destinies black as night
that you're brim-full of. Shepherds, I am so
alone in you. Yet, now, there's room for me.
Weren't you astonished: the big bread-fruit-tree
was casting shadow. Well, that shade *I* threw.
O you undaunted, if you only knew
how even now upon each gazing face
the future shines. Much will be taking place
in that clear light. To you I can speak out,
you have discretion; straight souls, free from doubt,
you hear tongues everywhere. Warmth speaks and rain,
wind, birds' flight, what you are; no one sound is
more than another, and no vanities
fatten themselves. You don't detain
things in that interval the breast, to be
tormented there. As his own ecstasy
streams through an angel, earthliness can make
its way through you. And should a thornbush take
fire suddenly, the Infinite could still
call to you from it; Cherubim would fill,
if any deigned to walk where your flocks graze,
those hearts of yours with no alarmed surprise:
you'd fall upon your faces and give praise,
and name this earth still and not Paradise.

But all this was. A new thing dawns to-day
for which the round earth seeks to grow more wide.
What is a thornbush now: God feels his way
into a virgin's womb. I am the ray
thrown by her inwardness, which is your guide.

THE BIRTH OF CHRIST

If you lacked simplicity, how then
should this fall to you that midnight skies
are ashine with? God, who stormed at men,
mild in you now comes to mortal eyes.

That he's not more great – does this surprise?

What is greatness? Sweepingly his fate
cuts across all human measurings.
No star, even, has a path so straight.
Look, these coming now are great, these kings

dragging to your lap, as presents, things

which, they hold, are greater far than all.
Maybe they astound you, gifts like these: –
look, though, how within your folded shawl
he excels already all one sees.

Amber, shipped across great distances,

golden ornaments and fragrant spice
such as makes the heavy senses swim:
these were pleasures over in a trice,
and regretted when their power grew dim.

But (as you will see): joy comes of him.

REST ON THE FLIGHT INTO EGYPT

These, who late so breathlessly had flown
from the scene where blood of infants flowed,
oh, to what a greatness they had grown,
imperceptibly, upon the road.

Scarcely had their furtive backward glancing
melted anguish, dissipated dread,
when they brought, on their grey mule advancing,
danger to whole towns that lay ahead;

for when they, in this huge land so small,
neared strong temples where the heathen prayed,
idols there, as if they'd been betrayed,
grew demented, crashed down, one and all.

Who could have supposed that all this mad
rage would greet their coming on the scene?
And they feared themselves, this power they had,
while the babe alone remainéd serene.

Yet, they had to sit down and recover
for a little, where a tree spread wide.
When – the tree that silently hung over
came, as though to serve them, to their side,

bowing down. That very tree, whose wreath
has until eternity the sleeping
Pharaoh's brow entrusted to its keeping,
stooped. Felt other crowns' new green up-leaping.
And they sat, as in a dream, beneath.

OF THE MARRIAGE AT CANA

Could she fail to take pride in this son
who for her turned plainest things to treasure?
When he came, was not high night as one
half deranged, though used to largest measure?

Was there not unheard-of glory later
in that time when he was lost and found:
when earth's wisest, knowing him for greater,
changed their tongues for ears? Did not the sound

of his voice remake the dwelling? Oh,
surely she'd a hundred times denied
outward shining to her joy and pride.
Following, she felt her wonder grow.

But when all those wedding-guests were seated
and they suddenly ran out of wine, –
she could not take in that he had greeted
with refusal her entreating sign.

Then he did it. Just what *she* had done
grew clear afterwards: for now at last
his real wonder-working had begun
and the die for sacrifice was cast

irretrievably. It had been, truly,
fore-ordained. But was it time yet? She:

she had forced the pace of things unduly
in the blindness of her vanity.

She was joyful with the others bidden
to the festive meal; nor understood
that the water of her tears, yet hidden,
turned, as this wine reddened, into blood.

BEFORE THE PASSION

Oh, willing this, you should not have been born
of woman's body: saviours should by right
be quarried from the mountains, brought to light
where out of what is hard the hard is torn.

When you lay waste the valley that you love
does it not grieve you? I am helpless, look;
I only have a milk- and tear-filled brook
and you were always over and above.

You were announced to me with so much splendour.
Why did you not rush wildly from my womb?
If you want tigers tearing you asunder,
why was I brought up in the women's room,

to weave for you a garment soft and clean
where not one trace of joining should be found
harsh to the touch: – thus my whole life has been,
and you have suddenly turned nature round.

PIETÀ

Full is my woe now, speechlessly it all
brims up in me. Rigid am I, as stone
at the stone's core.
Thus hard, I only see one thing:
that you have grown –
. . . and you have grown
into a grief so large,
it is beyond my heart to grasp
and reaches out.
Now you lie right across my womb,
now I can nevermore
give birth to you.

MARY AT PEACE WITH THE RISEN LORD

What they experienced then: is it not
beyond all secrets sweet,
and all still terrestrial:
when he, a little pale still from the grave,
disburdened came to her:
in all parts resurrected.
Oh, to her first. How they were both then
inexpressibly healing.
Yes, healing, just that. They did not require
to touch at all strongly.
He laid, for barely a second,
his soon to become
eternal hand on her woman's shoulder.
And they had started,
quietly as trees in the springtime,
immensely together,
this season of their
farthest-reaching communion.

OF THE DEATH OF MARY

I

The same great angel from whose lips she heard,
long since, the Saviour promised to her womb,
waiting her notice, stood there in the room.
'The time has come for you to appear.' His word,
still awful, found still the obedient,
wholly-consenting handmaid. But he, nearing
endlessly, radiant, was disappearing
as if into her countenance – and sent
for the disciples scattered far and wide
to climb once more together that sloped way
to the Last Supper house. All stepped inside
more heavily, and heart-sick: there she lay
on the small bed, who'd so mysteriously
been plunged in sorrow and electedness;
she lay as though unused, all ravageless,
and hearkened to the angels' psalmody.
But seeing now their candles and how they
all waited there, she forced herself to part
from this too-glorious sound, and gave away

both of her dresses, gave with all her heart,
lifting her eyes to each in turn . . . (O those
well-springs of tears, what rivers they had shed.)

Then she lay back in weakness on her bed
and drew Jerusalem and Heaven so close,
that, when her spirit came to separate,
it only had to stretch a tiny distance:
already He, who knew its whole existence,
was lifting it to its divine estate.

II

Before she came there, who would have suspected
that abundant Heaven was incomplete?
He had assumed his place, the Resurrected,
but for those four-and-twenty years the seat
next him was empty. And they had begun
to get used to this purest gap, now seeming
all but healed, since full of brightness streaming,
with such marvellous beauty, from the Son.

So she did not, crossing Heaven's threshold,
approach him, though this longing was transcendent;
there was no room, for He was there, resplendent
with radiance it hurt her to behold.
But when, a touching figure, – adding light
to light – she joined the souls newly assembled
and whom she modestly would have resembled,
from ambush in her burst out rays so bright,
the angel caught and blinded by them trembled
and cried out in a loud voice: Who is she?
There was astonishment. Then all could see
how God the Father stooped down and restrained
our Lord, so that a mild half-light remained
and wavered softly round the empty place
which now was as a little grief, a trace
of loneliness, left over from the dearth
and dry affliction he had borne on earth. –
All watched her. As if feeling: I must be
his longest pain, she leant round anxiously
and gazed: – and then rushed forward. But this drew
the angels to her side. With blissful song
they led her to him, helping her along,
and carried her for the last step or two.

III

But when Thomas the Apostle drew
near the sepulchre, belatedly,
forth there came to him the angel, who,
long foreseeing, spoke commandingly:

Push the stone aside. Does your heart wonder
where she is, that was so moved by her?
Look, she was a little while thereunder
buried like a bag of lavender,

that the earth might have such fragrance stealing
from each fold as finest cloths are lent.
All that's dead, decayed, (you can't help feeling)
has been stupefied by her sweet scent.

See the linen shroud, its blinding whiteness:
are there greens where bleaching can be done
half so well? The stainless body's brightness
was more purifying than the sun.

And so gentle was her vanishing
out of it, it scarcely seems forsaken.
But the heavens above are being shaken:
man, kneel down and look at me and sing.

DUINO ELEGIES

Written at various times and with long interruptions between January 1912 and February 1922; published June (special edition) and October (ordinary edition) 1923.

The dates of composition are as follows:

First Elegy:
Sent to Princess Marie von Thurn und Taxis from Schloss Duino, 21 January 1912.

Second Elegy:
Duino, end of January and beginning of February 1912.

Third Elegy:
Begun at Duino early in 1912; continued and completed in Paris, late autumn 1913.

Fourth Elegy:
Munich, 22 and 23 November 1915.

Fifth Elegy:
Château de Muzot, Sierre (Switzerland), 14 February 1922.

Sixth Elegy:
Lines 1-31, Ronda, January–February 1913; lines 42-44, Paris, late autumn 1913; lines 32-41, Muzot, 9 February 1922.

Seventh Elegy:
Muzot, 7 February 1922 (final version of the conclusion, 26 February).

Eighth Elegy:
Muzot, 7-8 February 1922.

Ninth Elegy:
Lines 1-6 (first paragraph) and 77-79, Duino, March 1912; the rest, Muzot, 9 February 1922.

Tenth Elegy:
Lines 1-15, Duino, beginning of 1912; continued and completed in a form subsequently rejected, Paris, end of 1913; new and final version of lines 16-end, Muzot, 11 February 1922. The rejected version of 1913 will be found in Poems 1906 to 1926*, p. 162.*

THE PROPERTY OF PRINCESS MARIE VON THURN UND TAXIS-HOHENLOHE

Rilke had known the Princess Thurn und Taxis since December 1909; he had been a frequent guest at her castle of Duino on the Adriatic coast, and had been staying there alone during her absence when he wrote the first two Elegies early in 1912. It was she, he declared, who restrained him, in his despair of ever being able to complete them, from publishing the then still fragmentary collection at the end of the first World War. He always professed to regard them as her 'property', and, when at last he came to publish them, so described them: as a painting loaned to an exhibition might be described as 'From the Collection of', 'Lent by', etc.

THE FIRST ELEGY

Who, if I cried, would hear me among the angelic
orders? And even if one of them suddenly
pressed me against his heart, I should fade in the strength of his
stronger existence. For Beauty's nothing
but beginning of Terror we're still just able to bear,
and why we adore it so is because it serenely
disdains to destroy us. Every angel is terrible.
And so I repress myself, and swallow the call-note
of depth-dark sobbing. Alas, who is there
we can make use of? Not angels, not men;
and even the noticing beasts are aware
that we don't feel very securely at home
in this interpreted world. There remains, perhaps,
some tree on a slope, to be looked at day after day,
there remains for us yesterday's walk and the long-drawn loyalty
of a habit that liked us and stayed and never gave notice.
Oh, and there's Night, there's Night, when wind full of cosmic space
feeds on our faces: for whom would she not remain,
longed for, mild disenchantress, painfully there
for the lonely heart to achieve? Is she lighter for lovers?
Alas, with each other they only conceal their lot!
Don't you know *yet*? – Fling the emptiness out of your arms
to broaden the spaces we breathe – maybe that the birds
will feel the extended air in more fervent flight.

Yes, the Springs had need of you. Many a star
was waiting for you to perceive it. Many a wave
would rise in the past towards you; or else, perhaps,
as you went by an open window, a violin
would be utterly giving itself. All this was commission.
But were you equal to it? Were you not still
distraught by expectancy, as though all were announcing
some beloved's approach? (As if you could hope
to house her, with all those great strange thoughts
going in and out and often staying overnight!)
Should you be longing, though, sing the great lovers: the fame
of all they can feel is far from immortal enough.
Those – you envied them almost, those forsaken, you found
so far beyond the requited in loving. Begin
ever anew their never-attainable praise.
Consider: the Hero continues, even his setting
was a pretext for further existence, an ultimate birth.

But lovers are taken back by exhausted Nature
into herself, as though such creative force
could not be exerted twice. Does Gaspara Stampa[1]
mean enough to you yet, and that any girl, whose beloved
has slipped away, might feel, from that far intenser
example of loving: 'Could I but become like her!'?
Should not these oldest sufferings be finally growing
fruitfuller for us? Is it not time that, in loving,
we freed ourselves from the loved one, and, quivering, endured:
as the arrow endures the string, to become, in the gathering out-leap,
something more than itself? For staying is nowhere.

Voices, voices. Hearken, my heart, as only
saints once hearkened: so, that the giant call
lifted them off the ground; they, though, impossibles,
went on kneeling and paid no heed:
such was their hearkening. Not that you could bear God's
voice, by a long way. But hark to the suspiration,
the uninterrupted news that grows out of silence.
Rustling towards you now from those youthfully-dead.
Whenever you entered a church in Rome or in Naples
were you not always being quietly addressed by their fate?
Or else an inscription sublimely imposed itself on you,
as, lately, the tablet in Santa Maria Formosa.
What they require of me? that I should gently remove
the appearance of suffered injustice, that hinders
a little, at times, their purely-proceeding spirits.

True, it is strange to inhabit the earth no longer,
to use no longer customs scarcely acquired,
not to interpret roses, and other things
that promise so much, in terms of a human future;
to be no longer all that one used to be
in endlessly anxious hands, and to lay aside
even one's proper name like a broken toy.
Strange, not to go on wishing one's wishes. Strange,
to see all that was once relation so loosely fluttering
hither and thither in space. And it's hard, being dead,
and full of retrieving before one begins to perceive
a little eternity. – All of the living, though,
make the mistake of drawing too sharp distinctions.
Angels (it's said) would be often unable to tell
whether they moved among living or dead. The eternal

[1] Gaspara Stampa (1523-1554), an Italian poetess of noble family who recorded her at first happy and then unrequited love in some two hundred sonnets.

torrent whirls all the ages through either realm
for ever, and sounds above their voices in both.

They've finally no more need of us, the early-departed,
one's gently weaned from terrestrial things as one mildly
outgrows the breasts of a mother. But we, that have need of
such mighty secrets, we, for whom sorrow's so often
source of blessedest progress, could we exist without them?
Is the story in vain, how once, in the mourning for Linos,
venturing earliest music pierced barren numbness, and how,
in the startled space an almost deified youth
suddenly quitted for ever, emptiness first
felt the vibration that now lifts us and comforts and helps?

THE SECOND ELEGY

Every Angel is terrible. Still, though, alas!
I invoke you, almost deadly birds of the soul,
knowing about you. Where are the days of Tobias,
when one of the shining-most stood on the simple threshold,
a little disguised for the journey, no longer appalling,
(a youth to the youth as he curiously peered outside).
Let the archangel perilous now, from behind the stars,
step but a step down hitherwards: high up-beating,
our heart would out-beat us. Who are you?

Early successes, favourites of fond Creation,
ranges, summits, dawn-red ridges
of all forthbringing, – pollen of blossoming godhead,
junctures of light, corridors, stairways, thrones,
chambers of essence, shields of felicity, tumults
of stormily-rapturous feeling, and suddenly, separate,
mirrors, drawing up again their own
outstreamed beauty into their own faces.

For we, when we feel, evaporate; oh, we
breathe ourselves out and away; from ember to ember
yielding a fainter scent. True, someone may tell us:
'You've got in my blood, the room, the Spring's
growing full of you' . . . What's the use? He cannot retain us,
we vanish within and around him. And those that have beauty,
oh, who shall hold them back? Appearance of something
keeps getting up in their faces and going away. Like dew
from the morning grass what's ours exhales from us, like the heat
from a smoking dish. O smile, whither? O upward gaze:
new, warm, vanishing wave of the heart – alas,
but we *are* all that. Does the cosmic space
we dissolve into taste of us, then? Do the angels really
only catch up what is theirs, what has streamed from them, or at times,
as though through an oversight, is a little of our
essence in it as well? Is there just so much of us
mixed with their features as that vague look in the faces
of pregnant women? Unmarked by them in the whirl of their
coming back to themselves. (How should they remark it?)

Lovers, indeed, if only they could, might utter
strange things in the midnight air. For it seems that everything's
trying to hide us. Look, the trees exist; the houses

we live in still stand where they were. We only
pass everything by like a transposition of air.
And all combines to suppress us, partly, perhaps,
as shame, and partly as inexpressible hope.

Lovers, to you, each satisfied in the other,
I turn with my question about us. You grasp yourselves. Have you proofs?
Look, with me it may happen at times that my hands
grow aware of each other, or else that my hard-worn face
seeks refuge within them. That gives me a little
sensation. But who, just for that, could presume to exist?
You, though, that go on growing
in the other's rapture till, overwhelmed, he implores
'No more'; you that under each other's hands
grow more abundant like vintage years;
swooning at times, just because the other
has so expanded: I ask you about us. I know
why you so blissfully touch: because the caress withholds,
because it does not vanish, the place that you
so tenderly cover; because you perceive thereunder
pure duration. Until your embraces almost
promise eternity. Yet, when you've once withstood
the startled first encounter, the window-longing,
and that first walk, just once, through the garden together:
Lovers, are you the same? When you lift yourselves
up to each other's lips – drink unto drink:
oh, how strangely the drinker eludes his part!

On Attic stelæ, did not the circumspection
of human gesture amaze you? Were not love and farewell
so lightly laid upon shoulders, they seemed to be made
of other stuff than with us? Oh, think of the hands,
how they rest without pressure, though power is there in the torsos.
The wisdom of those self-masters was this: hitherto it's us;
ours is to touch one another like this; the gods
may press more strongly upon us. But that is the gods' affair.
If only we too could discover some pure, contained,
narrow, human, own little strip of corn-land
in between river and rock! For our own heart still transcends us
even as theirs did. And we can no longer gaze
after it now into pacifying image, or godlike
body, wherein it achieves a grander restraint.

THE THIRD ELEGY

One thing to sing the beloved, another, alas!
that hidden guilty river-god of the blood.
Him she discerns from afar, her lover, what does he know
of that Lord of Pleasure, who often, out of his lonely heart,
before she'd soothed him, often as though she didn't exist,
streaming from, oh, what unknowable depths, would uplift
his god-head, uprousing the night to infinite uproar?
Oh, the Neptune within our blood, oh, his terrible trident!
Oh, the gloomy blast of his breast from the twisted shell!
Hark, how the night grows fluted and hollowed. You stars,
is it not from you that the lover's delight in the loved one's
face arises? Does not his intimate insight
into her purest face come from the purest star?

It wasn't you, alas! it wasn't his mother
that bent his brows into such an expectant arch.
Not to meet yours, girl feeling him, not to meet yours
did his lips begin to assume that more fruitful curve.
Do you really suppose your gentle approach could have so
convulsed him, you, that wander like wind at dawn?
You terrified his heart, indeed; but more ancient terrors
rushed into him in that instant of shattering touch.
Call him . . . you can't quite call him away from sombre consorting.
He certainly wants to, he does escape; disburdenedly settles
into your intimate heart, takes up and begins himself there.
Did he ever begin himself, though?
Mother, you made him small, it was you that began him;
for you he was new, you arched over those new eyes
the friendly world, averting the one that was strange.
Where, oh, where, are the years when you barred the way
for him, with your slender form, to the surging abyss?
You hid so much from him then; made the nightly-suspected room
harmless, and out of your heart full of refuge
mingled more human space with that night-space of his.
Not in the darkness, no, but within your far nearer presence
you placed the light, and it shone as though out of friendship.
Nowhere a creak you could not explain with a smile,
as though you had long known *when* the floor would behave itself thus . . .
And he listened to you and was soothed. So much it availed,
gently, your rising: his tall cloaked destiny stepped
behind the wardrobe then, and his restless future,
that easily got out of place, conformed to the folds of the curtain.

And he himself as he lay there in such relief,

dissolving, under his drowsy eyelids, the sweetness
of your light shaping into the sleep he had tasted,
seemed to be under protection . . . *Within*, though: who could avert,
divert, the floods of origin flowing within him?
Alas! there *was* no caution within that sleeper; sleeping,
yes, but dreaming, yes, but feverish: what he embarked on!
He, so new, so timorous, how he got tangled
in ever-encroaching creepers of inner event,
twisted to primitive patterns, to throttling growths, to bestial
preying forms! How he gave himself up to it! Loved.
Loved his interior world, his interior jungle,
that primal forest within, on whose mute overthrownness,
light-green, his heart stood. Loved. Left it, continued
out through his own roots into violent beginning
where his tiny birth was already outlived. Descended,
lovingly, into the older blood, the ravines
where Frightfulness lurked, still gorged with his fathers. And every
terror knew him, winked, was as though it were waiting.
Yes, Horror smiled at him . . . Seldom
did you, Mother, smile so tenderly. How could he help
loving what smiled at him? Long before you
he loved it, for even while you bore him
it was there, dissolved in the water that lightens the seed.

Look, we don't love like flowers, with only a single
season behind us; immemorial sap
mounts in our arms when we love. Oh, maid,
this: that we've loved, *within* us, not one, still to come, but all
the innumerable fermentation; not just a single child,
but the fathers, resting like mountain-ruins
within our depths; – but the dry river-bed
of former mothers; – yes, and the whole of that
soundless landscape under its cloudy or
cloudless destiny: – *this* got the start of you, maid.

And you yourself, how can you tell, – you have conjured up
prehistoric time in your lover. What feelings
whelmed up from beings gone by! What women
hated you in him! What sinister men
you roused in his youthful veins! Dead children
were trying to reach you . . . Oh, gently, gently
show him daily an honest, confident task done, – guide him
close to the garden, give him preponderance
over his nights . . . . . .

Withhold him . . . . . .

THE FOURTH ELEGY

O trees of life, what are your signs of winter?
We're not at one. We've no instinctive knowledge,
like migratory birds. Outstript and late,
we force ourselves on winds and find no welcome
from ponds where we alight. We comprehend
flowering and fading simultaneously.
And somewhere lions still roam, all unaware,
while yet their splendour lasts, of any weakness.

We, though, while we're intent upon one thing,
can feel the cost and conquest of another.
The Next's our enemy. Aren't lovers always
coming to precipices in each other, –
lovers, that looked for spaces, hunting, home?
Then, for the sudden sketchwork of a moment,
a ground of contrast's painfully prepared,
to make us see it. For they're very clear
with us, we that don't know our feeling's shape,
but only that which forms it from outside.
Who's not sat tense before his own heart's curtain?
Up it would go: the scenery was Parting.
Easy to understand. The well-known garden,
swaying a little. Then appeared the dancer.
Not *him*! Enough! However light he foots it,
he's just disguised, and turns into a bourgeois,
and passes through the kitchen to his dwelling.
I will not have these half-filled masks! No, no,
rather the doll. That's full. I'll force myself
to bear the husk, the wire, and even that face
of sheer appearance. Here! I'm in my seat.
Even if the lights go out, even if I'm told
'There's nothing more', – even if greyish draughts
of emptiness come drifting from the stage, –
even if of all my silent forbears none
sits by me any longer, not a woman,
not even the boy with the brown squinting eyes:
I'll still remain. For one can always watch.

Am I not right? You, to whom life would taste
so bitter, Father, when you tasted mine,
that turbid first infusion of my Must,
you kept on tasting as I kept on growing,
and, still arrested by the after-taste

of such queer future, tried my clouded gaze, –
you, who so often, since you died, my Father,
have been afraid within my inmost hope,
surrendering realms of that serenity
the dead are lords of for my bit of fate, –
am I not right? And you, am I not right, –
you that would love me for that small beginning
of love for you I always turned away from,
because the space within your faces changed,
even while I loved it, into cosmic space
where you no longer were . . . , when I feel like it,
to wait before the puppet stage, – no, rather
gaze so intensely on it that at last
a counterpoising angel has to come
and play a part there, snatching up the husks?
Angel and doll! Then there's at last a play.
Then there unites what we continually
part by our mere existence. Then at last
emerges from our seasons here the cycle
of the whole process. Over and above us,
then, there's the angel playing. Look, the dying, –
surely they must suspect how full of pretext
is all that we accomplish here, where nothing
is what it really is. O hours of childhood,
hours when behind the figures there was more
than the mere past, and when what lay before us
was not the future! True, we were growing, and sometimes
made haste to be grown up, half for the sake
of those who'd nothing left but their grown-upness.
Yet, when alone, we entertained ourselves
with everlastingness: there we would stand,
within the gap left between world and toy,
upon a spot which, from the first beginning,
had been established for a pure event.

Who'll show a child just as it is? Who'll place it
within its constellation, with the measure
of distance in its hand? Who'll make its death
from grey bread, that grows hard, – or leave it there,
within the round mouth, like the seeded core
of a nice apple? . . . . . . Minds of murderers
can easily be fathomed. This, though: death,
the whole of death, before life's start, to hold it
so gently and so free from all resentment,
transcends description.

THE FIFTH ELEGY

Dedicated to Frau Hertha Koenig[1]

But tell me, who *are* they, these travellers, even a little
more fleeting than we ourselves, – so urgently, ever since childhood,
wrung by an (oh, for the sake of whom?)
never-contented will? That keeps on wringing them,
bending them, slinging them, swinging them,
throwing them and catching them back: as though from an oily,
smoother air, they come down on the threadbare
carpet, thinned by their everlasting
upspringing, this carpet forlornly
lost in the cosmos.
Laid on like a plaster, as though the suburban sky
had injured the earth there.
And hardly there,
upright, shown us: the great initial
letter of Thereness, – than even the strongest
men are rolled once more, in sport, by the ever-
returning grasp, as once by Augustus the Strong
a tin platter at table.

Alas, and round this
centre the rose of onlooking
blooms and unblossoms. Round this
pestle, this pistil, caught by its own
dust-pollen, and fertilised over again
to a sham-fruit of boredom, their own
never-realised, so thin-surfacedly gleaming,
lightly sham-smiling boredom.

There, the withered wrinkled lifter,
old now and only drumming,
shrivelled up in his massive hide as though it had once contained
two men, and one were already
lying in the churchyard, and this one here had survived him,
deaf and sometimes a little
lost in his widowed skin.

And the youngster, the man, like the son of a neck
and a nun: so tautly and smartly filled

[1] This Elegy was largely inspired by recollections both of Picasso's painting *Les Saltimbanques*, the property of Frau Hertha Koenig, in whose house in Munich Rilke had lived with it from June till October 1915, and also of the real *saltimbanques*, who had meant so much to him during his years in Paris.

with muscle and simpleness.

O you,[1]
a pain that was still quite small
received as a plaything once in one of its
long convalescences. . . .

You,[2] that fall with the thud
only fruits know, unripe,
daily a hundred times from the tree
of mutually built up motion (the tree that, swifter than water,
has spring and summer and autumn in so many minutes),
fall and rebound on the grave:
sometimes, in half-pauses, a tenderness tries
to steal out over your face to your seldomly
tender mother, but scatters over your body,
whose surface quickly absorbs the timidly rippling,
hardly attempted look . . . And again
that man is clapping his hands for the downward spring, and before
a single pain has got within range of your ever-
galloping heart, comes the tingling
in the soles of your feet, ahead of the spring that it springs from,
chasing into your eyes a few physical tears.
And still, all instinctive,
that smile. . . .

Angel! oh, take it, pluck it, that small-flowered herb of healing!
Get a vase to preserve it. Set it among those joys
not yet open to us: in a graceful urn
praise it, with florally soaring inscription:
'Subrisio Saltat.'.[3]

Then you, my darling,[4]
mutely elided
by all the most exquisite joys. Perhaps
your frills are happy on your behalf, –
or over your tight young breasts
the green metallic silk
feels itself endlessly spoilt and in need of nothing.
You,
time after time, upon all of the quivering scale-pans of balance

[1] Addressed to the whole group of 'travellers'.
[2] Addressed to the youngest of them, a little boy.
[3] Abbreviated Latin (as on a chemist's jar) for *Subrisio Saltatoris*, 'acrobat's smile'.
[4] Addressed to the little boy's sister.

freshly laid fruit of serenity,
publicly shown among shoulders.

Where, oh, where in the world is that place in my heart
where they still were far from being *able*, still fell away
from each other like mounting animals, not yet
ready for pairing; –
where weights are still heavy,
and hoops still stagger
away from their vainly
twirling sticks? . . . . .

And then, in this wearisome nowhere, all of a sudden,
the ineffable spot where the pure too-little
incomprehensibly changes, veering
into that empty too-much?
Where the many-digited sum
solves into zero?

Squares, O square in Paris, infinite show-place,
where the modiste Madame Lamort
winds and binds the restless ways of the world,
those endless ribbons, to ever-new
creations of bow, frill, flower, cockade and fruit,
all falsely coloured, to deck
the cheap winter-hats of Fate.

. . . . . .

Angel: suppose there's a place we know nothing about, and there,
on some indescribable carpet, lovers showed all that here
they're for ever unable to manage – their daring
lofty figures of heart-flight,
their towers of pleasure, their ladders,
long since, where ground never was, just quiveringly
propped by each other, – were able to manage it there,
before the ringed onlookers there, countless unmurmuring dead:
would not those then fling their last, their for ever reserved,
ever-concealed, unknown to us, ever-valid
coins of happiness down before the at last
truthfully smiling pair on the quietened
carpet?

THE SIXTH ELEGY

Fig tree, how long it's been full of meaning for me,
the way you almost entirely omit to flower
and into the early-resolute fruit
uncelebratedly thrust your purest secret.
Like the tube of a fountain, your bent bough drives the sap
downwards and up; and it leaps from its sleep, scarce waking,
into the joy of its sweetest achievement. Look,
like Jupiter into the swan.
. . . . . We, though, we linger,
alas, we glory in flowering; already revealed
we reach the retarded core of our ultimate fruit.
In few the pressure of action rises so strongly
that already they're stationed and glowing in fullness of heart,
when, seductive as evening air, the temptation to flower,
touching the youth of their mouths, touching their eyelids, appears:
only in heroes, perhaps, and those marked for early removal,
those in whom gardening Death's differently twisted the veins.
These go plunging ahead: preceding their own
victorious smile, as the team of horse in the mildly-
moulded reliefs of Karnak the conquering King.

Yes, the Hero's strangely akin to the youthfully dead. Duration
doesn't concern him. His rising's existence. Time and again
he takes himself off and enters the changed constellation
his changeless peril's assumed. There few could find him. But Fate,
grim concealer of us, enraptured all of a sudden,
sings him into the storm of his surging world.
None do I hear like him. There suddenly rushes through me,
borne by the streaming air, his dark-echoing tone.

And then how gladly I'd hide from the longing: Oh would,
would that I were a boy, and might come to it yet, and be sitting,
propped upon arms still to be, and reading of Samson,
how his mother at first bore nothing, and, afterwards, all.

Was he not hero already in you, O mother, and had not
even in you his lordly choosing begun?
Thousands were brewing in the womb and trying to be *him*,
but, look! he seized and discarded, chose and was able to do.
And if ever he shattered columns, that was the time, when he burst
out of the world of your body into the narrower world,
where he went on choosing and doing. O mothers of heroes!
Sources of ravaging rivers! Gorges wherein,

from high on the heart's edge, weeping,
maids have already plunged, victims to-be for the son.
For whenever the Hero stormed through the halts of love,
each heart beating for him could only lift him beyond it:
turning away, he'd stand at the end of the smiles, another.

THE SEVENTH ELEGY

Not wooing, no longer shall wooing, voice that's outgrown it,
be now the form of your cry; though you cried as pure as the bird
when the surging season uplifts him, almost forgetting
he's merely a fretful creature and not just a single heart
it's tossing to brightness, to intimate azure. No less
than he, you, too, would be wooing some silent companion
to feel you, as yet unseen, some mate in whom a reply
was slowly awaking and warming itself as she listened, –
your own emboldened feeling's glowing fellow-feeling.
Oh, and Spring would understand – not a nook would fail
to re-echo annunciation. Re-echoing first the tiny
questioning pipe a purely affirmative day
quietly invests all round with magnifying stillness.
Then the long flight of steps, the call-steps, up to the dreamt-of
temple of what's to come; – then the trill, that fountain
grasped, as it rises, by Falling, in promiseful play,
for another thrusting jet . . . And before it, the Summer!
Not only all those summer dawns, not only
the way they turn into day and stream with Beginning.
Not only the days, so gentle round flowers, and, above,
around the configured trees, so mighty and strong.
Not only the fervour of these unfolded forces,
not only the walks, not only the evening meadows,
not only, after late thunder, the breathing clearness,
not only, evenings, sleep coming and something surmised . . .
No, but the nights as well! the lofty, the summer
nights, – but the stars as well, the stars of the Earth!
Oh, to be dead at last and endlessly know them,
all the stars! For how, how, how to forget them!

Look, I've been calling the lover. But not only she
would come . . . Out of unwithholding graves
girls would come and gather . . . For how could I limit
the call I had called? The sunken are always seeking
Earth again. – You children, I'd say, a single
thing comprehended here's as good as a thousand.
Don't think Destiny's more than what's packed into childhood.
How often you'd overtake the beloved, panting,
panting from blissful pursuit of nothing but distance!
Being here's glorious! Even you knew it, you girls,
who went without, as it seemed, sank under, – you, in the vilest
streets of cities, festering, or open for refuse.
For to each was granted an hour, – perhaps not quite

so much as an hour – some span that could scarcely be measured
by measures of time, in between two whiles, when she really
possessed an existence. All. Veins full of existence.
But we so lightly forget what our laughing neighbour
neither confirms nor envies. We want to be visibly
able to show it; whereas the most visible joy
can only reveal itself to us when we've transformed it, within.

Nowhere, beloved, can world exist but within.
Life passes in transformation. And, ever diminishing,
outwardness dwindles. Where once was a permanent house,
up starts some invented structure across our vision, as fully
at home among concepts as though it still stood in a brain.
Spacious garners of power are formed by the Time Spirit, formless
as that tense urge he's extracting from everything else.
Temples he knows no longer. We're now more secretly saving
such lavish expenses of heart. Nay, even where one survives,
one single thing once prayed or tended or knelt to,
it's reaching, just as it is, into the unseen world.
Many perceive it no more, but neglect the advantage
of building it grandlier now, with pillars and statues, *within*!

Each torpid turn of the world has such disinherited children,
those to whom former has ceased, next not yet come, to belong.
For even the next is far for mankind. Though this
shall not confuse us, shall rather confirm us in keeping
still recognisable form. This *stood* once among mankind,
stood in the midst of Fate, the extinguisher, stood
in the midst of not-knowing-whither, as though it existed, and bowed
stars from established heavens towards it. Angel,
I'll show it to you as well – there! In your gaze
it shall stand redeemed at last, in a final uprightness.
Pillars, pylons, the Sphinx, all the striving thrust,
greyly from fading or foreign town, of the spire!
Was it not miracle? Angel, gaze, for it's *we* –
O mightiness, tell them that *we* were capable of it – my breath's
too short for this celebration. So, after all, we have *not*
failed to make use of the spaces, these generous spaces, these
our spaces. (How terribly big they must be,
when, with thousands of years of our feeling, they're not overcrowded.)
But a tower was great, was it not? Oh, Angel, it was, though, –
even compared with you? Chartres was great – and music
towered still higher and passed beyond us. Why, even
a girl in love, alone, at her window, at night . . .
did she not reach to your knee? –

Don't think that I'm wooing!
Angel, even if I were, you'd never come! For my call
is always full of outgoing; against such a powerful
current you cannot advance. Like an outstretched
arm is my call. And its hand, for some grasping,
skywardly opened, remains before you
as opened so wide but for warding
and warning, Inapprehensible.

THE EIGHTH ELEGY

Dedicated to Rudolf Kassner

With all its eyes the creature-world beholds
the open. But our eyes, as though reversed,
encircle it on every side, like traps
set round its unobstructed path to freedom.
What *is* outside, we know from the brute's face
alone; for while a child's quite small we take it
and turn it round and force it to look backwards
at conformation, not that openness
so deep within the brute's face. Free from death.
We alone see *that*; the free animal
has its decease perpetually behind it
and God in front, and when it moves, it moves
within eternity, like running springs.
We've never, no, not for a single day,
pure space before us, such as that which flowers
endlessly open into: always world,
and never nowhere without no: that pure,
unsuperintended element one breathes,
endlessly knows, and never craves. A child
sometimes gets quietly lost there, to be always
jogged back again. Or someone dies and *is* it.
For, nearing death, one perceives death no longer,
and stares ahead – perhaps with large brute gaze.
Lovers – were not the other present, always
blocking the view! – draw near to it and wonder . . .
Behind the other, as though through oversight,
the thing's revealed . . . But no one gets beyond
the other, and so world returns once more.
Always facing Creation, we perceive there
only a mirroring of the free and open,
dimmed by our breath. Or that a dumb brute's calmly
raising its head to look us through and through.
For this is Destiny: being opposite,
and nothing else, and always opposite.

Did consciousness such as we have exist
in the sure animal that moves towards us
upon a different course, the brute would drag us
round in its wake. But its own being for it
is infinite, inapprehensible,
unintrospective, pure, like its outgazing.
Where we see Future, it sees Everything,

itself in Everything, for ever healed.

And yet, within the wakefully-warm beast
there lies the weight and care of a great sadness.
For that which often overwhelms us clings
to him as well, – a kind of memory
that what one's pressing after now was once
nearer and truer and attached to us
with infinite tenderness. Here all is distance,
there it was breath. Compared with that first home
the second seems ambiguous and fickle.

Oh, bliss of *tiny* creatures that *remain*
for ever in the womb that brought them forth!
Joy of the gnat, that can still leap *within*,
even on its wedding-day: for womb is all!
Look at the half-assurance of the bird,
through origin almost aware of both,
like one of those Etruscan souls, escaped
from a dead man enclosed within a space
on which his resting figure forms a lid.
And how dismayed is any womb-born thing
that has to fly! As though it were afraid
of its own self, it zigzags through the air
like crack through cup. The way a bat's track runs
rendingly through the evening's porcelain.

And we, spectators always, everywhere,
looking at, never out of, everything!
It fills us. We arrange it. It collapses.
We re-arrange it, and collapse ourselves.

Who's turned us round like this, so that we always,
do what we may, retain the attitude
of someone who's departing? Just as he,
on the last hill, that shows him all his valley
for the last time, will turn and stop and linger,
we live our lives, for ever taking leave.

THE NINTH ELEGY

Why, when this span of life might be fleeted away
as laurel, a little darker than all
the surrounding green, with tiny waves on the border
of every leaf (like the smile of a wind): – oh, why
have to be human, and, shunning Destiny,
long for Destiny? . . .
                                        Not because happiness really
exists, that precipitate profit of imminent loss.
Not out of curiosity, not just to practise the heart,
that could still be there in laurel. . . . .
But because being here is much, and because all this
that's here, so fleeting, seems to require us and strangely
concerns us. Us the most fleeting of all. Just once,
everything, only for once. Once and no more. And we, too,
once. And never again. But this
having been once, though only once,
having been once on earth – can it ever be cancelled?

And so we keep pressing on and trying to perform it,
trying to contain it within our simple hands,
in the more and more crowded gaze, in the speechless heart.
Trying to become it. To give it to whom? We'd rather
hold on to it all for ever . . . But into the other relation,
what, alas! do we carry across? Not the beholding we've here
slowly acquired, and no here occurrence. Not one.
Sufferings, then. Above all, the hardness of life,
the long experience of love; in fact,
purely untellable things. But later,
under the stars, what use? the more deeply untellable stars?
Yet the wanderer too doesn't bring from mountain to valley
a handful of earth, of for all untellable earth, but only
a word he has won, pure, the yellow and blue
gentian. Are we, perhaps, *here* just for saying: House,
Bridge, Fountain, Gate, Jug, Fruit tree, Window, –
possibly: Pillar, Tower? . . . but for *saying*, remember,
oh, for such saying as never the things themselves
hoped so intensely to be. Is not the secret purpose
of this sly Earth, in urging a pair of lovers,
just to make everything leap with ecstasy in them?
Threshold: what does it mean
to a pair of lovers, that they should be wearing their own
worn threshold a little, they too, after the many before,
before the many to come, . . . as a matter of course!

Here is the time for the Tellable, *here* is its home.
Speak and proclaim. More than ever
things we can live with are falling away, for that
which is oustingly taking their place is an imageless act.
Act under crusts, that will readily split as soon
as the doing within outgrows them and takes a new outline.
Between the hammers lives on
our heart, as between the teeth
the tongue, which, in spite of all,
still continues to praise.

Praise this world to the Angel, not the untellable: you
can't impress him with the splendour you've felt; in the cosmos
where he more feelingly feels you're only a novice. So show him
some simple thing, refashioned by age after age,
till it lives in our hands and eyes as a part of ourselves.
Tell him *things*. He'll stand more astonished: as you did
beside the roper in Rome or the potter in Egypt.
Show him how happy a thing can be, how guileless and ours;
how even the moaning of grief purely determines on form,
serves as a thing, or dies into a thing, – to escape
to a bliss beyond the fiddle. These things that live on departure
understand when you praise them: fleeting, they look for
rescue through something in us, the most fleeting of all.
Want us to change them entirely, within our invisible hearts,
into – oh, endlessly – into ourselves! Whosoever we are.

Earth, is it not just this that you want: to arise
invisibly in us? Is not your dream
to be one day invisible? Earth! invisible!
What is your urgent command, if not transformation?
Earth, you darling, I will! Oh, believe me, you need
no more of your spring-times to win me over: a single one,
ah, one, is already more than my blood can endure.
Beyond all names I am yours, and have been for ages.
You were always right, and your holiest inspiration
is Death, that friendly Death.
Look, I am living. On what? Neither childhood nor future
are growing less. . . . . Supernumerous existence
wells up in my heart.

THE TENTH ELEGY

Some day, emerging at last out of this fell insight,
may I lift up jubilant praise to assenting Angels!
May not one of the clear-struck keys of the heart
fail to respond through alighting on slack or doubtful
or rending strings! May a brighter radiance stream from
my streaming face! May inconspicuous Weeping
flower! How dear you will be to me then, you Nights
of Affliction! Why did I not, inconsolable sisters,
more kneelingly welcome you, more loosenedly render
myself to your loosened hair? We wasters of sorrows!
How we stare away into sad endurance beyond them,
trying to foresee their end! Whereas they are nothing else
than our winter foliage, our sombre evergreen, *one*
of the seasons of our interior year, – not only
season – they're also place, settlement, camp, soil, dwelling.

Strange, though, alas! are the streets of the City of Pain,
where, in the pseudo-silence of drowned commotion,
loudly swaggers the casting cast from vacuity's
mould: the begilded ado, the bursting memorial.
How an Angel would trample it down beyond trace, their market
    of comfort,
with the church alongside, bought ready for use: as clean
and disenchanted and shut as the Post on a Sunday!
Outside, though, there's always the billowing edge of the fair.
Swings of Freedom! Divers and Jugglers of Zeal!
And the figured shooting-range of bedizened Happiness: targets
tumbling in tinny contortions whenever some better shot
happens to hit one. Cheer-struck, on he goes reeling
after his luck. For booths that can please
the most curious tastes are drumming and bawling. Especially
worth seeing (for adults only): the breeding of Money!
Anatomy made amusing! Money's organs on view!
Nothing concealed! Instructive, and guaranteed
to increase fertility! . . . . . .
                                        . . . Oh, but then just outside,
behind the last hoarding, plastered with placards for 'Deathless',
that bitter beer that tastes quite sweet to its drinkers
so long as they chew with it plenty of fresh distractions, –
just at the back of the hoardings, just behind them, it's real!
Children are playing, and lovers holding each other, – aside,
gravely, in pitiful grass, and dogs are following nature.
The youth is drawn further on; perhaps he's in love with a youthful

Lament . . . He emerges behind her into the meadows, she says:
'A long way. We live out there . . . . . '
'Where?' And the youth
follows. He's touched by her manner. Her shoulder, her neck, – perhaps
she comes of a famous stock? But he leaves her, turns back,
looks round, nods . . . What's the use? She's just a Lament.

Only the youthfully-dead, in their first condition
of timeless serenity, that of being weaned,
follow her lovingly. Girls
she awaits and befriends. Gently, she shows them
what she is wearing. Pearls of Pain and the fine-spun
Veils of Endurance. – Youths
she walks with in silence.

But there, where they live, in the valley, one of the elder Laments
takes to the youth when he questions her: – 'We were once,'
she says, 'a great family, we Lamentations. Our fathers
worked the mines in that mountain-range: among men
you'll find a lump, now and then, of polished original pain,
or of drossy petrified rage from some old volcano.
Yes, that came from there. We used to be rich.'

And lightly she leads him on through the spacious landscape
of Lamentation, shows him the temple columns, the ruins
of towers from which, long ago, Lords of the House of Lament
wisely governed the land. Shows him the tall
Tear trees, shows him the fields of flowering Sadness
(only as tender foliage known to the living);
shows him the pasturing herds of Grief, – and, at times,
a startled bird, flying straight through their field of vision,
scrawls the far-stretching screed of its lonely cry. –
At evening she leads him on to the graves of the longest
lived of the House of Lament, the sibyls and warners.
But, night approaching, they move more gently, and soon
moon-like emerges the all-
guarding sepulchral stone. Twin-brother to that on the Nile,
the lofty Sphinx, the taciturn chamber's gaze.
And they start at the regal head that has silently poised,
for ever, the human face
on the scale of the stars.

His sight, still dizzy with early death,
can't take it in. But her gaze
frightens an owl from behind the pschent. And the bird,

brushing, in slow down-skimming, along the cheek,
the one with the ripest curve,
faintly inscribes on the new
death-born hearing, as though on the double
page of an opened book, the indescribable outline.

And, higher, the stars. New ones. Stars of the Land of Pain.
Slowly she names them: 'There,
look: the *Rider*, the *Staff*, and that fuller constellation
they call *Fruitgarland.* Then, further, towards the Pole:
Cradle, *Way*, *The Burning Book*, *Doll*, *Window.*
But up in the southern sky, pure as within the palm
of a consecrated hand, the clearly-resplendent *M*,
standing for Mothers. . . . '

But the dead must go on, and, in silence, the elder Lament
brings him as far as the gorge
where it gleams in the moonlight, –
there, the source of Joy. With awe
she names it, says 'Among men
it's a carrying stream'.

They stand at the foot of the range.
And there she embraces him, weeping.

Lone he ascends to the mountains of Primal Pain.
And never once does his step sound from the soundless fate.

And yet, were they waking a symbol within us, the endlessly dead,
look, they'd be pointing, perhaps, to the catkins, hanging
from empty hazels, or else
to the rain downfalling on dark soil-bed in early Spring. –

And we, who think of *ascending*
happiness, then would feel
the emotion that almost startles
when happiness *falls*.

SONNETS TO ORPHEUS

WRITTEN AS A FUNERAL MONUMENT FOR WERA OUCKAMA KNOOP

Written at the Château de Muzot, Sierre, Switzerland, 2-23 February 1922; published end of March 1923.

At the beginning of January 1922 Rilke's friend Frau Gertrud Ouckama Knoop had sent him a journal she had kept during the long and fatal illness of her daughter Wera, who died at the age of eighteen or nineteen, and whom Rilke had seen once or twice when she was a child. This beautiful girl had been an exquisite dancer, but, just before the beginning of her fatal glandular disease, had suddenly declared that she neither could nor would dance any longer, and, during the short time that remained for her, had devoted herself first to music and then to drawing, as though (in Rilke's words) 'the dancing which had been denied were more and more gently, more and more discreetly, still issuing from her'. His thoughts about Wera, whose fullness and love of life had seemed to reach their highest intensity when life was passing into death, crystallised, as it were, around the figure of Orpheus with his lyre, of which he had recently acquired a small engraving – Orpheus the mediator, at home in the realms both of the living and of the dead; and the result was this entirely unexpected series of sonnets, of which the First Part was written shortly before, and the Second Part shortly after, the completion of the *Duino Elegies*.

FIRST PART

I

A tree ascending there. O pure transcension!
O Orpheus sings! O tall tree in the ear!
All noise suspended, yet in that suspension
what new beginning, beckoning, change, appear!

Creatures of silence pressing through the clear
disintricated wood from lair and nest;
and neither cunning, it grew manifest,
had made them breathe so quietly, nor fear,

but only hearing. Roar, cry, bell they found
within their hearts too small. And where before
less than a hut had harboured what came thronging,

a refuge tunnelled out of dimmest longing
with lowly entrance through a quivering door,
you built them temples in their sense of sound.

II

And almost maiden-like was what drew near
from that twin-happiness of song and lyre,
and shone so clearly through her spring attire,
and made herself a bed within my ear.

And slept in me sleep that was everything:
the trees I'd always loved, the unrevealed,
treadable distances, the trodden field,
and all my strangest self-discovering.

She slept the world. O singing god, and stayed,
while you were shaping her, with no desire
to wake, and only rose to fall asleep?

Where is her death? Oh, shall you find this deep
unsounded theme before your song expire?
Sinking to where from me? . . . Almost a maid. . .

III

A god can do it. But can a man expect
to penetrate the narrow lyre and follow?
His sense is discord. Temples for Apollo
are not found where two heart-ways intersect.

For song, as taught by you, is not desire,
not wooing of something finally attained;
song is existence. For the god unstrained.
But when shall we *exist*? And he require

the earth and heavens to exist for us?
It's more than being in love, boy, though your ringing
voice may have flung your dumb mouth open thus:

learn to forget those fleeting ecstasies.
Far other is the breath of real singing.
An aimless breath. A stirring in the god. A breeze.

IV

Step now and then, you gentle-hearted,
into the breath not breathed for you,
let it blow over your cheeks, and, parted,
quiver behind you, united anew.

O you blissful, you all-entire,
you with whom starting of hearts appears.
Targets and bows for the darts of desire,
lastinger glances your smile through tears.

Don't be afraid of suffering, render
heaviness back to the earth again;
mountains are heavy, and seas, and the tender

trees that in childhood you set in their places
have grown too heavy for you to sustain.
Ah, but the breezes . . . ah, but the spaces . . .

V

Raise no commemorating stone. The roses
shall blossom every summer for his sake.
For this is Orpheus. His metamorphosis
in this one and in that. We should not make

searches for other names. Once and for all,
it's Orpheus when there's song. He comes and goes.
Is it not much if sometimes, by some small
number of days, he shall outlive the rose?

Could you but feel his passing's needfulness!
Though he himself may dread the hour drawing nigher
Already, when his words pass earthliness,

he passes with them far beyond your gaze.
His hands unhindered by the trellised lyre,
in all his over-steppings he obeys.

VI

Does he belong here? No, his spreading
nature from either domain has sprung.
Withes would they weave in a cunninger wedding,
hands to which roots of the willow had clung.

Going to bed, never leave on the table
bread or milk, forcing the dead to rise. –
He shall invoke them, he who is able
to mingle in mildness of closing eyes

their appearance with all that we view;
he for whom magic of earth-smoke and rue
shall be clear as the clearest link between things.

Nothing can weaken the image he saves,
whether from dwellings, whether from graves,
glorifying pitchers or bracelets or rings.

VII

Praising, that's it! As a praiser and blesser
he came like the ore from the taciturn mine.
Came with his heart, oh, transient presser,
for men, of a never-exhaustible wine.

Voice never fails him for things lacking lustre,
sacred example will open his mouth.
All becomes vineyard, all becomes cluster,
warmed by his sympathy's ripening south.

Crypts and the mouldering kings who lie there
do not belie his praising, neither
doubt, when a shadow obscures our days.

He is a messenger always attendant,
reaching far through their gates resplendent
dishes of fruit for the dead to praise.

VIII

Only Praising's realm may Lamentation
range in, naiad of the weeping spring;
watching over our precipitation,
till our tears are crystals, blazoning

that same rock that bears the gates and altars.
Round her quiet shoulders, as she broods,
look, the dawn of an awareness falters
she's the youngest of the sister-moods.

Triumph *knows*, and Longing is admitting, –
Lamentation learns still; nightly sitting,
counts, with maiden-hands, old tribulation.

Then, however inexpertly limned,
lifts our voices in a constellation
to the sky her breathing has not dimmed.

IX

Only by him with whose lays
shades were enraptured
may the celestial praise
faintly be captured.

Only who tasted their own
flower with the sleeping
holds the most fugitive tone
ever in keeping.

Make but that image the pond
fleetingly tendered
knownly endure!

Not till both here and beyond
voices are rendered
lasting and pure.

X

Welcome, whose meaning in me so long,
coffins of stone, has been quietly growing, –
you the Romans' gladdening water's flowing
through to-day as a wandering song;

you also, as open to all delight
as a wakening shepherd's eyes,
full of stillness and flowering nettle and flight
of delirious butterflies;

welcome to all we have snatched like this
from doubt, the mouths re-endowed with power
of speech, after knowing what silence is.

Knowing it or not, friends – which is our case? –
Both alike has the lingering hour
graved in the human face.

XI

Search the heavens. Is no 'Horse-man' reckoned
there in starry outline? For we share
much with that proud earth. And with a second,
driving, curbing, whom it has to bear.

Is not this, first hunted and then broken,
just the nature of the course we run?
Turf and turning. Pressure, nothing spoken.
New horizons. And the two are one.

Are they though? Or are they never able
both to choose the way they both pursue?
Severingly unlike are field and table.

Even those uniting stars beguile.
Still, it gladdens and suffices too
to believe the symbol for a while.

XII

Hail, the spirit able to unite!
For we truly live our lives in symbol,
and with tiny paces move our nimble
clocks beside our real day and night.

Still we somehow act in true relation,
we that find ourselves we know not where.
Aerialled station feels for aerialled station –
what seemed empty space could bear . . .

Purest tension. Harmony of forces!
Does not this displaying of our resources
keep us from impeding your intents?

All the farmer's toiling and arranging
never reaches where the seed is changing
slowly into Summer. Earth *presents*.

XIII

Banana, rounded apple, russet pear,
gooseberry . . . Does not all this convey
life and death into your mouth? . . . It's there! . . .
Read it on a child's face any day,

when it tastes them. What infinity!
Can't you feel inside your mouth a growing
mysteriousness, and, where words were, a flowing
of suddenly released discovery?

Dare to say what 'apple' has implied!
Sweetness, concentrated, self-repressing,
slowly yielding to the tongue's caressing,

growing awake, transparent, clarified,
double-meaning'd, sunshine-full, terrestrial: –
O experience, feeling, joy, – celestial!

XIV

Our life-long neighbours, flower, vine-leaf, fruit,
they do not merely speak the season's speech.
These things so brightly manifest, that reach
from darkness, gleam, it may be, with the mute

envy of those through whom the earth grows strong.
What do we know about the part they play?
To mix their unused marrow with the clay
has been their second-nature for so long.

But do they do it of their own accords?
Is it by sullen slaves that these clenched fruits
are laboured and thrust forth to us, their lords?

Are *they* the lords, who sleep beside the roots,
and grant us, what their plenty never misses,
this middle-thing, made of dumb strength and kisses?

XV

Stay . . . , this is good . . . But already it's flown.
. . . Murmurs of music, a footing, a humming: –
Maidens, so warm, so mute, are you coming
to dance the taste of this fruit we've known?

Dance the orange. Who can forget it,
the way it would drown in itself, – how, too,
it would struggle against its sweetness. And yet it
's been yours. Been deliciously changed into you.

Dance the orange. The landscape, create it
warm from yourselves, till its airs be enfolding
again the splendour they ripened! Loose,

glowingly, fragrance on fragrance! Relate it
all to the peel, so chastely withholding,
all to the joyfully plentiful juice!

XVI

The reason, friend, you feel so alone . . .
With our words and our pointings, little by little,
we're making – who knows? – perhaps the most brittle,
most perilous part of the world our own.

Who among us can point to a smell? –
Yet there's many a power we obscurely dread
which you can feel . . . You're aware of the dead,
and you shrink away from the conjurer's spell.

Look, our tasks are really the same:
dealt out a puzzle of parts, to endeavour
to make it a whole. Hard to help you. Never

plant me in your heart. I should grow too well.
But I will guide *my* master's hand and exclaim:
This is Esau here in his own rough fell.

XVII

Undermost he, the earth-bound
root of uprearing
multitudes, source underground,
never appearing.

Helmet and hunting-horn,
words of the aging,
rage between brothers-born,
women assuaging . . .

Branch on branch, time on time,
vainly they spire . . .
One free! Oh, climb . . . oh, climb . . .

One, though the others drop,
curves, as it scales the top,
into a lyre.

XVIII

Master, there's something new
droning and drumming.
It has its heralds too,
praising its coming.

Ill though our ears withstand
such perturbation,
now the machines demand
their celebration.

Source of our weakness
now, and in vengeful rage
ruining our heritage,

us shall these things at length,
us, who supply their strength,
serve in all meekness.

XIX

Change though the world may as fast
as cloud-collections,
home to the changeless at last
fall all perfections.

Over the thrust and the throng,
freer and higher,
echoes your preluding song,
god with the lyre.

Sorrow we misunderstand,
love we have still to begin,
death and what's hidden therein

await unveiling.
Song alone circles the land,
hallowing and hailing.

XX

But what shall I offer you, Master, say,
you who taught all creatures to hear? –
The remembered evening of one spring day,
in Russia: a horse drawing near . . .

White, coming up from the village alone,
on one fetlock a tethering-block,
to spend the night alone, on his own:
how gaily he tossed the shock

of his mane in time to his mounting mood
on that rudely encumbered race!
How they leapt, the springs of the equine blood!

He had followed the call of space.
He sang and he listened – your cycle swept
unbrokenly through him.
His image: accept.

XXI

Spring has come again. Earth's a-bubble
with all those poems she knows by heart, –
oh, so many . . . With prize for the trouble
of such long learning, her holidays start.

Stern was her teacher, he'd over-task her
from time to time; but we liked the snows
in the old man's beard; and now we can ask her
what green, what blue are: she knows, she knows.

Eager to catch you, Earth, happy creature,
play with the children now outpouring!
Conqueringly foremost the happiest springs.

All she has ever been taught by her teacher,
all that's imprinted in roots and soaring
difficult stems, – she sings, she sings!

XXII

We wax for waning.
Count, though, Time's journeying
as but a little thing
in the Remaining.

End of unmeasured
hasting will soon begin;
only what's leisured
leads us within.

Boys, don't be drawn too far
into attempts at flight,
into mere swiftness. – Look

how rested all things are:
shadow and fall of light,
blossom and book.

XXIII

Only when flight shall soar
not for its own sake only
up into heaven's lonely
silence, and be no more

merely the lightly profiling,
proudly successful tool,
playmate of winds, beguiling
time there, careless and cool:

only when some pure Whither
outweighs boyish insistence
on the achieved machine

will who has journeyed thither
be, in that fading distance,
all that his flight has been.

XXIV

Shall those primeval friends of ours, the unfated,
ever-unsuing gods, because they are nought for
the hard-faced steel we have sternly nursed, be repudiated,
or else within some map be suddenly sought for?

Those overmastering friends, who are always reaving
the dead from us, brush nowhere against our wheels.
Now we have left the welcoming bath and the old guest-meals
far behind, we find their messengers tardy beyond believing,

we that can overtake them. Lonely misunderstanders
one of another we wholly depend on at every turning,
nowadays the ways we led in lovely meanders

run right ahead. In boilers only are burning
the former fires and heaving the heavier-growing
hammers. But we are like swimmers whose strength is going.

XXV

Now it is you, though, you whom I never
knew but as some unnamable flower, I will try
once more to recall and show them, vanished for ever,
beautiful playmate of, ah, the invincible cry.

Dancer, who all of a sudden, her body rebelling,
stopped, as her youth had been bronzed into art,
mournfully hearkening. – Then, from the Ever-Impelling,
music entered into her altered heart.

Sickness was near. In grip of the shadows already,
darklier thrusted the blood, though defiantly ready
to surge to its natural spring-tide just as before.

Time and again out of darkness emerged with a mocking
earthly effulgence. Then, after terrible knocking,
entered the hopelessly open door.

XXVI

You that could sound till the end, though, immortal accorder,
seized by the scorn-maddened Maenads' intemperate throng,
wholly outsounded their cries when in musical order
soared from the swarm of deformers your formative song.

Wrestle and rage as they might on that fated career,
none was able to shatter your head or your lyre:
hard stones hurled at your heart could only acquire
gentleness, soon as they struck you, and power to hear.

Though they destroyed you at last and revenge had its will,
sound of you lingered in lions and rocks you were first to
enthral, in the trees and the birds. You are singing there still.

O you god that has vanished! You infinite track!
Only because dismembering hatred dispersed you
are we hearers to-day and a mouth which else Nature would lack.

SECOND PART

I

Breathing, invisible poem! That great
world-space, at each inhalation
exchanged for this human existence. Counter-weight
of my rhythmical realisation.

Single wave, to whose slowly
gathering sea I'm wrought;
you, of all possible seas most frugal and lowly, –
space incaught.

Of all these places in space, how many a one
has been within me already. Many a wind
seems like a son.

Do you know me, air, still full of my dwelling-places?
You, the one-time smooth-skinned
rondure and leaf of my phrases.

II

Just as the handiest paper snatches
sometimes for ever the master-stroke,
often only the mirror catches
smiles that nothing will re-evoke

from maidens approving the morning alone,
or the image obsequious lamp-light graces;
and later the real, the breathing faces
merely reflect what was once their own.

What have eyes not gazed into quivering flosses
glowing among logs that have ceased to blaze? –
Glimpses of living, beyond recall.

Earth, O Earth, who could tell your losses?
Only who sang with unfaltering praise
of the heart, born into the midst of it all.

III

Mirrors: no one has yet distilled with
patient knowledge your fugitive
essence. You spaces in time, that are filled with
holes like those of a sieve.

Squandering the empty ball-room's pomp,
deep as forests when twilight broods . . .
And, like sixteen-pointers, the lustres romp
through your virginal solitudes.

Pictures crowd you at times. A few
seem to be taken right within you,
shyly to others you wave adieu.

There, though, the fairest will always be,
till through to her lips withheld continue
Narcissus, released into lucency.

IV

This is the creature there has never been.
They never knew it, and yet, none the less,
they loved the way it moved, its suppleness,
its neck, its very gaze, mild and serene.

Not there, because they loved it, it behaved
as though it were. They always left some space.
And in that clear unpeopled space they saved
it lightly reared its head, with scarce a trace

of not being there. They fed it, not with corn,
but only with the possibility
of being. And that was able to confer

such strength, its brow put forth a horn. One horn.
Whitely it stole up to a maid, – to *be*
within the silver mirror and in her.

V

Flower-muscle, gradually releasing
the anemone's pale meadow-day,
till at length into her lap unceasing
sky-light pours its polyphonic ray;

muscle stretching out that starry-flowered
quietude for endless welcoming;
so at times by fullness overpowered
that the restward call of evening

almost fails to bring your far-extended
petal-edges back to you once more:
world of will and power uncomprehended!

We, the violent, are not so fleeting.
Through what lives though must we pass before
we reach that state of open-hearted greeting?

VI

You for Antiquity, rose throned in power,
were a calyx with only a single rim,
but for us of to-day you're the full, the numberless flower,
the theme whose depths we can only skim.

Grown so rich, you appear like draping on draping
about a body of air and fire;
though each of your leaves in itself is at once an escaping
and a disowning of all attire.

For centuries, name after sweetest name,
we have heard your fragrance singing:
suddenly it hangs in the air like fame.

And then we find to name it exceeds our powers . . .
And over to it go winging
memories yielded up by recallable hours.

VII

Flowers, whose kinship with ordering hands we are able
to feel at last (girls' hands, of once, of to-day),
who often, strewn all over the garden table,
tired and tenderly injured, lay

waiting for water to come, once more repealing
death already begun, – and now
uplifted again between the poles of those feeling,
magnetical fingers you have to allow

can be far kinder than delicate you had guessed
on coming round in the jug, to find
you were cooling and slowly exhaling the warmth of girls, like
    things confessed,

like tiring sins remembered in drowsy gloom,
which gathering of you committed, to bind
you to them once more, who blend with you in their bloom.

VIII

You few, the one-time sharers of childhood's treasure
in the city's scattered garden walks,
how we met and awoke in each other a hesitant pleasure,
and, like the lamb with the scroll that talks,

spoke without speaking. If sometimes happiness found us,
no one possessed it. Whose could it be?
And how it would melt among all those moving around us,
and the long year's anxiety.

Unconcerning carriages rolling and swerving,
houses surrounding us strongly – untruthfully, though, and never
a thing that knew us. Was anything real at all?

Nothing. Only the balls. Their glorious curving.
No, not even the children . . . Though one would ever
pass, ah, fleetingly! under the falling ball.

In memoriam Egon von Rilke

IX

Boast not, judges, of racks no longer required,
of throats no longer locked in the iron's embrace.
Not one heart has it heightened, that newly-acquired
spasm of mercy's milder grimace.

Things it has slowly collected, the scaffold one day
offers us back, like children their long-ago gifted
birthday toys. He'd enter the pure, the uplifted,
gate-wide open heart in a different way,

the god of genuine mercy. Mightily, spreading
flamelier out from his origin.
More than a wind for the great ships steadily heading.

Potent no less than that gentle unconscious awaring,
silently winning us over within
like the quietly playing child of an infinite pairing.

X

Long will machinery menace the whole of our treasure,
while it, unmindful of us, dares to a mind of its own.
Checking the glorious hand's flaunting of lovelier leisure,
now for some stubborner work sternlier it fashions the stone.

Not for an hour will it stay, so that for once we may flee it,
oiling itself in a quiet factory, fitly employed.
Now it is life, no less, and feels best able to be it,
having, with equal resolve, ordered, constructed, destroyed.

Even to-day, though, existence is magical, pouring
freshly from hundreds of well-springs, – a playing of purest
forces, which none can surprise without humbly adoring.

Words still melt into something beyond their embrace . . .
Music, too, keeps building anew with the insecurest
stones her celestial house in unusable space.

XI

Many a rule of death rose with deliberate rightness,
onwardly-conquering man, during your hunting past:
better than trap or net known to me, fluttering whiteness,
you they were wont to hang down in the cavernous Karst.

Gently letting you in, as were you a token
publishing peace. But then: vassal would twitch at your thong,
Night would cast from the caves pallid handfuls of broken-
flighted doves to the light . . .
Not even that, though, was wrong.

Far from the gazer remain every emotion but gladness,
not from the hunter alone, gathering, watchful and keen,
that which his suns have matured.

Killing merely is one form of our wandering sadness . . .
Pure in the spirit serene
's all we ourselves have endured.

XII

Choose to be changed. With the flame, with the flame be enraptured,
where from within you a thing changefully-splendid escapes:
nothing whereby that earth-mastering artist is captured
more than the turning-point touched by his soaring shapes.

That which would stay what it is renounces existence:
does it feel safe in its shelter of lustreless grey?
Wait, a hardest is warning the hard from a distance,
heaved is a hammer from far away.

He who pours forth like a spring shall be known of his Knowing;
ravished, it leads him through cheerful creation, that closes
often as not with beginning and opens with end.

Parting's child or descendant is each glad space they are going
gazingly through. And now, feeling her metamorphosis,
laurelled Daphne wants you, changed to a wind, for her friend.

XIII

Anticipate all farewells, as were they behind you
now, like the winter going past.
For through some winter you feel such wintriness bind you,
your then out-wintering heart will always outlast.

Dead evermore in Eurydice, mount with more singing,
mount to relation more pure with more celebrant, tongue.
Here, in this realm of the dwindlers and dregs, be a ringing
glass, which has, even though shivered to pieces, been rung.

Be – and, perceiving in that which is being's negation
merely the infinite ground of your fervent vibration,
beat, through this never-again, to the fullest amount.

To the stock of used-up, as well as of dumb and decaying
things within copious Nature, those sums beyond saying,
count yourself joyfully in and destroy the account.

XIV

Flowers, so faithful to Earth that has sent them hither,
whom we lend fate from the borders of fate – and yet
who knows, when we think we see them regretfully wither,
if it is not for us to be their regret?

To all that would soar our selves are the grand aggravation,
we lay them on all we encounter, proud of their weight;
what terrifying teachers we are for that part of creation
which loves its eternally childish state.

Could someone but take them right into his slumber and sleep
deeply with things, how differently, lightly he'd wander
back to a different day out of that communal deep.

Or, it may be, he would stay, and they'd blossom and praise
him, the converted, now one of them and all yonder
silent brothers and sisters in woodlands and ways.

XV

O fountain mouth, you mouth that can respond
so inexhaustibly to all who ask
with one, pure, single saying. Marble mask
before the water's flowing face. Beyond,

the aqueducts' long derivation. Past
the tombs, from where the Apennines begin,
they bring your saying to you, which at last,
over the grizzled age of your dark chin,

falls to the waiting basin, crystal-clear;
falls to the slumbering recumbent ear,
the marble ear, with which you still confer.

One of earth's ears. With her own lonely mood
she thus converses. Let a jug intrude,
she'll only think you've interrupted her.

XVI

Still the god remains an ever-growing
wholeness we have irritably burst.
We are sharp, for we insist on knowing,
he exists serenely and dispersed.

Even gifts of purest consecration
only find acceptance in so much
as he turns in moveless contemplation
to the end we do not touch.

Only those who dwell
out of sight can taste the spring we hear,
when the god has silently assented.

With its brawling we must be contented.
And the lamb's more silent instinct's clear
when it begs us for its bell.

XVII

Where, in what ever-blissfully watered gardens, upon what trees,
out of, oh, what gently dispetalled flower-cups do these
so strange-looking fruits of consolation mature?
Delicious, when, now and then, you pick one up in the poor

trampled field of your poverty. Time and again you find
yourself lost in wonder over the size of the fruit,
over its wholesomeness, over its smooth, soft rind,
and that neither the heedless bird above nor jealous worm at the root

has been before you. Are there, then, trees where angels will congregate,
trees invisible leisurely gardeners so curiously cultivate,
that, without being ours, they bear for us fruits like those?

Have we, then, never been able, we shadows and shades,
with our doing that ripens too early and then as suddenly fades,
to disturb that even-tempered summer's repose?

XVIII

Dancer: you transmutation
of all going-by into going: what you have wrought!
And your finishing whirl, that tree of mere animation,
how it took over the year you had flyingly caught!

Did not its crown, that your swaying might settle to swarming,
suddenly blossom with stillness? Above that, too,
was there not sunnily, was there not summerly warming
all the warmth that exhaled from you?

Nay, it was able, your tree of rapture, to bear.
Are they not, all its fruits that so peacefully shine,
jug streaked with ripeness, vase further ripened, still there?

And does not your mark in their paintings still meet the discerning –
that of your eyebrows' darker line
swiftly inscribed on the wall of your own swift turning?

XIX

Gold dwells somewhere at ease in the pampering bank,
mixing with thousands on intimate terms. But to any
coin that blind man begging, to even a penny,
seems but a desolate place, a chink in a dusty plank.

Money shines out from the shops in its own dimension,
plausibly masking in silk, carnation, and fur.
He, though, silently stands in the breath-suspension
of all the money breathing, asleep or astir.

Oh, how does it ever close at night, that perpetually open hand?
Fate to-morrow will fetch it back and display it,
bright, poor, endlessly fragile, year after year.

Could but at last some gazer, astoundedly coming to understand,
celebrate its persistence! – Only a singer could say it.
Only a god could hear.

XX

Inter-stellar spaces – ah yes, but how many times greater
spaces terrestrial are!
First, for example, a child . . . then a neighbour, a moment later, –
oh, how incredibly far!

Fate but through spanning us, maybe, with Being's measure
seems so strange to our eyes:
think of the spans to a man from a maid, whose pleasure
lingers with him she flies!

All is remote – nowhere does the circle close.
Look at that curious face on the welcoming table,
staring out of its dish.

Fishes are dumb, . . . so one imagined. Who knows?
May there not be some place where, *without* them, the dwellers are able
to speak what would be the language of fish?

XXI

Sing those gardens, my heart, poured as into a glass,
gardens you have not known, transparent, untrampled.
Waters and roses of Ispahan or Shiras,
blissfully sing them, praise them, the unexampled.

Show that by you, my heart, they are never missed:
pleasure for you their ripening figs are preparing,
you with their breezes, almost visibly bearing
fragrance of blossoming branches, can always tryst.

Know that no want exists for, no hand bereaving
takes from, the acted resolution: to *be*.
Silken thread, you have entered into the weaving.

Feel, with what pattern soever you're inwardly blended
(even a scene from the story of Agony),
feel that the whole, the praisable, carpet's intended.

XXII

Oh, but in spite of fate, life's glorious abundance
foaming over in parks and splendid estates, –
or in stone men, with all their straining redundance,
under balconies built over lofty gates.

Oh, the brazen bell that daily uplifts its solemn
hammer against the dullness of every day.
Or the one, the only, at Karnak, the column, the column,
surviving almost eternal temples' decay.

Now, though, the overflowings of that same font all
plunge but as speed from the yellow, the horizontal
day to the night so dazzlingly overwrought.

Rushing by but to vanish and leave no traces.
Lingering spirals of flight through ethereal spaces, –
not one, perhaps, is in vain. Yet as were they but thought.

XXIII

Call me to your lonely meeting-places
with the hour that always says you nay:
suppliantly near you, like dogs' faces,
time and time again, though, turned away,

when at last you think that it is yours.
Things thus snatched from you are most your own.
We are free – dismissed from those same doors
where we thought such welcome had been shown.

Anxiously we long to be foot-helder,
we, too youthful sometimes for the elder,
and too old for what has never been;

only right when under every star we
praise, for, oh, branch, axe and sweetness are we
of a peril ripening unseen.

XXIV

Oh, this delight, ever-new, from made-workable soil!
Hardly a hand lent the earliest darers assistance.
Cities rose none the less on gulfs to a blessed existence,
pitchers were filled none the less with water and oil.

Gods, – we plan them in bold provisional sketches
cross-grained Fate takes from us and flings to the past.
Still, they *are* the Immortals. Our spirit outstretches,
hearkening-out the one that will hear it at last.

We, but one race for millennia, growing ever greater,
age after age, with that child of the future whose birth
shall so entirely surpass and astonish us, later.

We, so immeasurably ventured, what aeons attend us!
And only taciturn Death knows what we are worth,
and how much it always pays him to lend us.

XXV

Hark, the earliest harrows striving
already; the rhythm of man once more
breaks the tense stillness around reviving
pre-vernal earth. What has come before

seems to return as unstaled as ever.
No new-comer, it comes like new.
Looked for again and again, you never
could capture it. Always it captured you.

Sunset splashes the wintered oaken
leaves with a brown that is yet to be.
Sometimes breezes exchange a token.

Black are the hedges. But heaps of dung
crouch more satedly black on the lea.
Hours grow more eternally young.

XXVI

How it thrills us, the bird's clear cry . . .
Any cry that was always there.
Children, playing in the open air,
children already go crying by

real cries. Cry chance in. Through crevasses
in that same space whereinto, as dreaming
men into dreams, the pure bird-cry passes
they drive their splintering wedge of screaming.

Where are we? Freer and freer, we gyre
only half up, kites breaking
loose, with our frills of laughter flaking

away in the wind. – Make the criers a choir,
singing god! that resurgently waking
may bear on its waters the head and the lyre.

XXVII

Does it exist, though, Time the destroyer?
When will it scatter the tower on the resting hill?
This heart, the eternal gods' eternal enjoyer,
when shall the Demiurge ravish and spill?

Are we really such tremblingly breakable
things as Destiny tries to pretend?
Does childhood's promise, deep, unmistakable,
down in the roots, then, later, end?

Ah, Mutability's spectre!
out through the simple accepter
you, like a vapour, recede.

We, though we wax but for waning,
fill none the less for remaining
powers a celestial need.

XXVIII

Oh, come and go, you almost child, enhancing
for one brief hour the figure of the dance
to purest constellation of that dancing
where, subject as we are to change and chance,

we beat dull Nature. For she only started
hearing with all her ears at Orpheus' song.
And you still moved with motion then imparted,
and shrank a little when a tree seemed long

in treading with you the remembered pace.
You knew it still, that passage where the lyre
soundingly rose, the unimagined centre,

and practised all your steps in hope to enter
that theme again, whirling to one entire
communion with your friend both feet and face.

XXIX

Silent friend of those far from us, feeling
how your breath is still enlarging space,
fill the sombre belfry with your pealing.
What consumes you now is growing apace

stronger than the feeding strength it borrows.
Be, as Change will have you, shade or shine.
Which has grieved you most of all your sorrows?
Turn, if drinking's bitter, into wine.

Be, in this immeasurable night,
at your senses' cross-ways magic cunning,
be the sense of their mysterious tryst.

And, should earthliness forget you quite,
murmur to the quiet earth: I'm running.
Tell the running water: I exist.

RILKE'S NOTES ON THE SONNETS TO ORPHEUS

FIRST PART

x In the second stanza the allusion is to the graves in the celebrated ancient cemetery of the Allyscamps near Arles, which are also mentioned in *Malte Laurids Brigge*.

xvi This sonnet is addressed to a dog. – By 'my master's hand' the relation to Orpheus is established, who here stands for the poet's 'master'. The poet wants to guide this hand, so that, for the sake of its infinite concernment and devotion, it may bless the dog too, which, almost like Esau [Rilke must have meant: like Jacob], has only put on its fell in order to receive within its heart some share in an inheritance which does not fall to it: that of the whole human condition, with its distress and its happiness.

xxi The little spring-song seems to me, as it were, the 'interpretation' of a singularly dancing music I once heard sung by the convent children at a morning service in the little Conventual Church at Ronda (in the South of Spain). The children, always in dance measure, sang a text I did not know to triangle and tambourine.

xxv To Wera.

SECOND PART

iv The unicorn has ancient, in the Middle Ages continually celebrated, significations of virginity: hence it is asserted that, although non-existent for the profane, it *was*, as soon as it appeared, within the 'silver mirror' which the virgin is holding before it (see tapestries of the xv. century) and 'in her', as in a no less pure, no less mysterious mirror. [Rilke is alluding to the celebrated tapestries of *La Dame à la Licorne* in the Musée de Cluny.]

vi The rose of antiquity was a simple 'eglantine', red and yellow, in the colours that appear in flame. It blooms here, in the Valais, in certain gardens.

viii Fourth line: The lamb (in pictures), which only speaks by means of the scroll in its mouth.

xi Referring to the manner in which, according to ancient hunting custom, the peculiarly white rock-doves in certain districts of the Karst, by means of cloths carefully suspended into their caves and suddenly shaken in a particular way, are scared out of their subterranean dwellings to be shot during their terrified escape.

xxiii To the Reader.

xxv Counterpart to the little Spring Song of Songs in the First Part of the Sonnets [i.e., xxi].

xxviii To Wera.

xxix To a friend of Wera's.

FROM

THE UNCOLLECTED POEMS OF 1906 TO 1926

None of these poems were ever collected and published in book-form by Rilke himself, although he allowed some of them to appear in periodicals. They will all be found, together with many more, in *Poems 1906 to 1926*, translated by J. B. Leishman and published by the Hogarth Press in 1957.

With many travels and truancies, Rilke had continued to make Paris his headquarters, but in July 1914 he had gone to visit friends in Germany and he was caught and kept there by the outbreak of war. In the summer of 1919 an invitation to lecture and give readings from his poems enabled him to obtain a visa for Switzerland, where, except for two visits, one short and one long, to Paris, and a short visit to Italy, he remained until his death in December 1926. From his arrival in the summer of 1919 his great ambition was to find some peaceful refuge where he could collect and concentrate himself and complete the *Duino Elegies*, and this refuge he eventually found, in 1921, in the little Château de Muzot, near Sierre, in the Rhône Valley between Brigue and Sion.

PRAYER FOR THE IDIOTS AND CONVICTS

You from whom quietly
Being has turned away
its vast face: one, maybe
not unbeing, will pray

under the stars that climb,
out on the dewy grass,
that time with you may pass,
for you have time.

When something makes you recall,
tenderly runs through your hair:
all has been now let fall,
all that was there.

Would but your speech desist
after the heart's grown old,
so that no mother be told
such can exist!

Now the moon's mounted to view
over the branches outthrown,
and, as though peopled by you,
stays there alone.

Paris, c. January 1909

Rolling pearls. Did something snap in the necklace?
But supposing I managed to thread them again: I'd need
you, strong clasp, to hold them together, beloved.

Was it not time? Like chill dawn waiting for sunrise,
I am waiting for you, pale with accomplished night;
I am one gigantic face, like a crowded house,
so as not to miss one single line of your lofty
central appearance. As a gulf hopes out for the open,
casting with outstretched
lighthouse shining spaces, – as a river-bed in the desert
for a burst of heavenly ravishing rain from the mountain, –
as a prisoner stands upright and longs for an answer
from the single star to come through his innocent window, –
as a cripple snatches the warm
crutches out of his hands to be hung up over the altar,

and lies there and can't get up till a miracle happens:
I lie, and, if you don't come, shall grovel here till the end.

I only want you. Is not the crack in the pavement,
when it feels the sprouting grass through its wretchedness, bound
to desire the whole of spring? The terrestrial springtime.
Does not the moon need the strange star's mighty appearance
to get itself imaged in village ponds? How can
the least thing happen, unless all future fullness,
time's completed sum, move to meet us half-way?

Are you not finally in it, ineffable? After a while
I shall cease to be fit for you. I shall grow old, or children
will have thrust me aside . . .

Begun Venice, early July 1912; completed in Spain, end of 1912

THE SPANISH TRILOGY

I

Out of that cloud, look, that so wildly hides
the star that peered this instant – (and myself),
out of that mountain-land beyond, possessing
night and her winds awhile now – (and myself),
out of this river in the vale, that catches
the gleam of torn sky-clearings – (and myself);
out of myself, Lord, and all that, to make
one single thing: myself here, and the feeling
with which the flock, penned in the fold, endure
the great dark no-more-being of the world
with sighing breath, – myself, and every light
in the dim multitude of houses, Lord,
to make a thing; from strangers (for, indeed,
I don't know one of them), and from myself,
myself, to make one thing: from all those sleepers,
those strangers, those old men up at the hospice,
coughing importantly in bed, those children,
heavy with slumber, at such strangers' breasts;
from much that's vague, and always from myself,
myself alone and all I do not know,
to make the thing, Lord, Lord, Lord, Lord, the thing,
that, cosmic-earthly, like a meteor
comprises in its weight only the sum
of its own flight, weighing only its arrival.

II

Oh, why must someone always be assuming
such load of alien things, like a poor porter,
heaving a more and more remotely filled
basket from stall to stall, and stumbling after
one whom he can't ask: Master, what's the feast for?

Oh, why must someone stand here like a shepherd,
exposed to such excess of influence,
with such a share in this place full of happening,
that, if he merely leant against a tree-trunk
in the landscape, he'd fulfil his destiny?
And yet his too large vision be denied
the quiet flock's appeasement, and each glance,
above, below, be full of world, world, world?
What gladly cleaves to others penetrating
as blindly and inhospitably as music
into his blood, to change there and pass on.

He'll rise up night by night and have the call
of birds outside already deep within him;
feel bold, to be receiving all those stars
into his gaze, not lightly – not like one
spreading this feast of night before a woman,
and spoiling her with all the heavens he's felt.

III

Let me, though, having once more the thronging of towns
and tangled skein of sounds and chaos
of vehicles round me, uncompanioned, –
let me, above the enveloping whirl,
remember sky and that earthy brim of the vale
where the homeward-faring flock emerged from beyond.
Let me feel stony, and let
the shepherd's daily task seem possible to me,
as he moves about and tans and with measuring stone-throw
mends the hem of his flock where it grows ragged.
His slow but laborious walk, his pensive body,
his glorious standing-still! Even to-day a god
might secretly enter that form and not be diminished.
Alternately lingering and moving like day itself,
while shadows of clouds
pass through him, as space were slowly
thinking thoughts for him.

Let him be for you what he may. Like a fluttering nightlight
into a mantling lamp, I place myself within him.
A light grows peaceful. Death
may cleanlier find his way.

Ronda, 6-14 January 1913

TO THE ANGEL

Strong, still light upon the verge of Being,
burning out into nocturnal space,
while we spend ourselves in dimly-seeing
hesitation round about your base.

Destiny will never let us sally
from the wandering inner maze below;
you appear above our bounding valley
like a glowing cone of alpine snow.

Downward-dropping lees from your eternal
happiness are more than we can share:
pure divider, standing, like a vernal
equinox, between the Here and There!

Could we hope to cloud your clear sedateness
with the mixture of our dim distress? –
You, resplendent with all kinds of greatness,
we, proficient but in pettiness.

Only pitiful in all our pleading;
when we look, no more than just awake;
when we smile, incapable of leading
anything that matters to mistake

what we are. And am I, then, complaining?
What could my complaint avail with you? –
Oh, though hands be pounding, throat be straining,
I've no hope of being harkened to!

You I'll never reach with lamentations
if my heart-beats cannot make you hear,
shine upon me! Let the constellations
look at me before I disappear!

Ronda, 14 January 1913

THE RAISING OF LAZARUS

One had to bear with the majority –
what they wanted was a sign that screamed:
Martha, though, and Mary – he had dreamed
they would be contented just to see
that he *could*. But not a soul believed him:
'Lord, you've come too late,' said all the crowd.
So to peaceful Nature, though it grieved him,
on he went to do the unallowed.
Asked them, eyes half-shut, his body glowing
with anger, 'Where's the grave?' Tormentedly.
And to them it seemed his tears were flowing,
as they thronged behind him, curiously.
As he walked, the thing seemed monstrous to him,
childish, horrible experiment:
then there suddenly went flaming through him
such an all-consuming argument
against their life, their death, their whole collection
of separations made by them alone,
all his body quivered with rejection
as he gave out hoarsely 'Raise the stone'.
Someone shouted that the corpse was stinking
(buried now four days ago) – but He
stood erect, brim-full of that unblinking,
mounting gesture, that so painfully
lifted up his hand (no hand was ever
raised so slowly, so immeasurably),
till it stood there, shining in the gloom.
There it slowly, clawingly contracted:
what if all the dead should be attracted
upwards, through that syphon of a tomb,
where a pallid chrysalidal thing
was writhing up from where it had been lying? –
But it stood alone (no more replying),
and they saw vague, unidentifying
Life compelled to give it harbouring.

Ronda, January 1913

THE SPIRIT ARIEL

(*After reading Shakespeare's Tempest*)

Sometime, somewhere, it had set him free,
that jerk with which you flung yourself in youth
full upon greatness, far from all respect.
Then he grew willing: and since then a servant,
after each service waiting for his freedom.
Half-domineering, half almost ashamed,
you make excuses, that for this and this
you still require him, and insist, alas!
how you have helped him. Though you feel yourself
how everything detained by his detention
is missing from the air. Sweet and seductive,
to let him go, and then, abjuring magic,
entering into destiny like others,
to know that henceforth his most gentle friendship,
without all tension, nowhere bound by duty,
a something added to the space we breathe,
is busied heedless in the element.
Dependent now, having no more the gift
to form the dull mouth to that conjuration
that brought him headlong. Powerless, ageing, poor,
yet breathing *him*, incomprehensibly
far-scattered fragrance, making the Invisible
at last complete. Smiling, to think you'd been
on nodding terms with that, such great acquaintance
so soon familiar. Perhaps weeping, too,
when you remember how it loved you and
would yet be going, always both at once.

(And there I left it? Now he terrifies me,
this man who's duke again. – The ways he draws
the wire into his head, and hangs himself
beside the other puppets, and henceforth
begs mercy of the play! . . . What epilogue
of achieved mastery! Putting off, standing there
with only one's own strength: 'which is most faint'.)

Ronda, beginning of 1913

Straining so hard against strong Night, they fling
their little heap of voices on the laughter
that will not burn. O disobedient world,
full of rejection! And the space you breathe,
the stars revolve in! For all this was free
to plunge through unknown cosmic space, and move
in measureless remoteness, far from us.
Instead of which it deigns to seek our faces
like love awakening, like eyes that open
to gaze in ours; and may be squandering
its being upon us, who are not worth it.
Angelic power, for all we know, is lessened
when constellated heaven defers to us,
suspended into our dim destiny.
In vain. For who has noticed it? And even
if someone has, who dares to press against it
as though nocturnal space were his own window?
Who has not disavowed it? Who has not
smuggled adulterated, pseudo-nights
into this native element, and been happy?
We slink away from gods to rotting refuse.
For gods never entice us. They have being,
nothing else, superfluity of being,
but neither scent nor nod. Nothing's so dumb
as a god's mouth. Beautiful as a swan
on its eternity of unplumbed surface,
the god will sail and dive and spare his white.

Everything else entices. The small bird,
at its pure work among the leaves, compels us;
the flower feels cramped at home and comes across;
what will the wind not do? Only the god,
column-like, lets us pass, distributing,
high up, where he takes the strain, to either side,
the light arch of his equanimity.

Paris, end of February 1913

Overflowing heavens of squandered stars
flame above your affliction. Leave off weeping
into your pillow, and weep into them, where, close to the weeping,
close to the fading face, expansive
ravishing cosmic-space begins. Who shall interrupt,
once you are there, that stream? No one. No one but you,
if you suddenly try to struggle out of that one-way traffic
of stars coursing to meet you. Breathe!
Breathe the darkness of Earth, and again
upgaze! Behold, without form or feature,
depth from above bending towards you: the fluid
face dissolved within Night leaving space for your own.

Paris, April 1913
From *Poems to Night.*

EMMAUS

Not while they walked, though he seemed strangely sure
when first he fell into their company,
and passed before them through the lowly door
with more than manliest solemnity;
not while they laid the table, rather flurried,
and half-ashamed of what he'd come to share,
and he stood tolerantly, with his unhurried
spectatorship reposing on the pair;
not even when, eager to break the ice,
they'd settled down, convivially waiting,
and he had grasped the bread, with hesitating,
beautiful hands, to do, within a trice,
what should convulse them into vast relation,
like terror leaping through a crowded street –
not till they'd seen, before that large donation,
the narrow limits of their meal retreat,
they knew; and, rapt into intenser living,
arose with bended head and trembling knee.
Then, when they saw he'd not yet finished giving,
forthreached for the two mouthfuls, quiveringly.

Paris, April 1913

THE HARROWING OF HELL

Painless at last, his being escaped from the terrible
body of pain. Upwards. Left it.
And lonely Dark was afraid,
and flung at the pallor
bats in whose evening flitting there flutters still
fear of colliding
with that chilled anguish. Dim restless air
depressed itself on the corpse, while gloomy aversion
rose in the powerful vigilant creatures of night.
His discharged spirit, perhaps, had thought of remaining
inactively in the landscape. The immeasurable act of his suffering
would last him awhile. There was measure,
he felt, in the cool nocturnal presence of things
he now, like a lonely space, began to enclose.
But Earth, parched up in the thirst of his wounds, split open,
Earth split open, and all profundity thundered.
He, passed master in torments, heard all Hell
howling for confirmation
of his completed pain: that her continuing torture
might tremble at hint of an end in the end of his endless.
And, ghost as he was, he plunged with the downward weight
of all his weariness: hastily strode
through the startled backward stare of pasturing shadows,
hastily lifted his eyes to Adam,
hastened down, disappeared, gleamed, vanished in plunging
of wilder depths. Suddenly (higher, higher), above the centre
of surging cries, stepped out on the top
of his tall unrailinged tower of endurance: breathless:
stood, surveyed his estate of Pain, was silent.

Paris, April 1913

ST. CHRISTOPHER

To serve the greatest is the thing preferred
by all great strength. He hoped in time to do him
service here at the ford. Without a word
he'd left two great lords that seemed little to him,
and given himself entirely to the third,

he did not know; impelled to undertake
that service, not by prayer or by fast,
but having heard, the Lord himself at last
would come to one that left all for his sake.

So he trod daily through the roaring flood,
father of bridges with their stony strides,
and gathered much experience of both sides,
and came to feel a farer with his blood.

And rested in his little house at night,
ready at every call to recommence,
breathing the toil from his relaxing might,
rejoicing in his spaciousness of sense.

Then, one night, came a thin, high call: a child.
To ferry it, he rose to his full height;
knowing, though, how timid children are, he smiled,
and stepped quite shrunkenly into the night;
stooped: there was nothing but the wind blowing wild.

He murmured: For what purpose could a child . . . ?
Withdrew with one great stride back to his rest,
and felt sleep coming and was reconciled.
But there it was again, full of request.
He peered again: only the wind blowing wild.

There's no one there, or else I've been beguiled,
he muttered, and returned once more to sleep,
till the same sounds, inexorably mild,
reverberated in some hidden deep:
he came giant-striding:
out there stood a child.

Paris, April 1913

Shatter me, music, with rhythmical fury!
Lofty reproach, lifted against the heart
that feared such surge of perception, sparing itself. My heart, – there:
behold your glory! Can you remain contented
with less expansive beats, when the uppermost arches
are waiting for you to fill them with organing impulse?
Why do you long for the face withheld, for the far beloved?
For, oh, if your longing lacks breath to extort resounding storms
from the trumpet an angel blows on high at the end of the world,
she also does not exist, nowhere, will never be born,
she whom you parchingly miss . . .

Paris, May 1913

Behind the innocent trees
old Fate is slowly forming
her taciturn face.
Wrinkles travel thither . . .
Here a bird screams, and there
a furrow of pain
shoots from the hard sooth-saying mouth.

Oh, and the almost lovers,
with their unvaledictory smiles! –
their destiny setting and rising above them,
constellational,
night-enraptured.
Not yet proffering itself to their experience,
it still remains,
hovering in heaven's paths,
an airy form.

Heiligendamm, August 1913

WIDOW

Deprived of their first leaves her barren children stand,
and seem, for all the world, to have been born
because she pleased some terror. She has worn
deep hollows in her head with each numb, gnawing hand.
Were she a stone outside, she'd be far less forlorn:
the great rain, purer than we understand,
would gather there, and birds would drink . . . Oh, whence
came Nature to neglect these moulds, and pour
the bounties that alleviate and restore
into some figure without sense?

Paris, autumn 1913

STANZAS FOR WINTER

Unyielding days draw on, that you must seek
to bear in the hard rind of your resistance;
defensive, never feeling on your cheek
the opened wind's discharging depth of distance.
The night is strong, but so far off, the weak
enquiring lamp takes charge of your existence.
Be cheerful: frost and rawness are preparing
the tension that's required for new awaring.

Did you feel fully all last summer's flowers?
The roses? (Oh, be honest – it repays!)
The re-awakefulness of morning hours?
The light-foot walk down spider-woven ways?
Dive deep into yourself, shake up, amaze
dearest Delight; somewhere in you she cowers.
And, finding anything that missed your heart,
be glad to re-perceive it from the start.

Perhaps a silver gleam of pigeons wheeling,
a passing bird-cry's half-presentiment;
sight of a flower (most are so unrevealing!);
just before nightfall, a presageful scent.
Nature's divinely full – too full for feeling
that's not divinely made equivalent.
One that could really feel her thrust and pull
would hold himself in with both hands, brim-full.

Hold in his multitudinous excess,
and never hope to take in any more;
hold in his multitudinous excess,
and never think of losses to restore;
hold in his multitudinous excess,
sated beyond his longing's power to soar:
with only this to wonder at, that he
could bear such overflowing sufficiency.

Paris, probably beginning of winter 1913-14

FROM THE SONNETS FOR FRAU GRETE GULBRANSSON

I

Voice in the burning thorn-bush: let the one
it's calling doff his shoes without delay,
bundle his cloak before his face, and say
into his cloak: Master, thy will be done!

Let no one be less ready to obey
for lack of comprehension. He will find
that Grace has cut into that undefined,
impassable command some narrow way.

Mary stepped after it, and children stepped
after the call, and maidens gently stole
from chamber-doors into uncertainty.

The hero wrests it with his fiery soul:
while others simply follow and accept,
as though they moved through air, through porphyry.

II

Even the lover's never qualified
for a survey of you, unbounded beings;
for who can read a face with which his seeing's
become so dazzlingly identified?

The poet hopes, through hinted counterpart
in this and that, to prove that you are here;
goes mounting on your track from sphere to sphere,
and fetches up in Heaven with a start.

Perhaps, though, he is then most near to you
when suddenly, as if in sweet affliction,
he cannot bid some garden-path adieu:

a lizard's whipped away there while he stands
imposing, almost with a benediction,
on the warm vineyard wall his empty hands.

Paris, 15 November 1913
The second and fifth of five sonnets inscribed in *The Life of Mary*.

O sure and swiftly guided plough! If pain
is where you plunge into another layer,
is not pain good? And that so long delayer
that breaks upon us in the midst of pain?

How much there is to suffer! Who could guess
there'd once been time for laughter and repose?
And yet I know, better than most of those
awaiting resurrection, blessedness.

Paris, autumn 1913
From *Poems to Night.*

Tears will not let me speak.
My death, blackamoor, heart-keeper!
tip me down deeper, steeper,
pour them off. For I want to speak.

Giant black heart-holder, would in the end,
because I'd spoken,
silence even then have been broken?

Rock me, old friend!

Paris, late autumn 1913

BROTHER AND SISTER

I

Oh, how often, and with, oh, what weeping,
eyelashes and shoulders we've caressed.
And in rooms around us night went creeping
like a wounded beast, by us distressed.

Were you purposed only for my seeing?
Would it with mere sisterhood not do?
Charming as a valley's seemed your being:
now it bends from arching heaven too,

and in never-ending revelation
comes into its own. Where shall I flee?
Ah, with such an air of deploration
you, uncomfortress, incline to me.

II

Let us not in this dark sweetness strain
to distinguish what has caused our tears.
Is it painful ecstasy appears
in our faces, or ecstatic pain?

Does renouncement feel more agonising
than an all-too wilful gift would do?
When at last the crowd of the arising
has unkinned us, and we, any two,
at the death-dispelling trumpet-chorus
stumble blindly from the stone uprent,
oh, how this desire so heavy for us
then will seem to angels innocent!

For it too is in the Spirit, wheeling
incandescent in the central blaze.
And you'll help me to my knees, and, kneeling
silently beside me there, will gaze.

Paris, end of 1913

THE GREAT NIGHT

I'd often stand at the window started the day before,
stand and stare at you. It still seemed to warn me off,
the strange city, whose unconfiding landscape
gloomed as though I didn't exist. The nearest
things didn't mind if I misunderstood them. The street
would thrust itself up to the lamp, and I'd see it was strange.
A sympathisable room up there, revealed in the lamplight:
I'd begin to share: they'd notice, and close the shutters.
I'd stand. Then a child would cry, and I'd know the mothers
in the houses, what they availed, and I'd know as well
the inconsolable grounds of infinite crying.
Or else a voice would sing, and what was expected
be just a little surpassed; or an old man coughed below,
full of reproach, as his body were in the right
against a gentler world. Or else, when an hour was striking,
I'd begin to count too late and let it escape me.
As a strange little boy, when at last they invite him to join them,
cannot catch the ball, and is quite unable
to share the game the rest are so easily playing,
but stands and gazes – whither? – I'd stand, and, all at once,

realise *you* were being friends with me, playing with me, grown-up
Night, and I'd gaze at you. While towers
were raging, and while, with its hidden fate,
a city stood round me, and undivinable mountains
camped against me, and Strangeness, in narrowing circles,
hungrily prowled round my casual flares of perception:
then, lofty Night,
you were not ashamed to recognise me. Your breathing
went over me; your smile upon all that spacious
consequence passed into me.

Paris, January 1914

Let me withstand your breakers of influence: hurl them
over my head! Have you not grandlier moulded
faces of shepherds than ever in royal wombs
peerless gone and coming of countless kings
stamped the crownly expression? Are galleons able
to hold, in the staring wood of their stock-still carving, a trace of
the ocean space, of the deep they dumbly encounter:
and, oh, shall a feeler fail, in a bursting effort of willing,
fail, O unyielding Night, to be finally more like you?

Paris, January 1914
From *Poems to Night.*

VOICE OF A POOR PERSON LED BY THE ANGEL

Now I've come to know it,
Father, I'll forgo it:
what I see is less
than what I always knew of –
the surging gloriousness
of all I've lost the view of.
Those feelings, can you guess
how widely they extended,
when mutely through your splendid
earthly nights I'd wait
in front of the night-shelter?
Dogs ran round my great
feelings helter-skelter.
Arches I slept under
taught my heart a new
soaring sense of wonder.
Snow inside my shoe
melted away as mild
as the tears do
of a comforted child.

Paris, winter 1913-14

Time-of-a-life-time Life, that can extend
from contradiction into contradiction!
Now hard and slow beyond all malediction,
now suddenly outspreading to ascend
wide angel-wings beyond all benediction:
O life-time, life-time, hard to comprehend!

Which of the daringly-devised creations
can beat us in our fiery enterprise?
We stand and strain against our limitations
and wrest things in we cannot recognise.

. . . . . .

Paris, winter 1913-14

Like the evening wind that blows
        through the shouldered scythes of reapers,
softly the Angel goes
        through the innocent blades of Affliction.

Hour on hour will race
        with the gloomily-galloping horseman;
keep the self-same pace
        as indefinable feelings.

Stands as tower by sea,
        meant to endure for ever.
All you feel is he,
        supple at heart of hardness,

so that in rocks of pain
        the long-crushed cluster of tears,
water-pure, may strain
        at last into amethyst crystals.

Paris, winter 1913-14

Beloved,
lost to begin with, never greeted,
I do not know what tones most please you.
No more when the future's wave hangs poised is it you
I try to discern there. All the greatest
images in me, far-off experienced landscape,
towers and towns and bridges and un-
suspected turns of the way,
and the power of those lands once intertwined
with the life of the gods:
mount up within me to mean
you, who forever elude.

Oh, you are the gardens!
Oh, with such yearning
hope I watched them! An open window
in a country house, and you almost stepped out
thoughtfully to meet me. Streets I discovered, –
you had just walked down them,
and sometimes in dealers' shops the mirrors,
still dizzy with you, returned with a start

my too-sudden image. – Who knows whether the self-same
bird didn't ring through each of us,
separately, yesterday evening?

Paris, winter 1913-14

It is impossible to decide whether this poem was written before or after the Benvenuta episode.

TURNING

The way from intensity to greatness
leads through sacrifice. Kassner

Long he'd outwrung it with gazing.
Stars collapsed on their knees
under that wrestlerish uplook.
Or he would kneelingly gaze
and his instancy's perfume
tired an immortal until
it smiled at him out of its sleep.

He gazed at towers so hard,
he filled them with terror:
building them up again, suddenly, all in a moment.
And yet how often the day-
over-laden landscape
sank to rest in his calm perception at evening!

Animals trustfully entered
his open glance as they pastured,
and the imprisoned lions
stared as into incomprehensible freedom.
Birds flew straight through him,
kindly soul. Flowers
gazed back into him
large as to children.

And report that a *seer* was there
stirred those less,
more doubtfully, visible
creatures, women.

Gazing, since when?
How long fervently fasting,
with glance that at bottom besought?

When, waiting, he lived in foreign lands; the inn's
distracted, alienated room

morosely around him; within the avoided mirror
once more the room,
and then, from his harrowing bed,
the room again: –
airy councils were held,
inapprehensible councils,
about his still, through the painfully cumbered body,
still perceptible heart:
councils unoverheard
judged that it had not love.

(Further consecrations withheld.)

For gazing, look, has a limit.
And the on-gazeder world
wants to mature in love.

Work of sight is achieved,
now for some heart-work
on all those images, prisoned within you; for you
overcame them, but do not know them as yet.
Behold, O man within, the maiden within you! –
creature wrung from a thousand natures, creature
only outwrung, but never,
as yet, belov'd.

Paris, 20 June 1914

LAMENT

Who'd hear your lament, heart? Ever forsakener
struggles your path through the incomprehensible
humans. All the more vainly, perhaps,
because it preserves its direction,
direction towards that future
for ever lost.

Once. You lamented? What was it? A fallen
berry of triumph, unripe!
Now, though, my triumph-tree is breaking,
breaking in storm is my gradual
triumph-tree.
Loveliest in my invisible
landscape, making me better
known to invisible angels.

Paris, beginning of July 1914

'MAN MUST DIE, BECAUSE HE HAS KNOWN THEM'

(*From the Sayings of Ptah-hotep, Papyrus Prisse, c. 2000* B.C.)

'Man must die, because he has known them.' Die
of their smile's ineffable blossom. Die
of their light hands. Die
of women.

Death-bringers, the youth shall sing them
when they move on high through his heart-space.
From his blossoming breast
shall sing them:
unattainables! Oh, their unlikeness!
Above the summits
of his feeling they rise and pass, outpouring
sweetly-changed night into the forsaken
vale of his arms. The wind
of their orience rustles the leaves of his body. His brooks
run sparkling away.

But the man
shall shudder in silence. He,
who has strayed pathless by night
in the mountain range of his feelings,
shall be silent.

As the sailor, growing old, is silent,
the terrors endured
playing about in him as in quivering cages.

Paris, July 1914

'If thou wishest to maintain a permanent friendship in the house to which thou art in the habit of going . . . strive against associating with the women . . . A thousand men seeking what is beautiful are destroyed by them. A man is made a fool of by their shining limbs, but they turn into things that are harder than quartzite sandstone. The pleasure is only for a little moment, and it (passes) like a dream, and a man at the end thereof finds death through knowing it' (E. A. Wallis Budge, *The Teaching of Ȧmen-Em-Ȧpt*, etc., 1924, p. 58).

In the different and abbreviated version which Rilke used (in Gressmann's *Altorientalische Texte und Bilder zum Alten Testament*, 1909, p. 201) the above passage concludes: 'A thousand men shall be destroyed because they have enjoyed a brief hour like a dream. A man must die because he has known them (i.e. women).'

FIVE HYMNS

August 1914

I

For the first time I see you rising,
hearsaid, remote, incredible War God.
How thickly our peaceful corn was intersown
with terrible action, suddenly grown mature!
Small even yesterday, needing nurture, and now
tall as a man: to-morrow
towering beyond man's reach. Before we know it, he's there,
the glowing god himself, tearing his crop
out of the nation's roots, and harvest begins.
Up whirl the human sheaves to the human thunder-storm. Summer
is left behind among the sports on the green.
Children remain there, playing; elders, recalling;
trustful women. The universal parting
mingles with moving fragrance of blossoming limes,
whose heavy scent will hold a meaning for years.
Brides are more chosenly walking, as though not only
one life had united with theirs, but a whole people
set their affections in tune. With slowly measuring gaze
boys encircle the youth that already belongs
to the more adventurous future: he, who has stood perplexed
in the web of a hundred contradictory voices, –
oh, how the single call has lightened his life! For what
would not be caprice beside this joyful, beside this unhesitant need?
A god at last! Since the God of Peace so often
eluded our grasp, the God of Battles has grasped us,
hurling his bolt: while over the heart full of home
screams his thunderous dwelling, his scarlet heaven.

II

Oh, to see men in the grip of something! Already
our drama had grown unreal,
the invented image no longer answered our hearts.
Now though, beloved, the time talks like a prophet, blindly,
full of primeval soul.
Hark! You have never heard it before. You are now the trees,
trees which the violent wind loudlier and loudlier rocks,
storming hither over the level years
from far ancestral feeling, from loftier deeds, from lofty

heroic ranges, soon to shine purer and nearer
in the newly-fallen snow of your jubilant glory.
How the animate landscape is being transformed! There pass
fragrant youthful coppice and older trees,
while saplings recently sprung bend after those on the march.
You that have once already, in bearing, experienced parting,
now, O mothers, shall feel joy of being givers again.
Give as though you were infinite! Give! Be a bountiful Nature
to these upspringing days. Send with a blessing your sons.
And, girls, to think that they love you! To think of being felt
in such hearts! That such frightful impulsion
wandered in gentle disguise, once, with your flowering selves!
Prudence restrained you: now a more infinite love,
like that of the mythical maids of long ago, is permitted:
the hoper standing as though in a hope-filled garden,
the weeper weeping as though in a constellation
named after one that wept. . . . .
. . . .

III

Only three days, and now . . . ? Am I really singing the terror,
really singing the god I admired from afar and imagined
one of the early, the now merely remembering gods?
Like a volcanic mountain he lay in the distance. Sometimes
flaming. Sometimes smoking. Melancholy and godlike.
Although now and then, perhaps, a neighbouring hamlet
quivered, we went on lifting the unscathed
lyre to other – oh, to what future? – gods.
When up stood he; stands; higher
than standing towers, higher
than the breathed air of days we have left behind.
Stands. Over-stands. And we? We're all of us glowing into oneness,
into a new creation he's animating with death.
I, too, exist no longer; my heart is beating
with the beat of the general heart, and the general mouth
is forcing my lips apart.

And yet, like a ship's syren, there howls within me at night
the vast interrogation 'Whither, whither, whither?'
Does the god from his lofty shoulder see where we are going?
Is he casting lighthouse-beams to a struggling future
that has long been looking for us? Is he a knower? Can he
possibly be a knower, this ravaging god?

Destroying everything known. So long, so lovingly,
trustingly known by us. Our houses are merely
lying about like ruins of his temple. In rising
he scornfully thrust them aside and stands up into the sky.

Sky of the summer still. Summer-sky. The summer's
intimate sky over the trees and ourselves.
Now: who can feel or proclaim its infinite guard
over the meadows? Who
does not stare into it strangely?

We are altered, altered to sameness: meteor-like,
there flashed into everyone's
suddenly no longer personal bosom a heart.
Hot, an iron heart from an iron cosmos.

IV

O friends, our ancient heart, our familiar heart
that was animating us yesterday, – who can foresee it
vanished for ever? No one
will ever feel it again, not one still living survivor
of this tremendous change.

For the older heart of an incompletely achieved
earlier age has ousted
the nearer, dearer, slowly, differently compassed
heart that was ours. And now
our task is just to re-forge that imperfect heart,
suddenly re-imposed, to consume its residual violence!
In praise; for is it not worthy of praise
to be freed from the prudence of private cares within *one*
adventuring spirit, in holy communion of danger
splendidly felt? In the field
life in millions mounts to its height, and in each
a coronational death steps to the princeliest square.
And yet, in the midst of your praising, praise without tinge of regret
the pain of not being those who are yet to come,
but far more nearly related,
still, to all that is gone: praise it, and mourn.
Don't be ashamed of mourning. Mourn! For, oh, not till then
will our unrecognisable, incomprehensible fate
be fulfilled: till mourned beyond measure, and yet,
in all its immeasurable mournfulness, longed for and kept like a feast.

V

Up and frighten the frightful god! Convulse him!
Too long he's been pampered by Joy of Battle. Let pain,
new, astoundedly staring Pain of Battle
hurl you ahead of his rage.
Though dominated by blood that has hurtled down
from far-away fathers on high, let your mood remain
ever your own, not aping
earlier, pristine moods, but proving
whether you are not pain. Pain in action. For Pain
has its triumph too, and a flag
flames up over your heads in the wind from the foe.
A flag? Yes, Pain's. The flag of Pain. That heavily
flapping cloth of Pain, with which every one of you's wiped
his sweating, hell-hot face. Where the face that belongs to you all
compresses itself into features – of the future, perhaps. If only
hate were not always there! But amazement, resolute pain,
magnificent rage that the blinded races around you
should have suddenly interrupted your peaceful vision:
they, – from whom, as from air and mine, you had gravely
won yourselves breath and earth. For in comprehending,
learning, entertaining within you
much, though it came from afar, you felt your peculiar task.
Now you're confined once more to what is your own. Though now
it has grown far greater. And though it be far from world,
accept it as world! Make use of it like a mirror,
catching the sun and casting the sun it has caught
upon those that have erred and strayed. (May your own error
burn itself out in the painful, terrible heart!)

First Hymn, Munich, 2 and 3 August 1914; the rest, beginning of August

Now it is you I'll praise, Banner, you, that from childhood
I gazed diviningly after, guessingly greeted,
when streaming files carried you sleepingly by:
tremblingly greeted, as though you might dream of my greeting.
You, now awake in battles, flaming with life, like a bride
that suddenly wakes, and, full of amazement, remembers
she's loved, leaps up, and with flowing
hair and gown, resplendently billowing maiden,
storms the night-guarded hill, leaving her feelings behind.
So that's what you are, then. Like a falcon a heron,
your mighty consciousness grasps you in mid-air. Wrings you
out of your folded sleep. How long you've contrived to dissemble!
Things are secretive. Look, and our heart, that
too's a secretive thing.

Munich or Irschenhausen, August 1914

Everything beckons to us to perceive it,
murmurs at every turn 'Remember me!'
A day we passed, too busy to receive it,
will yet unlock us all its treasury.

Who shall compute our harvest? Who shall bar
us from the former years, the long-departed?
What have we learnt from living since we started,
except to find in others what we are?

Except to re-enkindle commonplace?
O house, O sloping field, O setting sun!
Your features form into a face, you run,
you cling to us, returning our embrace!

One space spreads through all creatures equally –
inner-world-space. Birds quietly flying go
flying through us. Oh, I that want to grow,
the tree I look outside at grows in me!

It stands in me, that house I look for still,
in me that shelter I have not possessed.
I, the now well-beloved: on my breast
this fair world's image clings and weeps her fill.

Munich or Irschenhausen, August-September 1914

TO HÖLDERLIN

Lingering, even with intimate things,
is not vouchsafed us; the spirit plunges
from filled to suddenly fillable images; lakes
exist in eternity. Falling is here
fittest. Cascading down out of compassed feeling
into surmised beyond.

You, though, glorious invoker, for you a whole life was that
importunate image; when you expressed it,
a line locked up like destiny, even in the gentlest
there lurked a death, which you lighted upon, but the god
going before you guided you forth and afar.

Oh, you ranging spirit, you rangingest! Look how they all
dwell as at home in cosy poems and make
long stays in narrow comparisons. Participators. You only
move like the moon. And below there brightens and darkens
your own nocturnal, sacredly startled landscape,
the one you feel in partings. No one
surrendered it more sublimely, gave it more wholly,
dispensably, back to the whole. Such, too,
was your holy play, through the now uncounted years,
with happiness, as though it were not internal,
but lay about unclaimed
on Earth's soft turf, left by celestial children.
Oh, what the loftiest long for, you laid, with never a wish,
stone upon stone: it stood. And when it collapsed it left you
unbewildered.

Why, after such an eternal life, do we still
mistrust the terrestrial? Instead of earnestly learning
from fleeting Appearance the feelings
for, oh, what affections, in space?

Irschenhausen, September 1914 (ll. 1-6) and Munich, 25 October (ll. 7-end)

Exposed on the heart's mountains. Look, how small there!
look, the last hamlet of words, and, higher,
(but still how small!) yet one remaining
farmstead of feeling: d'you see it?
Exposed on the heart's mountains. Virgin rock
under the hands. Though even here
something blooms: from the dumb precipice
an unknowing plant blooms singing into the air.

But what of the knower? Ah, he began to know
and holds his peace, exposed on the heart's mountains.
While, with undivided mind,
many, maybe, many well-assured mountain beasts,
pass there and pause. And the mighty sheltered bird
circles the summits' pure refusal. – But, oh,
no longer sheltered, here on the heart's mountains . . .

Irschenhausen, 20 September 1914

Time and again, however well we know the landscape of love,
and the little church-yard with lamenting names,
and the frightfully silent ravine wherein all the others
end: time and again we go out two together,
under the old trees, lie down again and again
between the flowers, face to face with the sky.

Munich (?), end of 1914

LOVE'S BEGINNING

O smile, inaugurating smile, our smile!
How one it was! – Breathing the scent of lime-trees,
hearing park-stillness, suddenly looking up,
each in the other, wondering, till we smiled.

Within that smile was mutual reminiscence
of a young hare that we had just been watching
out on the lawn at play; such was its childhood,
that smile of ours. It took a graver impress
from motion of the swan that we saw later,
dividing the still lake into two halves
of soundless evening. – And the tree-tops, outlined
against the pure, free sky, already teeming
with future nights, had described outlines for it
against the ecstatic future in our faces.

Munich, spring or summer of 1915

ODE TO BELLMAN

Sound for me, Bellman, sound on. When has thus
summer's whole burden by a hand been weighed?
Even as columns their arcade,
you carry joy, which, if it's meant for us,

must needs be resting too on some support;
for, Bellman, we are not the hovering sort.
All we become submits to gravitation:
happiness, superabundance, resignation
have weight.

Bring life in, Bellman, serve that dish divine
with all its gaily-circling garniture:
pumpkin and pheasant and the white-tusked swine!
And, kingliest of caterers, ensure
that I hear field and leaf and star in pure
transparentness! And, crowning all, conjure
some yet more generous giving from the wine!

Ah, Bellman, and the woman dwelling near:
I think my feelings are no secret to her,
her scent so clings, her mind so gazes through her,
her thoughts to me, my thoughts to her, outsteer, –
and night is coming when I fade into her:
Bellman, I'm here!

Look, someone's coughing. Yet, in his distress,
has he not reached a kind of rhythmic beauty?
Lungs can't claim all our duty.
Life always was a piece of wantonness.
Suppose he died. Why, dying is so true.
Life he had pestered so would then have started
wanting the thing he used to want her to,
and sleep with him. So many have departed,
so rightly too.

Departing's all we've been,
yet in departure parting must be heeded.
Our part in partings – Bellman, let the needed
notes like the Great Bear's stars outstand serene!
So full of fullness to the dead we're speeded:
what have our eyes not seen!

Munich, 8 September 1915

Carl Michael Bellman, 1740-95, was one of the greatest of Swedish poets, and Rilke, who had recently been reading him with his Danish friend Inga Junghanns, declared that he wrote this poem under the influence of their last 'Bellman evening'. A great hunter, feaster and lover, Bellman combined passionate love of life with an intense awareness of death. He wrote most of his poems to be sung, either to traditional airs or to airs of his own composition, and he printed the music with the poems. He died of consumption.

THE DEATH OF MOSES

Not one, only the sombre, the fallen, angel
responded; took weapons, approached
the summoned with mortal intent. To hurtle
clattering, backwards, upwards,
crying into heaven: 'I can't!'

For calmly, without uplifting his bushy eyebrows,
Moses had simply noticed and gone on writing:
saving words and the name that endureth for ever.
And his eye was pure to the very depth of his power.

Therefore the Lord, tearing out half of heaven,
forced his way down to earth and bedded the mountain;
settled the ancient. Out of her ordered dwelling
summoned the soul, who up! and recounted
countless things in common, untellable friendship.

But at last she was satisfied, completed; admitted
that was enough. Then slowly the aged
God bowed down his aged face to the aged
mortal. Withdrew him out of himself in kisses
into his older age. And with hands of creation
re-established the mountain, now to be merely
one among all the mountains of earth, eluding
human detection.

Lines 1-14, Paris, summer 1914; lines 15-22, Munich, October 1915
'With reference to a passage in the Talmud about the death of Moses, translated by Herder.'

DEATH

There, a blue draught for somebody to drain,
stands Death, in a large cup without a saucer.
A rather odd position for a cup:
stands on the back of a hand. And still quite plain
and visible along the smooth glazed slope
the place where the handle snapped. Dusty. And 'Hope'
inscribed in letters half washed down the sink.

The drinker destinated for the drink
spelt them at breakfast in some distant past.

What kind of creatures these are, that at last
have to be poisoned off, it's hard to think.

Else, would they stay? Has this hard food, in fact,
such power to infatuate,
they'd eat for ever, did not some hand extract
the crusty present, like a dental-plate?
Which leaves them babbling. Bab, bab, ba. . .
. . . .

O falling star,
seen from a bridge once in a foreign land: –
remembering you, to stand!

Munich, 9 November 1915

REQUIEM ON THE DEATH OF A BOY

What names did I not memorise, till cow,
dog, elephant and all the ark
might have been met and passed without remark,
and then the zebra, – why, oh why?
  Who bears me now
mounts like a tidal mark
beyond all that. What peace can lie
in knowing that one existed in one's place,
but never pressed, where hard or soft withstands,
behind them to the comprehending face?

And these already started hands –

You sometimes said: He promises . . . a trace . . .
I promised, yes, but what I promised *you*
is not what overpowers.
Sometimes I'd crouch against the house for hours,
watching a skylark in the blue.
If I could have become just that, that gazing!
Carrying me, lifting me, my brows with raising
were right up there. No one was dear to me.
Affection was anguish, – then (oh see, if you can!)
I was not we
and was much bigger than a man,
as though I were myself the risks I ran,
as though the core of them was me.

A little core; I don't begrudge it, whether
to the streets or to the wind. I give it away.
For that we all sat so snugly there together
was a thing I never believed. Honour bright, I say.
You talked, you laughed, yet each one sitting by there
was not within the talk and laughter. You
all fluctuated in a way that neither
the sugar-bowl nor glass of wine would do.
The apple lay. How sometimes it would cheer
me to grasp the firm full apple with my hand,
or the strong table where the still cups stand:
the good cups, how they tranquillised the year!
My toys, too, sometimes kept me company;
behaved as other things did, hardly less
dependably, though not so restfully.
And thus in a perpetual wakefulness
they stood midway between my hat and me.
A wooden horse, a cock of painted clay,
the doll whose leg was broken on a stone:
I laboured for them day by day.
I made the sky small when they looked that way;
for that I felt quite early, how alone
a wooden horse is. But to make the thing:
a wooden horse of any size you showed.
It's painted and then tugged at with a string,
and gets the joltings of the real road.
Why was it not a lie, when this was called
a horse? Because one felt oneself a tiny
bit of a horse, grew maney, shiny,
sinewy, four-legged – (all, so that one might spring
to a man at last)? But was there not a trace
of wood in one as well, did not one try at
growing hard for it on the quiet,
and go about with a diminished face?

We kept exchanging, it would almost seem.
How I would murmur when I saw the stream,
and when it murmured, how I thither bounded!
And when I *saw* a ringing, I resounded,
and when it rang, I was the reason why.

I thrust into it all incessantly,
though not in need of me was all I'd fly to,
and only sadder for my company.
  Now I am suddenly said good-bye to.

See,
is a new learning beginning, a new asking?
Or must I now be tasking
myself with telling of you? – That troubles me.
The house? I never rightly understood.
The rooms? I tried to notice all I could.
. . . You, Mother, do you know *who* really
the dog might be?
Even that we gathered berries in the wood
seems to me now a strange discovery.

. . . . . .

There must be some dead children somewhere, though,
to come and play with me. They're always dying.
The same as I did, after a long lying
still in a room and never getting well.

Well . . . How that sounds here. Does it still make sense?
Here, where I am,
no one is ill, I think.
Since my sore throat, which I almost forget –

Here everyone is like a poured-out drink.

But those who drink us I've not seen as yet.

. . . . . .

Munich, 13 November 1915
The boy was Peter Jaffé, eight year old son of Professor Edgar Jaffé, who had died at Munich in October 1915.

THE GOD QUESTIONED

DEDICATION TO RENÉE

Am I not right thus provingly to bend them,
before I use them on the things that fly,
finding through trial which sons of men will lend them
to hurl my straightest eagerness most high?

Am I not right when I despise them nightly?
With them one only hits the game at hand;
targets for me, though, as I stride uprightly,
are those free-ranging storms above the land:

the very heavens, as they hover there,
I want to pierce, involuntarily feeling:
Where lies the bow for such a distant shot?
So long as love means, one should overbear
the other partner, I depart. Revealing
coolness in going, without part or lot.

Munich, 29 November 1915
Inscribed in *New Poems* for Renée Alberti.

THE GOD'S REPLY

SECOND DEDICATION TO RENÉE

You proving maiden, how exact you are!
The god shall be exacter in replying.
I had become a god of sighing.
But you, maybe, more bright than any star,

shall cheer me. Only end as you've begun,
and, leaving those found after all unfitted,
pursue, in radiance never intermitted,
your onward journey to the very one.

Sweep with that inner spaciousness you hide
through space to him, the goal of all your proving!
Nothing shall fetter your instinctive stride.
If he exists not, you'll have only missed
a lover to attain the god of loving:
for no one knows like you that I exist.

Munich, 29 November 1915
Inscribed in *New Poems: Second Part* for Renée Alberti.

SOUL IN SPACE

DEDICATED AS HER ABSOLUTE PROPERTY
TO HER ROYAL HIGHNESS
THE GRAND DUCHESS OF HESSE

Here I am, here I am, wrested,
reeling.
Can I dare? Can I plunge?

Even where I first intruded
many were capable. Now,
where the meanest are fully fulfilling might
in muteness of mastery: –
Can I dare? Can I plunge?

True, I endured through the timid body
nights; I befriended it,
finite earthen stuff, with infinity;
sobbingly,
lifted by me, overflowed
its innocent heart.

But now,
who'd be impressed if I said
'I am the soul'?
I must suddenly grow eternal,
clinging no more to an opposite, no more
comfortress; feeling with nothing but
heaven.

Scarce secret now;
or merely among those
secrets open to all
a tremulous one.

Oh, this procession of mighty embracings! Which
will encircle me, pass me on,
me, the clumsy
embracer?

Or have I forgotten, and can?
Forgot the exhaustive riot
of those hard-lovers? Hark,
hurtle upwards, and can?

Munich, January 1917

TO MUSIC

(THE PROPERTY OF FRAU HANNA WOLFF)

Music: breathing of statues. Perhaps:
stillness of pictures. You speech, where speeches
end. You time,
vertically poised on the courses of vanishing hearts.

Feelings for what? Oh, you transformation
of feelings into . . . audible landscape!
You stranger: Music. Space that's outgrown us,
heart-space. Innermost ours,
that, passing our limits, outsurges, –
holiest parting:
where what is within surrounds us
as practised horizon, as other
side of the air,
pure,
gigantic,
no longer lived in.

Munich, 11-12 January 1918
Written after a private concert at the house of the recipient.

How Childhood tries to reach us, and declares
that *we* were once what took it seriously.
We may have climbed beyond it a few stairs,
but it climbed too, and can mysteriously

emerge, when things we've placed beyond all doubt
suddenly make us hesitate and wonder.
Does not a voice say, that we now hold out
only because deep Childhood held us under?

Only through it do we remain akin
to the whole surmise, leave consideration,
that makes our lives as narrow as they are,

and become meeting-place of heart and star,
and object somehow cared about within
a world of store and night and agitation.

Munich, October 1918
Draft of a dedication?

ON ELIZABETH BARRETT-BROWNING'S SONNETS

When a heart's long made giving-up a duty,
and laid all hope and confidence aside,
and then awakes to hear itself accried:
'You overflowing fountain of all beauty!' –

How hard for it to bound on being unbound,
to hasten to returning happiness!
That heart, accustomed to a mute distress,
transmuting love is forcing into sound.

Here sounds a heart that sorrowed silently,
and fears to handle, as beyond its due,
the wealth of its victorious poverty.

Who's full? Whose giving is most unconfined? –
One who goes on seducing: for flesh, too,
achieves its incarnation in the mind.

Zürich, 3 November 1919
Inscribed in a copy of his translation of Elizabeth Barrett-Browning's *Sonnets from the Portuguese*: 'For Frau N. Wunderly-Volkart, in this book of hers'.

Be all that's here our home, however hard.
Who dares to pick and choose with destiny?
Suffering's perhaps to suffer sufferingly,
and menace, if we look away, will guard.

Switzerland, end of November 1919
Draft of a dedication.

FOR FRÄULEIN MARIA VON HEFNER-ALTENECK

To glorify the *world*: love makes no claim less
than this on hearts: loved, lover – who is who?
A nameless something praises here the Nameless,
as birds the season they're vibrating to . . .

Zürich, c. 1 December 1919
Inscribed in a copy of his translation of *The Four and Twenty Sonnets of Louise Labé*.

FROM THE POEMS OF COUNT C.W.

Karnak. We'd ridden, dinner quickly done with,
Hélène and I, to get the moonlight view.
The dragoman pulled up: the Avenue, –
the Pylon, ah! I'd never felt so one with

the lunar world! (Are you being magnified
within me, greatness, then beyond control?)
Is travel – seeking? Well, this was a goal.
The watchman at the entrance first supplied

the frightening scale. How lowly seemed his station
beside the gate's unchecked self-exaltation!
And then, for a whole life-time's meditation
did not the Column bring enough and more?

Ruin vindicated it: it would have been
too high for highest roof. It stood and bore
Egyptian night.
The following fellaheen

now fell behind us. To get over this
took time, because it almost stopped the heart
to know that such out-standing formed a part
of that same being we died in. – If I had
a son, I'd send him, when our only care
is finding truth to live by: 'Charles, it's there, –
walk through the Pylon, stand and look, my lad.'

Why could it not help *us* more helpfully?
That we endured it was enough indeed:
you in your travelling dress, the invalid,
and I the hermit in my theory.

And yet, the mercy! Can you still recall
that lake round which the granite cats were seated?
Mark-stones (of what?). So chained, as by repeated
spells, into that enchanted rectangle

one felt, that had not five been overturned
along one side (you too were overcome),
they would that moment, cattish, stony, dumb,
have held a court of judgment.

All discerned
was judgment. Here the ban upon the pond,
there on the margin the giant scarabee,
along the walls the epic history
of monarchs: judgment. And yet, quite beyond

all comprehension, an acquittal too.
As figure after figure there was filled
with the pure moonlight, the relief, outdrilled
in clearest outline, hollow, trough-like, grew

so much receptacle – for nothing less
than what, though never hidden, none could see,
for the world-secret, so essentially
secret, it baffles all secretiveness!

All books keep turning past it: no one ever
read in a book a thing so manifest
(I want a word – how can it be expressed?):
the Immeasurable submitted to the measure

of sacrifice. – Look there, oh, look: what's keeping,
that has not learnt to give itself away?
All things are passing. Help them on their way.
And then your life will not be merely seeping

out through some crack. Remain your whole life long
the conscious giver. Mule and cow, they throng
in close procession to the spot where he,
the god-king, like a stilled child, peaceably

receives and smiles. His mighty sacredness
is never out of breath. He takes and takes:
and yet such mitigation overtakes,
that the papyrus flower by the princess

is often merely clasped, not broken. –
Here
all ways of sacrifice abruptly end,
the Sabbath starts, the long weeks comprehend
its mind no longer. Man and beast appear

to keep at times some gains from the god's eyes.
Profit, though difficult, can be secured;
one tries and tries, the earth can be procured, –
who, though, but gives the price gives up the prize.

Schloss Berg am Irchel, end of November 1920

UNCOMPLETED ELEGY

Don't let the fact that Childhood has been, that nameless
bond between Heaven and us, be revoked by fate.
Even the prisoner, gloomily dying in a dungeon,
it has sat by and secretly nursed to the end, with its timeless
hold on the heart. For the sufferer,
when he staringly understands, and his room has ceased to reply,
because, like all the other possessions around him,
feverish, fellow-suffering, it's curable, – even for him
Childhood avails. For purely
its cordial bed blooms among nature's decay.

Not that it's harmless. The petting and prettyfying error
that be-aprons it and be-frills only deceived for a time.
It's no more certain than we and never more shielded;
no god can counterbalance its weight. Defenceless
as we ourselves, defenceless as beasts in winter.
More defenceless – no hiding places. Defenceless
as though itself were the thing that threatened. Defenceless
as fire, giants, poison, as goings-on
at night in suspected houses with bolted doors.

For who can fail to see that the guardian hands
lie, while trying to defend it, – themselves in danger? Who *may*, then?
'I!'
        – What I?
                        'I, mother, I *may*. I was fore-world.
Earth has confided to me what she does with the seed
to keep it intact. Those intimate evenings! We rained,
Earth and I, softly and Aprilly, into the womb.
O male, who shall make you believe in the pregnant concord
we felt together? For you no annunciation
of cosmic peace concluded round something growing! . . . '

Maternal magnanimity! Call of the comforters! Yet,
what you've described is peril itself, the entire
pure perilousness of the world, – and thus it turns to protection,
soon as you feel it completely. The fervour of childhood
stands like a centre within it: *out*-fearing it, fearless.

But anxiety! – Learnt all at once in that disconnexion
formed by us, by insolid humanity: draughtily
jerks itself in through the cracks: glides up from behind,
over its play, to the child, and hisses

dissension into its blood, – the swift suspicions that later,
always, only a part will be comprehensible, always
some single piece of existence, five pieces, perhaps, but never
combinable all together, and all of them fragile.
And forthwith splits in the spine the twig of the will
to grow up into a two-pronged doubting branch,
grafted on to the Judas-tree of selection.[1]

How it corrupts the doll, kind thing, that a moment ago most
gentle of toys, and makes it, still cuddled, inspire with
alien terror. – Not with itself, its piteous, pardonable strangeness,
no: with the child's affection, with what it's received.
Received during those long days of confidence, during those countless
hours of confessional play, while over against that unenvying
you it had fashioned the child proved and contrasted itself –
getting to know, through sharing its powers with a partner,
itself and its own so newly upspringing reserves.

Expanses of play! In ever more fruitful surrender,
ever more blissful discovery, on, as in ultimate outgrowth,
far beyond farthest descent, went that confident self!
Friendly with death, which, in lightly-made transformation,
it grew through hundreds of times . . . O doll,
farthest figure, – as stars upon distance
train to be worlds, you make the child into a star.
Is cosmic space too small for it? Space out of feelings
you stoundingly stretch between you, intensified space.

But all at once it occurs . . . What? When? – Unnameable, rupture –
What? – Betrayal . . . filled with the half of existence,
the doll will have no more, disowns, doesn't recognise.
Stares with refusing eyes, lies down, doesn't know; no longer
even a thing – look, how things
are ashamed of it,

. . . . .

Schloss Berg am Irchel, December 1920

[1] In his fair copy Rilke allowed the poem to end here and did not include what follows.

TO NIKÊ

In merely catching your own casting all's
mere cleverness and indecisive winning: –
only when all at once you're catching balls
an everlasting partner hurtles spinning
into your very centre, with trajecture
exactly calculated, curvingly
recalling God's stupendous pontifecture, –
only then catching's capability,
not yours, a world's. And if, not resting here,
you'd strength and will to throw them back again, –
no, – wonderfullier! – forgot all that, and then
found you'd already thrown . . . (as, twice a year,
the flocking birds are thrown, the birds that wander,
thrown from an older to a younger, yonder,
ultramarine warmth), – in that mood of sheer
abandon you'd be equal to the game.
Both ease and difficulty would disappear:
you'd simply throw. A meteor would flame
out of your hands and tear through its own spaces . . .

Muzot, 31 January 1922
Inscribed in *From the Early Work of R. M. Rilke* for Nanny Wunderly-Volkart.

(*Given to M.*)

. . . When will, when will, when will it have reached saturation,
this praising and lamentation? Has not all incantation
in human words been decanted by master-magicians? O vanity
of further experimentation! Is not humanity
battered by books as though by continual bells?
Perceiving, between two books, the silent heavens, or else
a segment of simple earth in evening light, rejoice!

Louder than storms, than oceans, the human voice
has cried . . . What infinite overbalance of stillness
there must be in cosmic space, since the grasshopper's shrillness
stayed audible over our cries, and the stars appear
silently there in the aether above our shrieking!

Would that our farthest, old and oldest fathers were speaking!
And we: hearers at last! The first of all men to hear.

Muzot, 1 February 1922
'Written on the evening before the Orpheus sonnets.'

PARALIPOMENA FROM THE 'SONNETS TO ORPHEUS'

I

Brew a magic to make us feel all limits dissolving,
spirit bending over the fire!
First, that mysterious limit of evil, revolving
round even the rester who only seems to respire.

Dissolve with a few more drops the confining
limit of times, that belies us so;
for, oh, how deeply to-day days when Athens was shining,
and Egyptian god or bird, persist in us though!

And do not pause till the verge of senseless misgiving
between the sexes has melted for good.
Open childhood and wombs of more givingly giving

mothers, who shaming the void with devotion,
unperplexed by the hindering wood,
may bring forth future rivers, enlargers of ocean.

Muzot, 15-17 February 1922

II

Seek no more than what the Attic stela
and its gently-chiselled image know:
almost cheerfully, as though they feel a
lightening of what here perplexes so.

Be content to feel the pure direction
in the river that returns no more –
possibly, alas! the chill reflection
of the jewels she sometimes wore.

Turn to things again, and prize them higher,
common things where consolation dwells.
Oh, the comforting of wind and fire!

Here and There – let both of them express
something strangely one for you. Or else
you'd separate the whiteness from the dress.

Muzot, 15-17 February 1922

III

They might have learnt through each other (or so it appears)
some of the sharable marvels of earth;
but, while he was slowly contending with oldening years,
she still was a child of the future, waiting for birth.

Her, perhaps, her, as she played among playmates so sweetly,
he had guessed at and longed for in boyhood, such ages ago,
foreknowing the encompassing heart that would hold him completely:
and now a mere nothing divides them, five decades or so.

O incompetent Hymen, unable to keep your own winning!
Holding your torch towards the ground
because it cast ashes on to that head greying slowly.

Shall he end in laments and praise what with her was beginning?
Or will in his quietest renouncement the way have been found
to fashion her into that figure surpassing him wholly?

Muzot, 16-17 February 1922

Possibly alluding to the passion which Goethe, at the age of seventy-four, conceived for the youthful Ulrike von Levetzow and commemorated in the *Marienbader Elegie*.

IV

For us, in the midst of change, in times unfestal, the best is,
failing in fêtes of our own, thought of an earlier day's.
Look, they are there for us too, all of the Villa d'Este's
plashing fountains, though now not every one of them plays.

Now, spite of all, they are ours, gardens such singers have chanted.
Let us possess them, for now owning's a debt they are owed.
Things which to us for the last time happy gods may have granted
find in a heedless renouncement no worthy abode.

Let not a god disappear. We need all of them time and again;
let every image once formed count with us even to-day.
Treat nothing deigning to speak deep in the heart with disdain.

Though we are other than those able to celebrate,
waters that turn our wheels, our more efficacious spray,
come to us over aqueducts gloriously great.

Muzot, 16-17 February 1922

V

What stillness around a god! How your ear perceives
within it each change in the playing fountain's leap
in and out of the marble-encradled water's sleep!
And a feeling steals over the laurel: three or four leaves

a butterfly brushes by, to career
into you, on the bearing air of the vale.
And memory begins to unveil
another time, when it seemed just as perfect, here,

this stillness around a god. But will this compare?
Wait! Is it not growing stiller and stiller, progressing
in stillness, until you can feel it pressing

your throbbing heart, whose beat has beaten a way
into some soundless pause in the day? . . .
He is there.

Muzot, 16-17 February 1922

VI

Who was ever so wake
as this wakening day?
Not just brooklet and brake,
but the roof, too, is gay,

with its tiles that outstand
in the blue of the sky,
as alive as a land,
and as full of reply.

Breathing thanks are conveyed.
All nocturnal affliction
has vanished with night,

whose darkness was made
– O pure contradiction! –
from legions of light.

Muzot, c. 23 February 1922

ANTISTROPHES

Women, that you should be moving among us,
here, among us, sadly;
not more sheltered than we, and, nevertheless,
able to bless like the blessed!

From where,
when the beloved appears,
do you fetch that never
quite realised future?
One to the last fixed star
familiar with distance
starts when he grows aware
of your glorious heart-space.
How, in the crowd, are you able to save it?
You, full of springs and night!

Was it really you, then,
that once were children
going to school,
cuffed by an elder brother?
You scathless!

While even as children we
disfigured ourselves for life,
you were like bread on the altar.

Snapping of childhood
left you intact. In a moment
you stood as though enlarged
to miraculous change in God.

Broken from mountain-brows,
often, mere boys, with sharp
jagged edges, perhaps
sometimes happily hewn:
we, like pieces of rock
startling down upon flowers.

Flowers of the deeper soil,
loved by every root:
you, Eurydice's sisters,
full of holy return
behind the ascending man.

We, vexed by ourselves,
gladly vexing, and gladly
vexed again by our need:
we, like weapons beside
watchfully sleeping rage.

You: protection almost where none
protect; in slumberous shade,
like some great tree, you rise, remembered,
for the flocking thoughts of the lonely.

Lines 1-4, Venice, summer 1912; lines 5-end, Muzot, 9 February 1922
Originally intended as the Fifth of the *Duino Elegies*.

We, in the wrestling nights,
fall from nearness to nearness:
she is a thawing pond,
we are a startling stone.

Muzot, 9 February 1922

VASE PAINTING

(BANQUET OF THE DEAD)

Look, our cups are interpenetrating,
clinklessly, and wine going through our wine
like the moon through her reflected shine
in a cloud. Oh, quiet world-outwaiting! . . .
And the unheard sound that we divine
plays here like a butterfly gyrating
round a warm stone with its concubine.

Mimic morsels daintily aspire,
freed, amoeba-like, though, from desire
for food, I'd leave them, did I lift them nigher,
just as distant from me as before;
and to change my posture would require
the dancer's step along the floor.

Muzot, between 11 and 15 February 1922

Some find it like wine, assuming the gleam of glasses
glowingly into its own interior light;
others inhale it like scent of flowering grasses,
or it vanishes from them in startled, uncatchable flight.

For many it purges their hearing, intensifying
every response a clarified earth can arouse.
Let no one slight it, in spite of apparent denying,
who has caught no more than a glimpse of the house;

or the door, perhaps, or the suddenly decorated
porch, or only that final bend where a sign
points straight on to the ever-illuminated
welcoming house, where, with food and wine,

hearts grow strong and sure, and *are* what they really intended
when they longed for day and for some receipt,
upbeating from slowly, wakefully, weepingly ended
nights at last with a terrifying beat.

For even those that have only longed have related
themselves to the whole with webs too fine to observe;
round their refulgent hearts have rotated
worlds of night in a consummate curve.

Muzot, c. 23 February 1922

Meaningful word, 'inclination'! Would we were aware of
it everywhere, not just in hearts where we think it's concealed!
That of a hill, when it slowly, with gathering share of
growth, inclines to the welcoming field:
let what we are by increasing of that be exceeded;
let but the small bird's liberal flight
gift us with heart-space, making a future unneeded!
All is abundance. Oh, there was quite
enough even then when Childhood almost defeated
with endless existence. Life had poured
more than sufficient. How could we ever be cheated,
ever betrayed, we with every reward
over-rewarded? . . .

. . . . .

Muzot, c. 23 February 1922
Sent to Anton and Katharina Kippenberg on 5 December 1923. The last poem resulting from the great surge of creative energy in February 1922.

THE TRAVELLER

WRITTEN ON A JOURNEY
FOR THE INEXHAUSTIBLY TRUSTING, COLLABORATING FRIEND
OF SO MANY YEARS WAYS AND CHANGES

How small, those two in the landscape, faring
side by side and mutually wearing
the things each tender hand contrives!
While the train, with too little time for comparing,
flings a wind of forswearing
over those endless lives.
Oh, the going-by, going-by of trains uncounted!
Fields and meadows revoked,
streets and steps and balconies stroked
with parting, even though still surmounted
by happy humanity! Would that some other
would raise them at least to their houses' height,
those infusers of joy into one another,
those open gifts to delight.

Do I not know them, those whom the fervent vibration
of hearts outbeating all limitation
suddenly sweeps through infinite spaces, apart,
to hover in heaven;
or even
those who are nothing loth
to glide from the watershed to the softness of vales?
Have I not always been gently telling their tales?
Am I not one of them, am I not both?
Am I not, day by day, their Whole-ward arise,
their ineffably pure outsetting,
and then, in midst of the dance, that little surmise
they're always forgetting?

Through them let us slowly endeavour
to guess at a grave, a grave in the earth,
at the weight, the worth
of the once under-foot and now over-heart for ever.
Never
can worse arrive. But the anxious graves are spurned,
they too, by the trains that pass,
and users of life
stand unconcerned
behind rattling glass.

Oh, to what climes
do we migrate, when we travel? Who waves us on?
Whence do we know that stability's gone,
and suddenly follow a beckoning
from thing to thing?
Who flings our heart ahead for us to pursue,
dear heart, that only in childhood we're equal to,
that carries *us* by and by.
(Who could ever satisfy its desire to fly?)

How does the landscape appear
to those swifter, loftier hearts, outleaping
our own – this landscape of cloudy or clear
waking or sleeping?
What has it spoken
to those free hearts that were broken
by our hesitation? . . .
How do the houses appear
to them, those graves, and the far too small
figures of lovers, apart, –
oh, and the leaves, lifted by winds of longing
in books of the lonely?

Train between Spiez and Sierre, 20 June 1923

Sent to Katharina Kippenberg, 17 July 1923, as his contribution to a commemorative volume (*Navigare Necesse Est*) presented to Anton Kippenberg on his fiftieth birthday, 22 May 1924. Rilke described it as an 'improvisation', written in his pocket-book as he was returning by train from Zürich to Sierre over the Lötschberg, and occasioned by the sight of a young man and woman standing side by side in the landscape which so transcended them.

IMAGINARY CAREER

A childhood, reckless of renunciation,
endless and aimless. O unconscious joy!
Then terrors, limits, schooling, subjugation,
and fallings-in with forces that destroy.

Defiance. Now the bent becomes the bender,
and wreaks on others his own overthrow.
Loved, feared, contender, triumpher, defender
and overcomer, blow for blow.

Then lonely in the vaster, rarer, colder.
Yet deep within the figure now displayed
a silent yearning for the earlier, older . . .

And then God hurtled from his ambuscade.

Schöneck, 15 September 1923
Written, at the request of Forest-Inspector Burri, for the *Festschrift* of the Free Association of Like-minded in Lucerne.

TEAR-VASE

Others receive your wine, others receive your oil
into the hollow vault arched by their rounded walls.
I, as a smaller measure, slimmest of all, recoil
to meet another requirement, catching the tear that falls.

Wine grows richer and oil translucifies in its holder.
What, then, happens with tears? – They gave me this heaviness,
gave me this dullness, gave me this shimmering shoulder,
gave me this brittleness, gave me this emptiness.

Schöneck, 16 September 1923

FOR FRAU AGNES RENOLD

We're merely mouth. Who'll sing the distant heart
that in the midst of all things has its seat?
In many little beats its mighty beat
is portioned out in us. And its great smart,
like its great jubilance, we can't sustain.
And so we keep on breaking loose again
and are mere mouth. Then comes a sudden chance
which secretly the great beat enters by,
so that we cry, –
and become being, change, and countenance.

Schöneck, end of September 1923
Inscribed in the *Book of Hours*, 'to make this book more personally and heartily her own'.

FOR NIKÊ

CHRISTMAS 1923

All that rushed in the river,
all that dripped in the cave,
give I with arms that quiver
back to the god who gave,

and the Feast of the Circle starts.

Frighted or onward smiled
every wind that shifted;
every latch uplifted
made me again a child, –

and I knew in my heart of hearts.

Oh, I know them indeed,
names and their metamorphoses:
still the original seed
deep in the ripeness reposes,

out of which all has bloomed.

Bonds for a god the word,
rising in bold conjurance,
weaves till it, undeterred,
stands in the glow of assurance

singing and unconsumed.

Muzot: lines 1-7, 31 January or 1 February 1922; lines 8-11, shortly afterwards; lines 12-20, shortly before Christmas 1923

Inscribed in the *Duino Elegies* for Frau Nanny Wunderly-Volkart.

FOR FRAU HELENE BURCKHARDT

Does Nature still feel that rough
jerk, when half the creation
tore from its staticalness?
Flowers, patient enough,
heard without emulation,
rested in rootedness.

Stand, for refusing to heed
wilful and wandering motion,
rich and immaculate.
Coursing within, outspeed,
filled with ecstatic commotion,
all the precipitate.

Wending interior ways
there at appointed station,
isn't that human fate?
Other existence will raise
tempest and turbulation:
let us be florally great!

Muzot, 22 December 1923
'Grateful remembrance: Christmas 1923.'

Strongest star, not needing to await
specious aid from Darkness, whom the rest
need to make their brightness manifest.
Star already setting, consummate,

when the others but begin their wheeling
through the gradually expanding night.
Star of love's priestesses, star whom feeling
kindles of itself into a light

ever-candid, never carbonising:
you that, sinking down the solar line,
overtake such infinite arising
with the purity of your decline.

Muzot, 20 and 22 January 1924
'(20 et 22 Janvier, à mon retour à Muzot, d'où la Vénus était admirablement visible le soir de ma rentrée)'. It was on 20 January that he returned from his first shattering visit to the sanatorium at Val-Mont, where about three years later he was to die.

FOR ROBERT AND FRAU JENNY FAESI

When from moments long unrecollected
rises in us what has long been mute,
fully-mastered, radiant, resurrected,
re-experienced in the Absolute:

there begins the word, as we conceive it;
us its value silently transcends.
For the spirit lonelying us intends
union through our fitness to achieve it.

Muzot, 24 January 1924
Inscribed in the *Duino Elegies*, 'in cordial affection'.

THE FRUIT

It climbed and climbed from earth invisibly,
and kept its secret in the silent stem,
and turned in the clear blossom into flame,
and then resumed its secrecy.

And through a whole long summer fructified
within that day and night travailing tree,
and felt itself as urging instancy
to meet responding space outside.

And though it now displays so shiningly
that rondure of completed rest anew,
within the rind it sinks resigningly
back to the centre it outgrew.

Muzot, end of January 1924

FOR HANS CAROSSA

Losing also is *ours*; and even forgetting
gathers a shape in the permanent realm of mutation.
What we release can circle; and, though we are seldom the centre,
each of those circles enrings us in its absolute curve.

Muzot, 7 February 1924
Inscribed in the *Duino Elegies*.

THE MAGICIAN

He calls it up. It shrinks together. Stays.
What stays? The Other; everything outside him
becomes a creature. And the thing displays
a swiftly made-up face that can deride him.

Prevail, magician, oh, prevail, prevail!
Create an equipoise. Cause no vibration:
you and the house have got to hold the scale
against the weight of all that augmentation.

Decision falls. The spell begins anew.
He knows, the call has countered the denial.
His face, though, stands at midnight, like a dial
with hands coincident. He's spell-bound too.

Muzot, 12 February 1924

DRAFTS FROM TWO WINTER EVENINGS

OFFERED IN FRIENDSHIP TO ANTON KIPPENBERG
FOR THE 22 OF MAY 1924

PRELUDE

Why do I suddenly see the antiquated
park-fountain framed in elm-tree shade,
whose quivering basin imitated
each motion that the background made?

Something would draw me – dreams young fancy weaves
of delicate oval or of light foot-fall.
Perhaps some vision of a cashmere shawl
was drowned in the reflected leaves.

Who knows, now that deceiving youth has hastened
away, away? What castles in the air
pure water's wonderfully chastened!
Water that sparkles on, and makes the dream more fair.

I

i

Nothing's remained like that. I was too small.
One afternoon. They suddenly thought of dancing,
and rolled up the old carpet to the wall.
(Oh, how it all keeps glimmering and glancing!)

They danced. One saw her – others not at all.
And sometimes one would even lose her too,
because the fragrance of her grew and grew
to a world one perished in. I was too small.

But could I ever, even when full-grown,
master the fragrance of that dress,
so as to fall out like a falling stone
from that intense relatedness? –

Nothing's remained like that. The hall, the dance,
the afternoon, and, then, her flowery scent!
Intact. Beyond the reach of change or chance.
My own for ever. A perpetual rent.

ii

Possession means, some possibility
of happiness flew over us. Not at all! –
Impossibility, rather; just an inkling
that this particular summer, garden-hall,
and music of unmeasured minutes tinkling
away, betrayed us purely, innocently.

You, long since grown-up, how I think of you!
Not as I did then, like a startled child,
but almost like a god taking his pleasure.
For if such hours can remain undefiled,
what structures may not life, beyond all measure,
erect within us out of scent and view?

iii

That hour, the whole of it – the budding roses
and the bracelet round her arm;
oh, the sweetness it encloses,
changeless, unexpiring charm!

I stood there dazed, enraptured, smitten
by my own heart's overplus,
in my hand a partly bitten
blossom of convolvulus.

Can life exceed the pure unfolding
then accomplished once for all,
as it dangled from its own withholding
down as from a garden wall?

iv

I'll never forget you, despite
  what fate may decree,
early, delectable light,
  earth's first-fruits to me.

All the promise you made, her own part
  has been to fulfil,
ever since you broke open my heart
  with unviolent skill.

Fleetingest, earliest form
  that had power to charm!
Now I've experienced storm
  I can celebrate calm.

v

I've told as I have done
of fruit, perhaps, because I once beheld you
stoop under the net to pick a strawberry;
and if no flower ever fades in me,
is it, perhaps, because joy once impelled you
to gather one?

No one else knows
how off you'd leap,
and suddenly, breathlessly, turning towards me, stand.
I sat by you asleep,
and your left hand
lay like a rose.

vi

Could I ever fly from your realm in the sequel?
Are you not still, wherever I go,
always beyond and ahead of me? Oh,
shall we ever be equal?

The datedness of your clothes cannot cast one breath
of detraction over your image: you were so right.
Your flitting's so much a part of me . . . Will it quite
disappear in my death?

Or have I already hurled back
at Nature a refutation of my disappearing, –
your influence over me? My long excited careering
along your track?

vii

Another thing's possible too: rejection,
standing with boys, apart;
instead of exaggerating a girl's reflection
within the heart.

Can the young men later on be compared
with that mild violence?
Even the friend remains in a silence
not to be shared.

Let hardness and tenderness silently test you.
Many a one that quietly came
will often have unexpectedly blessed you,
blessed your name.

II

i

How did it happen? Love alone succeeded
when nothing else at school succeeded yet.
Infinitude remains, unsuperseded,
undescribed, between our rise and set.

It secretly achieved its consummation
in one whose tongue could not yet make it clear,
although his heart could join the great gyration
of all the creatures round love's nameless year.

What were meals, school, playtime, impositions,
what was waking, what was sleep,
when in one ordered octave intuitions
of every future sound would leap?

ii

Oh, enjoyment then was undivided,
and the heart would have its way:
life, as yet, still stood there undecided,
looking on at boyish play.

Left with more than manageable treasure,
even then his winnings were foretold;

life's part, later on, would be to measure, –
now it was enough to hold.

For, hidden from the girl, a god was coming
to feel within this child his fullest span,
as he founded in the boy's succumbing
the endurance of the man.

Muzot, February 1924

FOR WITOLD HULEWICZ

Happy who know that behind all speeches
still the unspeakable lies;
that it's from there that greatness reaches
us in the forms we prize!

Trusting not to the diversely fashioned
bridges of difference we outfling:
so that we gaze out of every impassioned
joy at some wholly communal thing.

Muzot, 15 February 1924

Inscribed in the *Duino Elegies* for his Polish translator: 'To that faithful and active intermediary, Witold Hulewicz (Olwid), with gratitude: Rainer Maria Rilke'.

Since to bear you over such abysses
soaring rapture would so often serve,
build at last the unimagined bridge's
boldly calculable curve.

Miracle's not unexplained endurance
of some peril that encountered us:
not till we achieve in clear assurance
does it really get miraculous.

No presumption is there in assisting
this ineffable relatedness;
intimater grows the inter-twisting,
insufficient simple passiveness.

Stretch your practised powers until their tension
spans the distance between two
contradictions . . . For the god's intention
is to know himself in you.

Muzot, mid-February 1924

EROS

Masks! Masks! Or blind him! How can they endure
this flaming Eros gods and men obey,
bursting in summer-solstice on the pure
idyllic prologue to their vernal play?

How imperceptibly the conversation
takes a new, graver turn . . . A cry . . . And, there!
he's flung the nameless fascination
like a dim temple round the fated pair.

Lost, lost! O instantaneous perdition!
In brief divinity they cling.
Life turns, and Destiny begins her mission.
And within there weeps a spring.

Muzot, mid-February 1924

EARLY SPRING

Harshness gone. And sudden mitigation
laid upon the field's uncovered grey.
Little runnels change their intonation.
Tentative caresses stray

round the still earth from immensity.
Roads run far into the land, foretelling.
Unexpectedly you find it, welling
upwards in the empty tree.

Muzot, mid-February 1924

MUTABILITY

Quicksand of hours! Perpetual quiet disappearance
even of the blessedest pile into dust.
Life's always blowing. Already with no coherence
those uncarrying columns outthrust.

Decay: does it yield more cause, though, for lamentation
than the fountain's return to the mirror its ripples bespread?
Let us hold ourselves between the teeth of Mutation,
till it gets us completely into its gazing head.

Muzot, c. end of February 1924

Gods, for all we can tell, stride as richly bestowing
now as in former years;
gently their wind as well reaches our harvests, blowing
over more loaded ears.

Quite to forget it will fail quite to elude the relation:
they will perform their share.
Suddenly, silently there, prizing your proudest creation,
ponders their different scale.

Muzot, end of February 1924

The sap is mounting back from that unseenness
darkly renewing in the common deep,
back to the light, and feeding the pure greenness
hiding in rinds round which the winds still weep.

The inner side of Nature is reviving,
another *sursum corda* will resound;
invisibly, a whole year's youth is striving
to climb those trees that look so iron-bound.

Preserving still that grey and cool expression,
the ancient walnut's filling with event;
while the young brush-wood trembles with repression
under the perching bird's presentiment.

Muzot, beginning of March 1924

Springs, with emergent leap
almost too keen:
what speeds them from the deep,
divine, serene? –

Prepares a splendour there
in precious stone,
to cheer us when we fare
through fields alone?

We show we hardly know
the gesture's worth
when we dismember so
water and earth!

Muzot, (probably) April 1924

On the sunny road, within the hollow
cloven tree, that now for generations
has been a trough, inaudibly renewing
a little film of water, I can still my
thirst by letting all that pristine freshness
ripple from my wrists through all my body.
Drinking were too much for me, too open:
this, though, this procrastinating gesture
fills my consciousness with sparkling water.

So, if you came, I could be contented
just to let my hands rest very lightly
either on your shoulder's youthful rounding
or upon your breasts' responsive pressure.

Muzot, beginning of June 1924

The one birds plunge through's not that trusty space
where each confided form's intensified.
(Out in the open there you're self-denied,
and go on vanishing without a trace.)

Space spreads transposingly from us to things:
really to feel the way a tree upsprings,
cast round it space from that which inwardly
expands in you. Surround it with retention.
It has no bounds. Not till its reascension
in your renouncing is it truly tree.

Muzot, 16 June 1924

World was in the face of the beloved, –
but was poured out all of a sudden:
world is outside, can't be comprehended.

Why did I not drink, then, when I raised it,
drink from the full face of the beloved,
world, – so near, I tasted its bouquet?

Oh, I did! I drank insatiably.
Only, I was so brim-full already
with world, that when I drank I overflowed.

Ragaz, mid-July 1924

FROM THE THEMATIC MATERIAL: NIGHTS

Night. You face dissolved in the darkest
depths, oh, face against mine,
forcing the mounting scale of my starkest
stare to decline:

Night, that quivers under my straining
gaze, without being afraid;
inexhaustible source, remaining
after the colours fade;

full of young constellations, throwing
fire from their flying dress
to the interspace of silently flowing
adventurousness:

though the mere fact of your being there
almost annihilates me,
one with the dusky earth, I dare,
even in you, to be.

Muzot, 2 and 3 October 1924

FOR FRÄULEIN MARGA WERTHEIMER

All that our mind reclaims from wilderingness
will serve one day some liveliest endeavour;
if sometimes only thoughts, they'll none the less
dissolve in that great blood that keeps for ever
its onwardness.

And if it's feeling, who shall calculate
what in pure space its consequences are,
where some whit more of lightness or of weight
can start a system or displace a star?

Muzot, 5 October 1924
Inscribed in a copy of his translation of E. B. Browning's *Sonnets from the Portuguese*: 'with gratitude, in association with the hours of mutual work at Muzot (Autumn 1924): Rainer Maria Rilke.'

MAUSOLEUM

King's heart. Core of a lofty
lording-tree. Balsam fruit.
Golden heart-nut. Urn-poppy,
midst of the middle shrine
(where the echo rebounds
like a splinter of stillness
when you bestir,
feeling your previous
stance was too loud there . . .),
nation-abandoning,
stellar-minded,
long now invisibly
gyring king's heart.

Where, become what,
that of the lightsome
paramour? –
Smile, that so lightly
grafts on the hesitant rondure of gladdening fruits;
or, it may be, the moth's
preciousness, gauze wing, feelers . . .

Where, though, where the once singing them,
onesomely singing them,
poet's heart? –
Wind,
invisible,
wind-withinness.

Muzot, October 1924

Give me, O Earth, for keeping
tears, of your purest clay.
Pour, O my being, the weeping,
lost within you, away.

Let the withheldness flow where
that will receive which should.
Nothing is bad but the nowhere,
all that exists is good.

Muzot, 30 October 1924

THE GOLDSMITH

Coaxing chain-links, castigating rings,
'Wait! Go slowly!' is my constant cry:
'Outside there'll be happenings by and by.'
Things, I keep repeating, Things, Things, Things,
as I ply my smith-craft: for till I
reach them, none can set up on its own
or undertake the tiniest career.
All, by grace of God, are equal here:
I, the gold, the fire, and the stone.

'Gently, ruby, drop that raging tone!
This pale pearl is trembling, and the flowing
tears have started in the beryl-stone.
Now you've rested, it's sheer terror, going
round among you, as you leap from sleep.'
Bluely coruscating, redly glowing,
how they sparkle at me from the heap!

Gold, though, seems to know what I require,
for I've tamed its spirit in the fire;
still, I have to coax it carefully
round the gem; and suddenly, in grasping
that, the savage creature thrusts its rasping
claws with metal hatred into me.

Lines 1-11, Paris, 5 August 1907; lines 12-end, Muzot, late autumn 1925

The only example of such re-handling of an early poem. Lines 1-11 were his first attempt at *The Reliquary* in *New Poems: Second Part.*

FOR FRAU JOHANNA VON KUNESCH

The years go by . . . And yet, as in a train,
we're going, while they, like scenery we pass,
remain beyond this rattling window glass
which frost bedims and sunshine clears again.

How happenings and spaces harmonise:
one became mead, one tree, one went on high
to help create the heavens . . . Butterfly
and flower are really there, nothing lies;

transforming isn't lying . . .

Muzot, 10 December 1925

Inscribed in *The Life of Mary* at the request of the recipient's son-in-law, Achill von Karwinsky.

MUSIC

FOR HERR LORENZ LEHR

Sleeping . . . To grow, at the pure suscitation,
so wide awake, it's we, outstripped by such
awakenedness, that sleep . . . O trepidation!
Strike earth: it sounds dull, earthen, being so much
deadened by our objectives' limitation.
Strike stars: each has a stellar revelation!

Strike but one star: numbers beyond divining
fulfil themselves unseen: atomic powers
are multiplied in space. And sounds are shining.
And what with us is ear, for their bright showers
is somewhere eye as well: in realms not ours
these domes complete the arcs of their designing.

Music *stands* somewhere, just as somewhere too
this light brings ears a tinkling intimation . . .
Only for our perception seem the two
so separate . . . Between this and that vibration
vibrates unnamed excess . . . What smuggled through
to fruits, and in the cycle of gustation
reveals its worth? What message has a scent?
(Each step we take, whatever our intent,
dissolves the boundaries of revelation.)

Music: you water of our fountain-basin,
you beam that falls, you sound that mirrors, you
whom touch into blest wakefulness can hasten,
you rest inflowing brings completeness to,
you more than us, . . . from every whereunto
exempt . . .

Muzot, 18 December 1925
Inscribed in the *Duino Elegies* for the cellist Lorenz Lehr.

FULL POWER

Oh, if we could but escape counters and strikers of hours!
Out with hunters at dawn, hot with their youthful powers,
shouting above the bark.
Coolness joyfully spraying from bushes we beat our way through,
till we really felt, in the earliest airs, in the free and the new,
the aim that had found its mark.

That was what we were meant for: lightly appearing delight.
Not in a rigid room, after a negative night,
one more negative day.
These are eternally right: these with their deeply confirmed
closeness to life attract the completely affirmed
creature they're waiting to slay.

Muzot, 9 June 1926

FOR COUNT KARL LANCKOROŃSKI

'*No intellect, no ardour is redundant*':
to make one through the other more abundant
is what we're for, and some are singled out
for purest victory in that contention:
no signal can escape their tried attention,
their hands are wieldy and their weapons stout.

No sound must be too soft for their detection,
they must perceive that angle of deflection
to which the dial-pointer scarcely stirs,
and must, as might be with their eyelids, utter
reply to what the butterflies out-flutter,
and learn to fathom what a flower infers.

No less than others they can be extinguished,
and yet they must (why else were they distinguished?)
feel even with catastrophe some kin,
and, while the rest are helplessly bewailing,
recapture in the strokes of each assailing
the rhythm of some stoniness within.

They must be stationed like a shepherd, keeping
his lonely watch: one might suppose him weeping,
till, coming close, one feels his piercing sight;
and, as for him the speech of stars is clear,
for them must be as intimately near
what climbs in still procession through the night.

In slumber also they continue seers:
from dream and being, from laughter and from tears
a meaning gathers . . . which if they can seize,
and kneel to Life and Death in adoration,
another measure for the whole creation
is given us in those right-angled knees.

Ragaz, 10 August 1926

Described by Rilke as an 'improvisation' and inspired by the penultimate line of a short poem by Count Lanckoroński.

R. M. R.

4 DECEMBER 1875 - 29 DECEMBER 1926

ROSE, OH THE PURE CONTRADICTION, DELIGHT OF BEING NO ONE'S SLEEP UNDER SO MANY LIDS.

Epitaph composed by himself before 27 October 1925 and inscribed on his tombstone in the churchyard at Raron.

INDEXES OF FIRST LINES AND TITLES

(German and English)

INDEX OF FIRST LINES IN THE BOOK OF HOURS

(GERMAN)

AW=*Ausgewählte Werke*, Band I (1948); SW=*Sämtliche Werke*, Band I (1955); P=*Selected Works, Vol. II: Poetry* (1959)

INDEX OF FIRST LINES IN THE BOOK OF HOURS

(ENGLISH)

AW = *Ausgewählte Werke*, Band I (1948); SW = *Sämtliche Werke*, Band I (1955)
P = *Selected Works, Vol. II: Poetry* (1959)

INDEX OF TITLES AND FIRST LINES
(GERMAN)

AW = *Ausgewählte Werke*, Band I (1948); SW = *Sämtliche Werke*, Band I (1955) and (where the page-reference is followed by a ii) Band II (1956-7); P = *Selected Works, Vol. II: Poetry* (1959)

INDEX OF TITLES AND FIRST LINES

(ENGLISH)

AW = *Ausgewählte Werke*, Band I (1948); SW = *Sämtliche Werke*, Band I (1955) and (where the page-reference is followed by a ii) Band II (1956-7); P = *Selected Works, Vol. II: Poetry* (1959)